D1193135

Peaceful at Heart

Peaceful at Heart

Anabaptist Reflections on Healthy Masculinity

Edited by Don Neufeld and Steve Thomas

RESOURCE *Publications* · Eugene, Oregon

PEACEFUL AT HEART
Anabaptist Reflections on Healthy Masculinity

Wipf & Stock
An Imprint of Wipf and Stock Publishers
199 W. 8th Ave., Suite 3
Eugene, OR 97401

www.wipfandstock.com

PAPERBACK ISBN: 978-1-5326-4477-1
HARDCOVER ISBN: 978-1-5326-4478-8
EBOOK ISBN: 978-1-5326-4478-8

Manufactured in the U.S.A.

Book design by Mary E. Klassen

Contents

Preface
A Pastoral Vision for Engaging Men

You're holding a book by men for men who are seeking healthy masculinity.

This book comes at a time when men and masculinity are in the spotlight. We see many men behaving badly on the news—abusing power, violating women, and mistreating others. But most men I know aren't like this. In my work as a pastor and with Mennonite Men,[1] I see those seeking to be good men but wondering what that means as we wrestle with issues of gender identity, conventional masculinity, power and privilege, and expectations in the grind of daily living.

Along with many men, I have questions about masculinity. What kind of man am I? What do I wish for my sons as men? How do I want men to relate to my daughter? What does it mean to *be a man*? Who are we as males? Why isn't there more agreement on a description of masculinity? Aren't we just talking biology? How are men essentially different from women (if at all)? Where can we find healthy models of masculinity?

Depending on who we ask, we get different answers to these questions. Leaders in men's work offer various perspectives. Those in the mythopoetic men's movement draw on a rich tradition of stories and rituals, gatherings of men, and psychological archetypes for male formation. Those in the conservative evangelical men's movement reassert traditional male roles and "godly manhood," calling men to take responsibility for how they live. Those more attuned to feminist concerns examine social constructions of masculinity, critique patriarchal systems, question traditional roles, and call men to establish gender equality. Each of these groups have their contributions and some limitations.

In this book we ask what our shared Anabaptist Christian tradition offers for understanding healthy masculinity. The book

---

1 This book is part of the expanding work of Mennonite Men, the men's organization of Mennonite Church Canada and Mennonite Church USA. Our mission is *Engaging men to grow, give and serve as followers of Jesus* with a vision of building God's peace. Visit MennoniteMen.org to see resources and retreats we offer men.

begins by laying the context for answering this question by looking at masculinity from clinical and historical angles in part 1. Part 2 offers a variety of perspectives on masculinity to demonstrate that there is no singular masculinity but multiple masculinities, socially constructed and remarkably varied, even among Anabaptist men. The diverse backgrounds and styles of this part reflects the nature of our subject: a rough collage of pieces pulled together as images of what it's like to be men. Part 3 turns to the Bible in fresh ways and Anabaptist touchstones of discipleship, community, and peace as lenses for envisioning healthy masculinity. These chapters call men to follow the way of Jesus in community for God's peace. Part 4 offers practices for the lives of men, focusing on power, race, and peace in our relationships with others and God. Finally, by way of afterwords, three Anabaptist women leaders reflect on what they read in this book by Anabaptist men. We learn from their experiences and perspectives what needs further attention to benefit our lives together.

In this collection men speak from a wide range of backgrounds. While readers may not agree with everything, we invite readers to listen with a spirit of receptivity, seeking to learn and grow. As with any book, this volume has its limitations. Given its scope, focusing on the experiences of individual men and their expressions of masculinity, it points to but does not assess the complicated nature of hegemonic masculinity (largely defined by white, middle-class, heterosexual males in dominant culture) nor systemic patriarchy with the power and privileges it grants certain men while subordinating women. We acknowledge that more work needs to be done on these issues to address gender identity and equality. We hope this book prompts further conversation, study, and change in these areas as people of all identities come together to create "one new humanity" (Eph. 2:14–15) in God's shalom.

In our vision of healthy masculinity, we image men who:

- Embrace who they are as beloved children of God.
- Respect females as beloved daughters of God.
- Follow the way of Jesus, the image of God and model human being.
- Serve the mission of reconciliation for "one new humanity" (Eph. 2:15).
- Work to establish God's love and justice for marginalized people.

- Allow the Spirit to make us "strong, loving and wise" (2 Tim. 1:7).
- Are peaceful in heart and peaceful in life, extending God's shalom.

When we embody these characteristics in our process of human maturation, I believe gendered distinctions diminish and that men and women become more alike than different as we reflect our true selves in the image of God. We end up with a healthy personhood for a whole new humanity.

I wish for all men what my spouse, Linda, and I prayed for our children each night. At the end of our bedtime prayer with our children, we closed with these words: "May they know who they are as your beloved children and be filled with your Spirit who makes them strong, loving, and wise." We sought to imprint these words in their hearts and minds. (Our daughter took this a step further and had "strong, loving, and wise" tattooed on her body.) I look to the day when men will embrace who they are and be known by these marks as they embody and build God's peace.

Steve Thomas
Coordinator for USA
Mennonite Men

Contributors

David Augsburger, professor emeritus of pastoral care and counseling, Fuller Theological Seminary, Pasadena, California.

Gareth Brandt, professor of spiritual formation at Columbia Bible College and author of *Under Construction: Reframing Men's Spirituality* (Herald, 2009).

Scott Brubaker-Zehr, Mennonite pastor in Waterloo who completed his DMin thesis, "Understanding Men's 'Experience of God,'" in 2013.

Leonard Dow, former lead pastor of Oxford Circle Mennonite Church in Philadelphia, Pennsylvania, and currently works for Everence as Stewardship Development Specialist.

David Evans, associate professor of history and intercultural studies at Eastern Mennonite University, Harrisonburg, Virginia, and coeditor of *Between the World of Ta-Nehisi Coates and Christianity* (Cascade, 2018).

Kurt Horst, lead pastor at Whitestone Mennonite Church in Hesston, Kansas, and Conference Minister, Mennonite Church USA.

Hyung Jin Kim Sun, aka Pablo, PhD student at Emmanuel College in Toronto and a pastor at Iglesia Menonita Nueva Vida in Toronto.

Harry Lafond, retired executive director of the Office of the Treaty Commissioner of Saskatchewan, former chief of the Muskeg Lake Cree Nation, and active in the Catholic church as a partner with Mennonites in Saskatchewan along the path toward reconciliation.

Cyneatha Millsaps, executive director of Mennonite Women USA and former pastor of Community Mennonite Church, Markham, Illinois.

Don Neufeld, clinical social worker in private practice in the Niagara area of Ontario.

Pieter Niemeyer, attends Toronto United Mennonite Church and works in various faith based social justice initiatives.

Carol Penner, assistant professor of theological studies at Conrad Grebel University College, Waterloo, Ontario.

Jamie Pitts, associate professor of theology at Anabaptist Mennonite Bibilical Seminary, editor of *Anabaptist Witness*, and director of the Institute of Mennonite Studies, Elkhart, Indiana.

John Powell, African American leader with a long history of being engaged in antiracism, justice, and reconciliation work.

Hugo Saucedo, educator and university professor from San Antonio, Texas.

Sara Wenger Shenk, president of Anabaptist Mennonite Biblical Seminary, Elkhart, Indiana, and former associate professor of Christian practices at Eastern Mennonite Seminary, Harrisonburg, Virginia.

Steve Thomas, US coordinator for Mennonite Men and a Mennonite pastor in Goshen, Indiana.

Marty Troyer, aka the Peace Pastor, pastor of Houston Mennonite Church and peace promotor in Houston, Texas.

Thomas R. Yoder Neufeld, professor emeritus, New Testament and biblical peace studies, Conrad Grebel University College at the University of Waterloo, Waterloo, Ontario.

Introduction

Don Neufeld

This book contains information *about* men, but firstly and most importantly this is a book of wisdom *for* men. This is a book for men's lives, for how men see themselves in the mirror at the end of the day, in the quietness of personal reflection, and how men experience themselves in their relationships—with intimate partners, with family, with friends and community, with broader humanity, and with creation. Written from an Anabaptist Christian perspective, this is a book for how men experience their relationship with God.

This is a book primarily by men because men need to hear from other men, to speak into the lives of other men, and to listen to other men. This is a journey of us as men, a call for personal reflection and for joining as brothers in this journey—not about pointing fingers at men as objects or the "other." We men must take inventory of our historical manifestations, recognizing both the honorable and the shameful, the evidence of God breaking into the world in and through men, and the evidence of how far we can wander from the longings of the Creator's intentions for humanity. We must envision a preferred picture of living well as men.

Historically men have dominated public discourse on almost all topics, and social justice advocates of the last half century have rightly called for a broader and more inclusive conversation that privileges women and minority voices that have long been marginalized. Men, though, have seldom reflected consciously on our existence as men relative to each other and more significantly to those who are "other"—a privilege of being the dominant voice. While a relative silencing of the traditionally dominant voices of men may be necessary to allow others to be heard, this silencing cannot be permanent. Within the larger discussion of gender and justice, men must do our own work in contextualizing our lives in the rich tapestry of interconnected humanity and creation.

Masculinity is a cloak that we wear, a collection of assumptions, qualities, behaviors, and characteristics customarily assigned to those of the male gender. Masculinity is a mixture of biology and socialization, defined at any particular time in history by the leading voices within culture, family, and religious traditions. Each individual boy from birth is immersed into a world of expectations and messages unique to the characteristics of their individual context of family, moment in history, geography, culture, race, financial and social class, and numerous other factors that align in their lives. This context interacts with unique biology passed from the parental lines, the DNA containing the genetic information that defines how we function, grow, and reproduce as organisms.

The presumptions of the expression of masculinity within persons born with male bodies are in flux more than ever before. As each generation of males comes of age, the dynamic interplay of a number of factors finds expression in our lives. An acceleration of consciousness in our world about gender in the last half century has broadened our understandings and highlighted variabilities that are much more extensive than previous generations recognized. This has been unsettling for many but represents freedom and possibility for those who do not fit the normative messages of acceptable masculinity. It opens the door to a different future for all men.

In these times of globalization, the fracturing of families, and the toppling of the prominence of religious dogma, masculinity—along with many aspects of our social fabric—has come under considerable scrutiny. With good reason, voices advocating for justice have exposed the debris field of history perpetrated by those (primarily) men wielding the most power—power fueled by assumptions of entitlement and superiority that are too often blessed by a reading of sacred texts by those who benefit most from such a reading. Men's relationship to the dynamics of power and privilege is the flash point of critical attention to masculinity and has become the primary framework for understanding men. While revealing important understandings of men's behavior and critical for identifying necessary changes, this framework is ultimately inadequate for representing the fullness of men's experience. We need to look more deeply and broadly to formulate a helpful future for men.

In the face of the rapid deconstruction of assumptions that framed traditional masculinity, men experience confusion and shame and are challenged to consider a different future. Increasingly freed from constrictive definitions of the past, men have the opportunity to embrace a broader and richer masculinity. We can name traditional male characteristics and men who have lived with integrity that have served our world well and build on the lifegiving aspects of these. We must recognize that positive intentions and traits, however, have too often become entangled with destructive motives, supported by self-serving societal structures, leading to reprehensible outcomes. The line between these is frequently blurred, and men have failed to name such evils for what they are, work to deconstruct the oppressive forces of patriarchy and sexism, and adequately hold inappropriate actions to account.

This book is a calling to renew a vision of peace and to embrace a peacefulness within our male humanity. Peace, as envisioned in the biblical term "shalom," is a broad spectrum of wholeness, completeness, and wellness that undergirds relationships of mutuality and love. As nineteenth century author Henry David Thoreau famously wrote in *Walden*, "The mass of men lead lives of desperation. . . . A stereotyped but unconscious despair is concealed even under what are called the games and amusements of mankind." Many men know this too well in their lives, and society generally does not provide opportunity for men to name this reality and seek appropriate remedy. Others, due to male socialization that fails to nurture self-reflective focus in men, are oblivious to this lurking reality that undermines their hopes and intentions.

Further, men are barraged with varying and duplicitous messages about violence, which are overtly or tacitly encouraged in tale and sport and are justified by political and religious opportunists. Violent self-defense is generally legitimized, and male led violence is heroized when used in protection of family or country. Questions about the nature or nurture roots of male violence are at the forefront of discussions of masculinity: Is violence inevitable within masculinity? What structural forces are manifestations of masculinity that in turn continue to reinforce men's use of violence? What intrapersonal dynamics set the stage for violence, and how might peace theology reshape these dymanics in the personal lives of men? How does God's call for peacemaking speak to men and violence?

Sexual violence is a particularly disturbing and destructive curse in our world, and it is perpetrated primarily by men. The powerful combination of violence and sexuality as a tool for conquest, domination, and humiliation has been pervasive in history and continues to play a tragic role in human interactions in its many subtle and blatant forms, which are too often ignored and sometimes even sanctioned in society. The pervasive messages of male entitlement regarding sexual expression and the failure of men to honor and respect the full humanity of women and children fuel and enable systemic sexual violence. In addition to being perpetrators, boys and men can also be victims of sexual violence, a reality often underreported and relegated to the dark corners of men's experiences of shame. This critical area of conversation needs attention beyond the pages of this volume, though we hope that this volume will contribute to that larger dialogue and may be further impetus for moving forward discussions regarding sexual violence.

We made commitment to give voice within these pages to men who have experienced their maleness and the weights of masculinity from outside the white heterosexual norm of North American society. We acknowledge that any attempt to include diverse voices will always fall short, and we encourage the broadening of the conversation beyond the pages of this book. We also acknowledge the diverse experiences of white heterosexual men and hope that all men find their lives represented in important ways within these writings.

As a social worker for over twenty-five years, I came to the vision for this book as I sought after resources for my own development as a clinician and for the men who I encountered in my work—as individuals, with their partners and families, or in therapeutic group settings. Having been schooled in a feminist-informed masters program and practicing for eighteen years in child welfare services, I was constantly reminded that men are problems and that masculinity is toxic. As I have searched for resources since 2010, I have discovered three primary responses to men. First, the dominant voices in the gender justice world affirmed the sentiment I had lived thus far in my career, that men are responsible almost exclusively for all forms of injustice and violence, driven by men's apparent insatiable need for power and control. Next was the so-called Christian Men's Movement, reacting to the radical changes in society and calling men back to a "biblical" vision of men being real men. Finally, there were the men's advocacy groups who, with varying degrees of militancy, counter the rhetoric of feminism and defend men from what is felt to be unfair characterizations of men and privileging of women.

None of these perspectives on their own speak adequately to the lives of the men I encounter or to the lives of the male members of my family and church community. Though each has important perspectives to ponder, none reflects sufficiently the various stories of men or offers an adequate vision for change. As I pursued my search for resources and found few that were adequate, I began to wonder what further sources of understanding might be valuable.

This project arose as an inspiration from that longing. I was struck by the resonance between the challenges of masculinity and the Anabaptist theological tradition that I had been immersed in all my life.

Anabaptism, a peace church tradition with roots in the Reformation, holds an understanding of Christian faith anchored in Jesus's life and ministry. Characteristic of this understanding has been an emphasis on Jesus's teachings on peace, his call to discipleship, and his invitation to live faithfully within community. I came to the realization that each of these themes held important contributions for discussions on men and gender, and I set out again to find available resources within this community. As before, although I found much of interest dispersed in various places and forms, I could not locate any substantial treatments of masculinity from this perspective. I came to the realization that if Anabaptist thought was going to speak to men's specific needs, it would require an initiative to gather various Anabaptist men's voices together.

This volume brings to the table men from within Anabaptism, of various experience and expertise, to a conversation on masculinity. We made an intentional decision early in the process to bring together a number of voices rather than to rely on any one man as the expert. Practicing community, inspiring each other in our thinking, and holding each other accountable to the dynamic interplay of past and future, of violence and grace, of strength and vulnerability, of wisdom and humility, we together offer these thoughts to men and to those who journey with men as lovers, parents, children, pastors, family members, or service providers. The afterwords to the volume include some of these cojourneyers—three women who reflect on these visions of healthy masculinity. This volume is not intended to be exhaustive but rather to resource and inspire further development of the meaning of healthy masculinity.

I am grateful to those who have contributed to this volume and to those who have supported this project along the way. To the many dialogue partners with whom I have shared this dream and who endorsed its vision, propelling me forward, I say a hearty thank-you. In particular, Dan Epp-Tiessen contributed significantly to getting this project off the ground; Mennonite Men, under the leadership of my coeditor Steve Thomas, played a signifint role in the process; the Institute of Mennonite Studies at Anabaptist Mennonite Biblical Seminary has provided helpful editorial direction; and the Schowalter Foundation provided partial funding for this project. And to the men who have inspired me—my father, my opa, my sons, The Guys, and the many men who have invited me to their intimate places as they have shared the joys and sorrows with me in my practice—thank you!

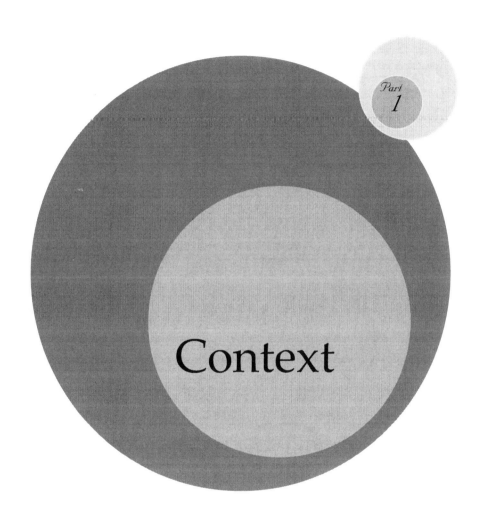

Part
1

Context

Masculinity and Human Need

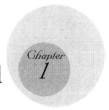

Don Neufeld

Ever since I took an Old Testament anthropology class at Canadian Mennonite Bible College in January 1985, the Hebrew word *nephesh* has remained in my awareness. Professor Waldemar Janzen told us that this word, used 754 times in the Old Testament, is generally translated "soul." He said that, among other things, *nephesh* conveys a sense of humanity's relationship of dependency with creation and on the Creator. This dependency, or we might even say neediness, extends beyond the biological to our relationship with life itself and our sense of personhood: the biblical text speaks of an inherent desire or longing that seeks fulfillment or completion. Scripture affirms this need as a positive and life-giving dynamic in human existence.

The significance of this word has become clearer to me now, more than thirty years later, as I have reflected on men's sense of self and expectations around masculinity. As a social worker and therapist, I have been struck by the breadth and complexity of human existence—by its great joys and deep sorrows, both of which engage my interest as I focus on men's stories. When I broaden my perspective on men to include my own life and the lives of the boys and men who have been part of my life, I recognize the complexities of need and fulfillment that thread through our experience. I see with greater clarity the challenges men face as we navigate expectations and expressions of masculinity.[1]

In *From Violence to Blessing: How an Understanding of Deep-Rooted Conflict Can Open Paths to Reconciliation*, Vern Neufeld Redekop, professor of conflict studies at St. Paul University (Ottawa), develops a theory of human identity needs, a framework for understanding the deep emotions and strong motivations that characterize the human quest for identity, and the role of these emotions and

---

1 Descriptions, especially when applied to large collections of subjects, do an injustice to the intricacies of life and the nuances of individual instances. All characterizations occur on a continuum, and I acknowledge the limitations of my attempts to generalize about the experiences of men and boys. I also acknowledge that, to a greater or lesser degree, the experiences of girls and women overlap with the experiences of men, and differences in many instances are a matter of degree rather kind.

motivations in conflicts. Human needs in their universality, considered from a developmental and social engagement standpoint, go beyond minimum requirements for biological existence. The core components of meaning, connectedness, security, recognition, and action inform our sense of self.

According to Redekop, although the needs categories are universal, the particular things that satisfy these needs are specific to our culture, values, and experience.[2] As young children, we depend on our caregivers—usually our parents—to define how these core developmental needs are met, and our brains are highly plastic as they wire together the neurons that grow in response to stimuli. In childhood, when caregivers are available and attentive and our environment is relatively peaceful, our core needs are generally satisfied, and we experience relative safety, contentment, and joy. In contrast, chaos, trauma, and neglect create distress and are the roots of a multiplicity of mental health challenges as we develop through childhood and into adulthood. Our self-perception arises out of an accumulation of data from sources within (intuition, senses, thoughts) and without (messages from family, community, religious leaders, media).

Although these identity needs are universal and not gender specific, culture and the values that are associated with how these needs get addressed come with highly gendered expectations that from early on differentiate male and female experiences of life. At times intentionally and explicitly, and at other times inadvertently and subtly, parents, siblings, extended family, neighbors, teachers, coaches, religious institutions, and the media communicate and reinforce acceptable standards of behavior for boys and girls. From the color of his bedroom furnishings to the ways adults respond to him (compared to his female toddler counterparts) when he falls and cries, messages accumulate that define for the growing boy what is acceptable and unacceptable in his preferences, in his behavior, in his emotions and expressiveness. Powerful forces shape his values, nurture his internal picture of acceptability, and police his compliance with particular behaviors. These forces prescribe the nature of the need satisfiers he should pursue. Many of the messages, anchored in culture, time, and place, help give structure and predictability to life: his identity, gained through living a life of integrity, productivity, and play within a family and community, provides meaning, belonging, security—a place in this world!

---

2 Redekop, *Violence to Blessing*, 32.

From the earliest chapters in the Bible, the unfolding story of humanity is characterized by a stubborn refusal to accept God's invitation to a relationship of trust and dependency, to a life lived within God's good intentions for creation. Adam and Eve, spurred on by the serpent's crafty manipulation of their perceptions of need and fulfillment, are convinced that God is holding back on them, and they seek to satisfy their desires by choosing another way (Gen. 3). According to the narrative in 1 Samuel, God's people insist on having a king and an army in order to be like the surrounding nations, a move that reveals their unwillingness to rely on God to lead and protect them. In order to win them over to the truth, God condescends and even integrates these developments into the continuing story of God's call to them to be a faithful people.[3] Ultimately, what is demonstrated over and over is the foolishness of human attempts to define our own way over against the wishes of a loving God. The results are tragic.

In a similar way, much of what defines masculinity in our society are desperate and distorted attempts to meet core human needs. Though the needs are legitimate, the means used to meet those needs are too often out of alignment with the intended ends. Again, the results are tragic.

In what follows, I draw on Redekop's categories of universal need as a way to consider characteristics of healthy and unhealthy masculinity.

Action

In our society, men are often defined by our activities, especially by our employment and our play. The world of employment for many men not only occupies a significant part of our daily lives; it is also a hallmark of our identity. We are known by our occupation and are respected for our ability to gain and hold a job that enables us to support ourselves and those who are dependent on us. We pursue education, monitor the economy and job trends, and maximize our employability and exposure in order to land the right job and secure our future. In years past, many men took up these adult responsibilities as early as possible, and they continued to carry them for many years. But changes in the economy and trends in employment now mean that this security is elusive, and many more men are joining the part of the workforce that is more volatile, unpredictable, and therefore unsettling to a self-image that

---

3 See Boyd, "The Heavenly Missionary."

values this manifestation of male responsibility. The job market is also a function of an economy that by its very nature privileges and rewards some at the expense of others. While some men excel in this realm and find ways to contribute to their families and to the larger community, others are ground down by unjust systems, poverty, and exclusion. Still others, because of various forms of disability, are marginally employable at best and thus lose access to the identity that comes from this source.

Especially for those of us who enjoy a prosperity that allows us to spend time in activities not devoted to meeting basic instrumental needs, play is another arena of masculine identity formation. Whether in athletic and recreational pursuits or in hobbies and interests, men fill significant amounts of time and spend inordinate amounts of money chasing their preferred pastimes. Many of these pursuits are life-giving to boys and men, contributing to health and personal development, expressing competitive drives and a quest for excellence, accomplishment, camaraderie, and creativity, while providing entertainment and spectacle for others.

Boys and men generally are oriented to doing and fixing. From earliest stages of their growth, they receive messages and are given tasks that encourage development of skills and endorse effective problem solving. Often in the context of helping others and at times involving significant risk and sacrifice of self, boys and men receive accolades and honor for achieving positive ends that are demanded of some of them (conscripted military service) and readily offered by others (chivalrous deeds of sacrifice).

What is a source of healthy identity for men may also entail hazards and can become oppressive when weighted heavily by certain expectations of masculinity. When satisfying work become workaholism, boundaries between self and work blur, and men compulsively extend their commitment to their work to the detriment of their well-being and that of those close to them. Jobs may become a diversion to avoid something they see as less desirable. Workaholism is especially insidious because it is often identified with productivity, dedication, and sacrifice, and it receives social sanction and copious reward. One effect is that statistically boys and men do the riskiest work; assumptions about men's duties and the relative disposability of boys and men contribute to a situation in which men account for approximately 92 percent of workplace deaths.[4]

Play for men is often highly competitive and at moderate levels motivates accomplishment. Too often, though, it pushes men into risky choices and leaves them broken. Foundational to competition is comparison, and comparisons can create fragile frameworks on which the egos of boys and men are suspended. Such competition may demand blood and sacrifice, even to the point of putting life at risk. Messages about masculinity propel pursuit of glory and prestige, setting standards for success and acceptability, and punishing with shame and ridicule those who do not measure up. Boys and men are tested for toughness and courage, and limited regard is given the gladiators that end up broken or dead.[5]

Action as a way to prove oneself, especially when other components of self are compromised or under threat, is a prerogative our culture gives to men. Many sectors in our society, fueled by a vision of masculine honor and pride, tacitly permit or even valorize the ramping up of power demonstrated in direct action or threat of action. Patriarchal assumptions produce templates of permission and expectation that drive men to express power in ways that mark them as masculine. Sociologist Michael Kimmel has developed the concept of "aggrieved entitlement": ultimately, when one's assumed rights are threatened, one's aggression toward an available scapegoat can escalate from self-righteous mocking to violent rage.

The characterization of men as people of action more than talk or relationship limits a broader, richer envisioning of the lives of men and boys. As important as action is, the faulty belief that men are less capable of softer relational skills dumbs down expectations, inhibits nurture of boys as relational beings, and relieves men of the challenges of stretching their default position to include vulnerabilities and complexities of human connection. Actions that inform healthy identity can also become merit markers that reward those who perform well and in acceptable ways and crush those who do not measure up to prevailing standards of masculinity.

Recognition

Closely related to action, especially for men, recognition is the component of self-identity that places our well-being in the hands

---

4 United States Department of Labour Bureau of Labor Statistics, Economic News Release, Table 1.
5 "Football High."

of others. Humans generally long to be valued by those around us, especially by our family and friends. The quantity and quality of that recognition feeds our souls, and we rise to opportunities to impress others with our personalities and our abilities. Warm and supportive response from others, even a smile or a kind word from a stranger, inspires a sense of belonging and being valued, bringing out the best of our humanity as we reciprocate with similar recognition for those around us. Mutuality of recognition and valuing supports our sense of dignity and self-worth, of the significance of our existence in this world, of the uniqueness of our individual expression of humanity. It inspires our pursuit of goals, soothes our pain, and leads us to welcome the stranger. Recognition by our intimate partners is an especially longed-for and powerful stabilizer of our human hearts.

A set of characteristics is valued in the members of each social environment, and contravention of these values usually leads to criticism, distancing, and even exclusion. Early on, children strive to comply with the expectations that lead to affirming responses from parents and other important people in their lives and to avoid the frowns or punishments they incur when they stray. Although the complexity of this compliance-contravention dance evolves over our lifetimes, no one is exempt from the effects of the ways those around us recognize us. This powerful influence in our lives provides healthy instruction in learning to get along with others and live in harmony with our human community.

Masculinity as a set of values and behaviors is a prescriptive lens that determines our value as men and forms how we are recognized in the world of human interaction. As a broad vision of possibilities, the expressions of maleness represented as masculinity are a helpful template to support the development of values and behaviors that can be life-giving. As boys watch their fathers and other men in their lives, they learn what it means to be a man and emulate behaviors that bring affirmation from others. As their own impulses resonate with positive displays and expressions in other men, they yearn to embody what is valued in their family and community, and this impulse is reinforced through positive recognition.

This need for recognition plays a powerful role in enhancing human life, but inherent in it are combustible elements for men who fail to achieve the recognition they crave. Recognition can be merit based, and failure to reach acceptable levels of merit, or to receive recognition for what we believe we deserve, can crush our sense of self. Masculinity itself can be seen as a performance, with markers defining what men must achieve and maintain. If one is exposed as lacking in key areas of masculine prowess—or for many the dreaded idenfication with some feminine characteristic (e.g., throwing "like a girl")—the effect can be shattering. The resulting shame and humiliation can deflate all sense of self-esteem and hope, and those who experience it may become self-destructive and resort to unhealthy coping through addictive pursuits or isolation from others. For too many men, in increasing numbers, suicide becomes a way out.

While some men turn inward or away from others in their shame, others react by escalating their defense of self through the inflation of their egos and demonstrations intended to elicit appreciation from those around them. Terrence Real describes this phenomenon: "A common defense against the painful experience of deflated value is inflated value; and a common compensation for shame, for feeling less than, is a subtle or flagrant flight into grandiosity, or feeling better than."[6] A soothing of this sense of failure through gaining acknowledgment from others can ease this angst, but failure to gain that acknowledgment leads to ever-increasing attempts to achieve, demand, or even compel recognition from others. In an often-repeated pattern, men employ escalating amounts of pressure, intimidation, and eventually violence to win recognition from others. This dynamic underlies a significant portion of violence perpetrated by men who are seeking recognition and reacting to perceived threats to their selfhood.

Pervasive messages about the respect men should expect from this world fuel much of the offense men feel about perceived lack of recognition. These messages suggest that men are entitled to deference from others, especially women and people "below them" in position or power. If they assume that the context for gaining value is a zero-sum game in which losers leave with nothing, men may posture and clamor for recognition in a contest that pits them against each other. When a critical sense of self rides on this pursuit of recognition, and society gives permission and even honor to men who express their bravado aggressively, we should not be surprised when violence is the result.

Ultimately, a man who perceives that he has failed to gain recognition in the socially acceptable ways and who is deeply wounded by rejection (although often unable to name or acknowl-

---

6 Real, *I Don't Want to Talk about It*, 55.

edge this wound) begins to find justification for punishing the source of the offense or anyone representing that wounding. The deeper the pain and offense, the greater the violence he believes is warranted, and his enraged mind sees as inconsequential the collateral damage to bystanders or those who attempt to prevent him from carrying out this vengeance.

Given the vulnerabilities and sensitivities of our sexual selves as humans, such men may turn to sexualized violence as a particularly attractive tool for humiliating and punishing those they perceive as a threat to their sense of entitlement to respect and for building up their egos by conquering others.

These dynamics play out individually and collectively. Together, men pump up each other's sense of entitlement and offense, inciting each other to prove their worth and value, and punishing offenders. This collective response can include punishing men who challenge or undermine group standards of masculinity. The brotherhood holds great power of recognition and marginalization, with attendant sacrifice to maintain inclusion. The alternative is to be willing to go it alone or find another reference group able to provide the needed recognition.

Security

Personal physical safety is a basic and easily understood need and is something that humans share with all created beings. Protection from external threats to our existence is a matter of survival. For men, the traditional role of protector of others who are more vulnerable has been a source of honor. A massive industry exists to support the human quest for personal and collective safety in its many dimensions, and we highly value and fiercely defend our security. Traditionally the primary jurisdiction of men, this world of power and posturing has been an important proving ground for qualities associated with masculinity, and it is an arena in which millions of men's lives have been extinguished. Whether in protecting against threats in the natural environment or against human enemies on the battlefield, men have offered themselves out of chivalrous concern for others, to secure their own privilege and survival, and in pursuit of the recognition gained through bravery and sacrifice. The adulation given for courage and heroism is an intoxicating draw for boys and men.

Human security, though, is much broader than physical protection from injury and death. Human existence requires meeting physical needs for food, shelter, and clothing, and for emotional and psychological security. Community, family, and individual well-being entails respect for human rights, including rights to think independently, gather with others, and practice one's religion. As we have moved from basic sustenance and survival in earlier eras of human existence, our broader expectations about security of persons have required greater exercise of ingenuity and initiative. Men have pursued the expansion of human life to all corners of the globe, where they have sought to create conditions in which their dependents can thrive. In a world of limited resources, security for one group has often meant scarcity for others, and men have traditionally been tasked with defending their group's advantage, even when it has meant maiming and killing outsiders. This role, repeated through thousands of generations of men, has molded a male identity that is ingrained and persistent and underlies a male propensity to use force.

We won't attempt to sort out how much this propensity for violence is innate and how much is the result of formative messaging, but the reality is that reliance on aggression and violence is integral to masculine culture. Whether arising from noble impulses to advance our species or from less noble drives to protect privilege for self or compatriots, perpetuating violence in a quest for security for some undermines security for all.

Connectedness

According to attachment theory, strong bonds with caregivers from the earliest stages of human life through adolescence are indispensable for the genesis of a healthy self.[7] The interactions of dependent children with responsive caregivers nurture connectedness, dependability, and trust, allowing them to explore their surroundings secure in the knowledge that their caregiver will be there to protect and sustain them. Out of their attunement to their children, parents offer love, encouragement, support, and instruction, increasing their children's confidence, success, knowledge, sense of meaning, and ultimately assurance of their value to others. When this context is healthy, they emerge from this incubator of development as strong and independent adults, with a richness of identity, a knowledge of self as separate from but interconnected with others, and an ability to form healthy relationships and join in collaborative activities of life in community.

---

7 Johnson, *Love Sense*, 32–33.

While we may assume that such nurture is more important in the lives of girls and women, boys and men are no less in need of connection and no less able—at least at birth—to experience healthy connection. Societal assumptions about masculinity and about differences between boys and girls lead to subtle and not-so-subtle carving out of the very dimensions of humanity in boys and men that make for healthy connecting. As is documented in Terry Real's *I Don't Want to Talk About It* (a book that I recommend to many men who come to me for counseling), "studies indicate that from the moment of birth, boys are spoken to less than girls, comforted less, nurtured less. Passive trauma in boys is rarely extreme; it is however pervasive."[8] Real continues, "Boys 'become' men by lopping off, or having lopped off, the most sensitive parts of their psychic and, in some cases, physical selves. The passage from boyhood to manhood is about ritual wounding. It is about giving up those parts of the self that do not fit within the confines of the roles."[9] Truncating these aspects of experience stunts the development of emotional intelligence in boys and men and sets them up for relational chaos and wounding. These experiences further reinforce aversion to vulnerability, that elusive though essential ingredient in human closeness and intimacy.

Too often lacking skills required to form and maintain healthy relationships, and despite being taught that they should not depend on others for their well-being, men live with the confusing reality of their longing for connection with others. These natural yearnings struggle to find expression in relationships with other men and with women, both in friendship and in more intimate forms. Norms delimiting acceptable expressions of affection between men make showing warmth awkward, which creates a conundrum for men who find themselves attracted romantically to other men. Historically, societal condemnation of such relationships, enforced in law (secular and religious) and vigilante justice, have pushed gay men into the margins, into denial, and ultimately for many, into suicide. These societal sanctions also lead heterosexual men to fear being identified as gay, were they to develop close relationships with other men. They fear the optics of often-stereotyped emotional and behavioral displays that could make them targets of scorn and even physical violence.

8 Real, *I Don't Want to Talk about It*, 110.
9 Real, *I Don't Want to Talk about It*, 132.

Boys and men are schooled in a set of expectations and entitlements that are to characterize their intimate relationships. Whether these scripts are internalized through role modeling and messaging by parents and other adults in their lives or perhaps with more impact through portrayals in media, boys enter teen years and young adulthood pumped on hormones and full of anticipation, feeling natural and healthy impulses to connect with an intimate other. Variable in personalities, abilities, and confidence, boys carry internal longings and social expectations that propel them into the world of romance and connecting. The traditional moral frameworks that guide these activities have developed in a patriarchal context, and the attendant ideals are applied and enforced unequally for men and women. The result is a situation that involves both privilege and precariousness for young men. Assumptions about male dominance and the centrality of genital sexual expression skew these pursuits toward conquest ("scoring") and status.[10] Presumptions of entitlement, combined with a sense of shame surrounding failure to prove one's masculinity in this area, can trigger desperation and even violent attack on any—usually women—perceived to be the source of the humiliation.

The limited emotional palette characteristic of immature masculinity and a dearth of socially sanctioned supports and outlets, leave many men struggling in relationships. Confronted by the relative emotional and relational strength of women (the outcome of female socialization or the variabilities of emotional health in their partners), men strive to build their relational edifices on foundations that are often precarious. Empathy, that ability to genuinely feel with another human by entering into their experience, is sometimes in especially short supply as a result of curtailed emotional development in boys and men. With this relative lack in their relational toolbox, many men are limited in their ability to be sensitive to others, and they operate out of internal impulses without the regulating effect of the feedback of others. Relational struggles result in feelings of insecurity, loneliness, embarrassment, shame, and fear that—combined with a limited ability to tune in to and name their feeling states—leave men emotionally distressed and lost. Reticent to seek assistance that would demand vulnerability, many "lead lives of quiet desperation," as Henry David Thoreau once put it.

The wounds resulting from neglectful or traumatic relationships in childhood and an accumulation of struggles associated

---

10 See the section on "recognition" above.

with efforts to reach healthy outcomes in platonic and intimate relationships leave many men troubled and searching for ways to soothe their pain. They turn to readily available substances (drugs, alcohol, food) and activities (gambling, risk taking, porn, sex, and even rage) to medicate their hurt and regulate unacceptable feeling states. The resulting addictions, much more prevalent in men than in women, bring only fleeting relief and high costs for men and those around them. Addictions specialist Gabor Mate says, "The first question is always not 'Why the addiction?,' it's 'Why the pain?'"[11] A further testimony to the critical linkage between addictions and men's relational challenges is the growing understanding that "the opposite of addiction is not sobriety; the opposite of addiction is connection."[12] The route to healing is through development of healthy relational skills and nurturing healthy connection with others.[13]

Meaning

As we turn to the next category, meaning, we begin to see how interconnected the five dimensions of Vern Neufeld Redekop's human identity needs framework are. Action, recognition, connectedness, and security each inform meaning and are informed by meaning. Although the components are universal, the needs satisfiers are specific to particular groups and even individuals and are flavored by a vast array of influences. The beliefs and values that we associate with male existence, collectively known as masculinity, occur on a wide continuum, and in myriad ways they support healthy emotional and relational existence or undermine it. Even the term *healthy* is value based, and the meanings people give to the word differ widely. The relative weight given to various ideas about masculinity inform parenting and general socialization, which provide a growing boy with the meaning he is to take on in his life as a male. To varying extents, male children and youth consciously or unconsciously accept these values as their own, and these values are in turn manifested in behaviors and create meaning for them.

In the last half-century, in many sectors of North American society, the traditional meanings given to male existence have been under significant critique, and resulting changes have unsettled previously accepted expressions of masculinity. Old assumptions

11 Maté, "What Is Addiction?"
12 Hari, "Everything You Think You Know."
13 Johnson, *Love Sense.*

and beliefs about male dominance and privilege have been directly challenged by women seeking equality and by marginalized people who have exposed the injustices perpetrated especially by white male power. Globalization and accompanying social and economic trends have brought a blurring of the relatively rigid boundaries and markers that used to define and differentiate people, and one outcome for men is what might be called a loss of job description. In some sectors of society, these changes have been especially disturbing and have provoked a backlash, an attempt to revert to more traditional ways of being men. For others, these radical changes have made room for the emergence of creativity and freedom. Some embrace the new meanings, and some resist, while others are simply overwhelmed and trying to find their way. Organizations advocating for men voice critiques of or support for these changes while challenging a perceived injustice men are experiencing with the emergence of a new order. In a context in which the road ahead is not well marked out, conscious engagement with beliefs, values, and expressions of masculinity becomes more necessary. Regardless of where we come out in our understanding of maleness, taking up these challenges constitutes an important opportunity.

Christian beliefs and values are a significant source of meaning for many men, particularly in explicitly Christian communities and families but also residually in society at large in North America. Certain understandings about men's roles and responsibilities, especially relative to corresponding beliefs about women, have dominated expressions of masculinity through the centuries of European settlement in North America.[14] The lessening of the influence of these dominant narratives, under the barrage of critique both external (from secular sources and other religious traditions) and internal (from, for example, Christian feminist and queer theology), has brought both resistance and embrace. A variety of organizations loosely fitting under the umbrella of the Christian men's movement have represented a reassertion of traditional positions, calling men back to "real manhood."

A social worker therapist's perspective

Through over twenty-five years of practice as a social worker, I have tracked with interest a growing attention to gender justice and men's experiences of self and relationship. My undergraduate

---

14 For fuller account of these influences, see the chapters in this volume by Jamie Pitts and Tom Yoder Neufeld.

education in theology and social sciences and my graduate education in social work took place in progressive and feminist-informed settings. My faith community and family experiences were all relatively open to new understandings about the roles of men and women and included a strongly egalitarian leaning. I welcome the positive values that undergird most of these developments and appreciate the implications for women and marginalized groups.

At the same time, I am increasingly aware that corresponding work for healthy change for men has been lacking, and the general atmosphere of suspicion toward men has not invited us to participate in the process of change. A broad characterization of men as motivated individually and collectively by a desire to maintain their power and control by dominating women and minorities fails to adequately differentiate between universal human need in men's lives and the "misguided blueprint for living"[15] that underlies men's frequently inadequate and often tragic attempts to meet those needs. The characterization of male motivation as primarily self-serving and as disregarding the humanity of others and the labeling of masculinity as "toxic" rely on shaming men into contrition and ultimately produce resistance to healthy change.

In *Becoming Ethical*, Alan Jenkins puts it this way:

> Here we must recognize a distinction between *shaming* and *facing shame*. When a man faces shame, he comes to his own realizations through recognizing a contradiction between his ethics and his actions. By contrast, shaming others is a political act, an attempt to coerce or compel through the attribution of shame and, not surprisingly, tends to further exacerbate avoidance of responsibility. Our work cannot be ethical if it employs shaming practices. Our job is to provide *safe passage* to assist the man to discover and face the inevitable sense of shame which will accompany his own realisations about the nature and effects of his abusive practices.[16]

This approach—inviting men to own their behavior by providing a safe environment through the avoidance of shaming practices—has informed my therapeutic practice and inspired my advocacy for men. Acknowledging and nurturing men's longings for healthy selfhood, while holding men accountable for their poor

---

15 Jenkins, *Becoming Ethical*, 4.
16 Jenkins, *Becoming Ethical*, 20 (italics original).

choices and harmful behaviors, gives them the dignity of their humanity and provides opportunity for healthy change. Development of respectful relationships becomes a context for engaging in difficult discussions about the need to dismantle systems of patriarchy and assumptions of privilege.

The above survey of human identity and the exploration of healthy and unhealthy manifestations of masculinity bent on fulfilling those needs provide a grounding for a compassionate response to men. The irony in my work with men is that, despite all the displays of strength and privilege in pursuit of security that have been the purview of men through the centuries, they experience great insecurities. An awareness that a significant portion of the bad behavior of men is compensation for, and effort to ward off, such insecurities leads us to embrace another approach to change. We find fertile ground for nurturing change by empowering men through fostering healthy values for self and others and teaching tools of empathy and connecting, in the context of affirming their core longings for well-being.

I began this chapter by reflecting on the biblical theme of healthy human dependency on Creator and with creation and by setting out the framework of human identity needs theory, which also points to our interdependence with others, with our environment, and with God. One tragic result of the traditional messages about masculinity has been that many men are unable to recognize their neediness, and are averse to expressing need ("I don't need to stop and ask directions!"), with the result that they are isolated, suffer in silence, display reactive anger, and even resort to suicide. Our loving Parent has created us for and invites us to relationship with Godself, with the creation God has so abundantly provisioned, and with each other. Responding to this invitation requires the humility that recognizes our neediness as humans, a step that is especially difficult when we are burdened by the assumptions of traditional masculinity.

Believing and affirming that we are created as needful beings, we can rest in the conviction that God delights in seeing us thrive in the healthy filling of our needs. We can also reject the deceiver's attempts to persuade us to pursue alternatives that bring only fleeting or precarious satisfaction of those needs. As a Christian faith community, our mission is to embody God's invitation, God's welcome. We are to reflect the character of our God, whose grace is unmerited and whose love is unconditional.

I am grateful to have been immersed all my life in the Anabaptist theological tradition, which emphasizes how God works in our lives through community, calling us to faithful discipleship and offering us peace as a path and an outcome. I believe these emphases are particularly helpful for linking our understandings of Christian faith with our human needfulness. They are particularly suited to addressing men's experiences of need and fulfillment.

Community

Where traditional ideas about masculinity lead men toward isolation and independence, community offers connectedness through belonging and inclusion within diversity, affirmation of interdependency and mutuality, a context for teaching and dialogue that inform meaning, a recognition that comes with being loved unconditionally and affirmed in the use of our gifts, and a place to contribute to a larger good alongside our brothers and sisters.

Discipleship

A response to God's unmerited grace, rather than the attempt to achieve God's approval through merit, discipleship releases men to welcome opportunities to learn and grow, in the belief that healthy fulfillment of needs is not about competition for a scarce resource. Discipleship enhances meaning in men's lives, gives definition to action in the context of personal and corporate mission, makes accountability operational, and encourages living faithfully in community.

Peace

In a societal context of duplicitous and inconsistent messages about the efficacy of violence, a Christian message of peace offers a consistent vision for peace as an inner gift of God through salvation that produces both the means and the end of living peaceably with our neighbors. This peaceableness rests on a radical re-visioning of the nature of security, a broadening of action to include peacemaking, and an enhancement of our sense connectedness with all humanity, including our enemies.

The following pages of this volume flesh out the implications of these Anabaptist faith perspectives for our lives as men and help us more fully envision what healthy masculinity looks like. Although I am under no illusion that this effort will end bad behavior by men and bring endless contentment, I do believe that it can put men in a healthier place, able to live with more joy and satisfaction, and empowered to come alongside women and oppressed peoples in undertaking the good work of bringing greater levels of justice and well-being for all.

Bibliography

Boyd, Greg. "The Heavenly Missionary," in sermon series "Cross Centered," Woodland Hills Church, St. Paul, MN, March 26, 2017, http://whchurch.org/sermons-media/sermon-series/cross-centered

"Football High: High School Football Has Never Had a Higher Profile . . . but Is Winning Worth the Risks?" PBS Frontline video, April 2011, http://www.pbs.org/wgbh/pages/frontline/football-high/

Hari, Johann. "Everything You Think You Know about Addiction Is Wrong," TEDGlobalLondon, https://www.ted.com/talks/johann_hari_everything_you_think_you_know_about_addiction_is_wrong.

Jenkins, Alan. *Becoming Ethical: A Parallel, Political Journey with Men Who Have Abused.* Dorset, England: Russell, 2009.

Johnson, Sue. *Love Sense: The Revolutionary New Science of Romantic Relationships.* New York: Little, Brown, 2013.

Maté, Gabe. "What Is Addiction?" YouTube, https://www.youtube.com/watch?v=T5sOh4gKPIg.

Real, Terrence. *I Don't Want to Talk about It: Overcoming the Secret Legacy of Male Depression.* New York: Scribner, 1997.

Redekop, Vern Neufeld. *From Violence to Blessing: How an Understanding of Deep-Rooted Conflict Can Open Paths to Reconciliation.* Ottawa, ON: Novalis, 2002.

United States Department of Labour Bureau of Labor Statistics. Economic News Release. Table 1: Fatal Occupational Injuries Counts and Rates by Demographic Characteristics, 2015–16, https://www.bls.gov/news.release/.

Chapter 2

Masculinities
Interdisciplinary Orientations

Jamie Pitts

What makes a man a man? Is it his body, his genitals and chromosomes, his muscles and brain? Is it some essential difference from women, from boys, or even from less "manly" men? How do economic status and race and religion define him as a man? What kind of sexual inclinations and activities make a man a man? Can people born with female genitalia become men by changing their clothes, their social roles, their bodies?

Although most cultures throughout history have used the categories "men" and "women" to identify humans and distinguish between them, their answers to these questions have varied. As the order of the questions indicates, Western culture tends to define men and women in the first place through medical descriptions of bodies. But when people have sought to determine what makes a man a man or a woman a woman, cultural descriptions—of a person's race, class, religion, or personal history, for example—have always been intertwined with biological ones.

More broadly, the category "gender" has been used since the mid-twentieth century to refer to the biological material of our bodies, their structure and capacities, as well as to cultural norms for bodies: about how bodies can and should be, about what they should and should not do. Attitudes and acts related to biological reproduction (reproductive organs, sexual attraction and intercourse, childbearing and child rearing) are usually central to how we define gender, but so are practices related to social reproduction. How we engage in our society's efforts to sustain and reproduce itself (work, education, government, war, art, etc.) is highly gendered: our engagement in these efforts is channeled along gendered lines, and our engagement tells others about our gender.

Answers to questions such as *What makes a man a man?* are, therefore, highly complex and require attention to multiple disciplines and arenas of inquiry. The answers, moreover, are unlikely to be definitive: they are likely to vary at least somewhat across cultures and times. If even our understanding of our bodies' biological material is culturally dependent (as I will explain in more detail later), then so is our understanding of gender.

I realize that a complex, dynamic, and culturally specific definition of gender may raise some anxieties as it opens the possibility of challenging long-held notions, cherished roles, and established practices. At the same time, I hope that readers of this book will receive this definition as good news. If gender is complex, dynamic, and culturally specific, then ancient patterns of organizing society and defining individuals along gendered lines may be open to change. For example, the common equation of men with domination and violence need not be the last word. Mennonite and other men can explore what it means to be men who are peaceful at heart.

In this chapter, I examine this understanding of gender and, specifically, of masculinity (cultural conceptions of what makes a man a man) through an interpretive summary of recent research from several disciplines: history, sociology, anthropology, biology, and theology. By interpretive summary, I mean that I will attempt to summarize the recent research, but not simply as a list. I will organize my summary to support the thesis that there are multiple masculini*ties*—that there are and have been multiple and often conflicting answers to questions about what makes a man a man, and that these answers depend on a variety of factors specific to particular times and places. Masculinity, like other identity traits, is to an important extent constructed by our society's assumptions about sex, gender, bodies, and social roles. Since there are different societies constructing masculine identities, there are different masculinities (and, as we will see, multiple masculinities within a particular society). Although we cannot simply choose willy-nilly among these masculinities, we can do the hard work of transforming our own masculinities to exhibit the fruit of the Spirit (Gal. 5:22–23)—and trust that the Spirit is enabling and guiding this work.

The chapter is organized in three parts. In the first part, I discuss the relationship between biological and cultural designations of maleness and manhood through a discussion of birth certificates. I then turn in the second part to examine the role of iconic masculinities—icons held up as masculine exemplars—and related masculinities. In the third and final part of the chapter, I provide an overview of historical Christian understandings of masculinity, especially in relation to sexuality. In each part I draw on a range of interdisciplinary studies, as well as my own experiences of becoming a man in late twentieth- and early twenty-first-century North

America. My experience, of course, is limited, and the reader should consult other sources—including the other essays in this volume—in order to develop a fuller picture of men and masculinities.

Birth certificates and the body

I was born in 1980 at St. Luke's Episcopal Hospital in Houston, Texas. My birth certificate, issued by the State of Texas, makes several claims about me: in addition to listing the time, date, and place of my birth, it says that my sex is male, my race is white, and that I was born to married parents who were themselves born in the United States. How am I to understand these claims? Are they indisputable and unchangeable biological facts about me? Would a birth record from a different era make different claims about me? If so, then would those claims change who I am?

Before addressing those questions, I want to consider who made the claims on my birth certificate. The doctor whose name and title are included on the certificate presumably filled out a form about me, and this form was sent to state authorities for processing. The authorized certificate was then sent to my parents, and it remains in my possession. The certificate serves nostalgic purposes, but it also enables me to prove my identity and citizenship in order to get a United States passport or a Social Security card, apply for government benefits, and so on. Notice how both in the certificate's origins—state-certified medical staff and state institutions—and in its later use, it is ultimately the government that guarantees that I am who the paper says I am. It is the government that claims I was born in a major urban center in the United States, that I am a white male, and that I come from married American parents. For many significant practical purposes, the government's claims about my identity are taken at face value.

We may see the state's collection of such information and its issuance of vital records as one of a child's earliest initiations into a specific identity. The child's identity is, to an important extent, constructed by state statistics: the child's future rests in part on being identified and identifiable as a citizen of a specific country, as of a certain race and sex, as having married parents, and so on. The state's claims about the newborn are claims about that newborn's identity, claims that will shape much of the newborn's life. The claims initiate the newborn into an enduring identity.

It might be objected that the state is simply recording facts about newborns—birth certificates report facts—and not constructing or initiating anything. The difficulty in accepting this view is that birth certificates and their categories have a history.[1] Most countries did not begin keeping vital statistics until the nineteenth century. The United States only began doing so in a uniform way in 1902.

The category of race used in government recordkeeping is notoriously malleable, reflecting various cultural assumptions and prejudices. (More broadly, the widespread use of racial categories is tied to the history of European colonization.) Until 1989, the US government determined a baby's race by the race (or national origin) of the parents. If the parents were of different races, and one of the parents was white, then the baby was assigned the nonwhite race. If neither of the parents was white, then the baby was assigned the father's race—unless the mother was Hawaiian or part Hawaiian, and then the baby was counted as Hawaiian. After 1989, the mother's race was used to determine the baby's race. Clearly, race is not a simple category to be read off of a child's body.

Can we say the same about biological sex? Most babies are born with either male or female genitalia. Male sex organs include the penis, scrotum, and testicles, and female organs include the clitoris, vulva, and vagina. These organs can be identified without thorough examination. Yet some children are born intersex, with any of several variations in sex characteristics that do not fit binary male/female categories.[2] For much of history, intersex people were identified from birth as the gender their external organs most resembled, but since the nineteenth century, surgical options have been available to make a body conform to one gender or another.

Uncertainty surrounding ambiguous genitalia led to a search for other clear biological markers for sex. Since the discovery of chromosomes and hormones in the late nineteenth and early twentieth century, both have been proposed as failsafe guides to determining sex and gender—but neither sex chromosomes nor sex hormones are simply identifiable as male or female. Recent advances in neuroscience lead some to hope to find definitive gender differences in brain structures and capacities. But men's and women's brains are very similar, and the character and the

---

1 Brumberg, Dozor, and Golombek, "History of the Birth Certificate," 407–11; National Center for Health Statistics, "Section 4—Technical Appendix," 4–6.
2 For the following information from the biological sciences, see Wiesner-Hanks, *Gender in History*, 5; Messer, "Contributions from Biology." The argument that culture irrevocably shapes how we understand bodies has been made forcefully by Judith Butler in books such as *Gender Trouble*.

significance of the slight variations are unclear. In any case, like everyone else, scientists may be guided by their assumptions about gender. The biological sciences are unlikely to provide us with unambiguous answers.

Our bodies are not endlessly malleable: we cannot avoid all pain or stop depending on food, shelter, and companionship, or sprout wings and fly. Nevertheless, it is clear that cultural patterns of gender identification and division play a major role in determining the significance of bodily differences. No straight lines can be drawn between certain body parts and, for example, a propensity to violence or emotional nurture.[3] These correlations have developed over millennia, and in somewhat different ways in different cultural settings.

Coming back to my birth certificate, we begin to see that the State of Texas's claim that I am male is not merely a biological designation; it is also a cultural designation of my gender, a designation that would shape my identity and future. The government, of course, does not act alone. I was born into a patriarchal society, and some trace of this fact is evident on my birth certificate from the fact that my mother and I have my father's last name.

Patriarchy ("rule by fathers") likely developed several thousand years ago as humans began to settle in agricultural communities. Communal settlements gave rise to property and to inheritance claims, which men tended to monopolize. This pattern probably disrupted more egalitarian patterns associated with earlier hunter-gather societies, some of which may have been led by women. Regardless, it seems that agriculture and patriarchy became dominant together, with important and enduring consequences for gender. From that time on, some specific tasks and capacities would be associated with men and others with women. Men gained long-term advantages over women in economics, politics, and cultural domains such as religion, art, and literature.

My birth certificate thus initiated me into a gender identity associated with certain social positions and forms of power. From birth I was identified as male, with all the privileges, possibilities, and limitations that designation has in our male-dominant society. Similar comments could be made about how my birth certificate identified me racially ("white"), as an American citizen, and more subtly, as belonging to a certain socioeconomic class (visible in my parents' address). These identifications were perpetuated by

---

3 On men and violence, see Edwards, "Femenism."

myriad other practices. To keep the focus on gender: my family and friends would dress me in blue, not pink; provide me with toy guns, not dolls; and praise me as handsome and strong, not pretty and delicate.[4] But even if those practices had varied, the state's identification of me would be almost unshakeable.

Masculine icons: Fathers and sons, women and stars

The term "masculinity" began to be used to define manly character in the eighteenth century. Prior to the eighteenth century, terms such as "manly," "manful," and "manhood" were more widely employed to designate personality characteristics that men were expected to exhibit and practices they were to engage in.

Norms for masculinity develop through comparisons among men (and males) and between men and women. In most cultures, the distinction between men and boys is crucial—boys become men in various ways—as are distinctions among "manly men" and men who are judged as less manly (as more like women) because of their occupation, socioeconomic status, citizenship status, race, bodily characteristics (for instance, penis size, stature, musculature, or voice pitch), interests, or behavior (especially sexual interests and behavior). Different profiles of ideal or normative masculinity develop in different cultures and become standards against which men and others in those cultures are measured and evaluated.

Some of these ideals are shared among many of the world's cultures and in many times and places, while others vary widely and change more or less rapidly. The existence of multiple ideals of masculinity—and multiple ways of varying from and resisting the ideal—leads scholars to talk about "masculinities," the many and sometimes conflicting ways of embodying manliness.

One way to think about ideal masculinity is to think about masculine icons, the distinct masculine images or sets of masculine characteristics a given culture holds up as ideal.[5] These characteristics can include high socioeconomic status, great physical strength and intellectual ability, sexual prowess, and specific racial identities. Masculine icons are emblems of the elite, and elite men tend to perpetuate their culture's icons in order to preserve their own status. Recent North American icons include white collar men

---

4 In the first half of the twentieth century, pink and blue were both used for North American girls and boys, and some sources insisted that pink as the "stronger" color should be the primary color of boys' clothing. See Paoletti, "Pink Is for Boys."
5 Yarrow, "Masculinity as a World Historical Category of Analysis," 114–38.

who combine technical rationality (scientific, political, or business knowledge) and competitive cunning and movie and sports stars whose performances of strength and daring earn them luxury lifestyles. Working class masculinities tend to become iconic at a culture-wide level only when filtered through media and celebrity.

Fatherhood in many cultures is held up as a core marker of masculine identity: to be a real man, you have to be a father. Boys are taught to imitate their fathers, and fatherhood is an assumed part of many versions of iconic masculinity. Fathers are instructed in how to perform their role, though this instruction—and the character of iconic fatherhood—has varied widely over time. Are fathers meant to be stern and aloof or warm and available? Our media and our families hold up both kinds of fathers as masculine icons.

A central component of most societies' icons of fatherhood is successful participation in patriarchal society. In North America, iconic fathers are "breadwinners": they are sexually potent husbands, heads of households, and gainfully employed homeowners. Their families bear their names, names passed down through the generations, along with property and wealth.

In spite of their evident power, masculine icons do not dominate unilaterally. Rather, in a given time and place there may be multiple, competing masculine icons. It is also likely that most men are not iconic; they do not live up to their culture's masculine ideals. Some of these men are liable to support and pursue iconic masculinity, some will resist the icons of their day, and some will acquiesce in their marginal status. All these responses to masculine icons contribute to making masculinity dynamic and changing.[6]

My life can be narrated as a series of responses of veneration for a succession of masculine icons, starting with my father. He is a lawyer, and at an early age I wanted to be a lawyer, too. I was particularly drawn to the intellectual prestige and power associated with graduating from a top university and law school and mastering legal argumentation. But other icons took center stage as I became more involved with school and media. The walls of my childhood bedroom were covered with posters of male athletes, representing physical and financial power far beyond that of my familial exemplars. I later developed intense interests in films about war, gangs, and the American West; in first-person shooter computer games; and in a wide variety of musicians, most of them male. These sources gave me icons who constructed and reinforced my

---

6 Connell, *Masculinities*, 76–81.

sense that to be a man was to be physically powerful and capable of violent domination; intuitively and individualistically intelligent and creative; (hetero)sexually successful; wealthy and famous (or trying to be!); and, in everything, competitive and highly conscience of image and status.

This sense of masculinity was complicated and eventually undermined by some of the very icons who contributed to its emergence. For example, I admired black musicians from Marvin Gaye to Mos Def who criticized white supremacy, war, and economic exploitation. Similarly, interactions with women—from my mother to school friends to feminist authors and colleagues—and with sexual minorities helped me begin to interrogate the ways many features of my masculine icons promoted the subordination of such people.

Iconic masculinity tends to be arrayed against women and anyone who can be denigrated as "feminine." In contemporary North America, this latter category usually includes some of the following: gay and bisexual men, trans men, single men, men who are not fathers, men who become fathers out of wedlock, poor and unemployed men, immigrants, men who are not considered white, and men with disabilities. Public discourse and private insults often associate these men with women, casting them as "effeminate" or as undeveloped, unmanly "boys." In many versions of iconic masculinity, women are to be conquered and controlled, and womanly men are to be humiliated and dominated.

The concept of masculine icons can help us understand how answers to the question *What makes a man a man?* will vary depending on time and place. There is no one basic pattern of masculinity that we can identify in a given cultural setting. Rather, there are multiple masculinities, some of which become associated with a dominant male elite and so achieve iconic status; other masculinities can be described in relation to iconic masculinities—as complicit with it, as subordinated and marginalized by it, or as resistant to it. There can be conflict among a culture's icons, and how a given individual relates to conflicting icons opens up certain possibilities for change and forecloses others.

Christianity, sexuality, and masculinity

Up to this point I have omitted discussion of Christianity and of my own Christian faith. That omission has enabled me to discuss a wide range of other sociological factors that shape masculinity, such as the state, family, media, and the arts. I could, however, have written about church practices of initiating bodies into manhood—through baptism, for instance. Before the state began to track vital statistics in the nineteenth century, most birth records in the West were collected by churches at baptism. Infant baptism identifies children with a specific name—often one that bears the marks of patriarchal naming conventions—and gender and religious identity. (Baptism is called christening in some traditions.) I could also have written about Christian masculine icons—pastors, youth leaders, mentors, missionaries, Christian musicians, and so on—or about how Christian identity has been a significant feature of many masculine icons.

In what follows I instead provide a brief history of Christianity and masculinity, focusing especially on the relationship between Christian understandings of masculinity and sexuality. Icons will be a feature of the account, but I emphasize historical developments—again in conversation with my personal story—in order to display continuities and divergences in one tradition's conception of masculinity over time. Since the editors, authors, and intended readers of this book are identified in some way with the Christian tradition, it is particularly important to grasp this history. My hope is that this section will help readers better comprehend how their faith has shaped their understanding of gender and gain some tools for enriching and transforming this understanding. I begin with a short sketch of my experience of Christianity, gender, and sexuality as a teenager and then move to put this sketch in historical context.

I became deeply involved with my Episcopal church's youth group after a conversion experience when I was eleven years old, in 1991, during the so-called culture wars that pitted conservative Christians against liberal ones. Although my church did not major in the culture wars, anxieties around key conservative issues including abortion, sexual mores, and school prayer were never far from the surface. I left the Episcopal church for a nondenominational charismatic church when I was seventeen, but the message about sex, sexuality, and gender that I took away from these conservative churches was similar.

In brief, that message was that sexual intercourse, most other romantic touching, and even sexual thoughts were to be reserved exclusively for marriage between a man and a woman. (I have attended weddings where the couples' first kiss was at the altar.) Prior to marriage, any sexual experience, any sexual desire, was viewed as sinful. This conviction posed a problem for men in particular.

Men, I learned, are possessed and indeed defined by their desire to seek sexual stimulation as often as possible. Men compulsively indulge in sexual fantasy ("lust"), masturbation, pornography, and even sexual intercourse outside of marriage. We were taught that all Christians should set their sights on marriage, and we were promised that within its bonds our sexual appetites would be fulfilled. When focused entirely on a marriage partner, those appetites would no longer be sinful—but until we married, we had to wage war against the temptation that constantly besieges men.

On the other hand, women were depicted as having little or no sex drive but instead were defined by their desire for emotional connection. This desire could lead women to make themselves sexually available outside of marriage, against their better judgment, but any such sexual contact would be extremely damaging to them spiritually and emotionally. Men were not in the same kind of danger, but all premarital sexual activity would create lasting bonds to past partners that would haunt the marital bed. I frequently heard testimonies from older teens and young adults about how God had freed them from lust and the legacies of past sexual relationships.

The message I heard has deep roots both in Christian tradition and in broader cultural attempts to make sense of the complex realities associated with sex, attraction, desire, and gender. But these are not the only roots in our history.[7] The strangeness of the message I heard becomes evident when we compare it to past precedent.

We start with a brief review of the New Testament and its background. The first thing to point out is that ancient Christians, like ancient Jews, Greeks, and Romans, had understandings of sex and gender very different from ours. They believed there was one physical sex that could manifest itself in two genders, with a spectrum of possibilities defined in terms of heat, activity, and perfection (men were hotter, more active, and more perfect).[8] Something like this "one-sex" view lies behind the Genesis creation stories, with their claims that men and women alike are created in God's image (1:27) and that men and women are partners who are related as

---

7 For overviews of the biblical and historical material, see Thatcher, ed., *Oxford Handbook of Theology, Sexuality, and Gender,* chapters 11–19; Wiesner-Hanks, *Gender in History,* 121–26.

8 Men were viewed as capable of losing their manliness and becoming slaves, barbarians, or even women—a real possibility, if you share a single sex. This perspective was supported by the common idea that women's genitals are simply the inverse of men's. The ancient one-sex theory was displaced in recent centuries by the view that there are two sexes that correspond to two genders. See Thatcher, *God, Sex, and Gender,* 6–14.

closely as possible to each other (2:18–24).[9] Only after the first couple's disobedience does hierarchy between men and women come into play (3:16), suggesting that patriarchal domination is an effect of sin, not intrinsic to God's purposes for humanity.

Tom Yoder Neufeld's chapter in this volume treats the delicate topics of God's and Jesus's masculinities, so I will limit my comments here to noting the following: (a) God is not a biological, sexed being, so gendered descriptions of God are inherently metaphorical (and we must attend to biblical depictions of God that draw on feminine imagery); (b) God's "fatherhood" in Scripture explicitly undermines human patriarchies;[10] (c) salvation in Christ is not gendered but is open to all through the shared path of discipleship; and (d) Jesus disrupted many of his society's assumptions about masculinity—for instance by remaining single and at times downplaying the importance of marriage, by speaking with women as equals, by weeping openly, and by being executed by the state as a criminal.

Jesus's legacy of complex masculinity shaped his movement and the churches that came out of it. Paul seems to have followed Jesus's teaching on marriage, as evident in the strong preference he expresses for singleness (1 Cor. 7), and he included women missionaries and leaders in his evangelistic movement. Many readers therefore take Galatians 3:28 ("There is no longer male and female; for all of you are one in Christ Jesus") as a programmatic early Christian thesis on gender: gender is not a decisive identity marker for Christians. There are difficult passages in both Old and New Testaments that seem to reinforce or recommend patriarchy, and it is safe to say that the early church inherited a mixed theological legacy with regard to gender, sex, and sexuality.

As Christianity grew and eventually became the official religion of the Roman Empire, many Christians assimilated to powerful Roman cultural patterns related to gender and sexuality. For some, Christian senators and other powerful men served as masculine icons: they were effective rulers of cities, armies, their own house-

---

9 Note that the term "helper" (2:18: *ezer*), used to describe woman in the second creation story, is mostly used in the Hebrew Bible to describe God's relationship to humans (e.g., Exod. 18:4; Deut. 33:7; 33:26; 33:29), so clearly it implies no subordination.

10 God in the Bible is depicted as an adoptive (not procreative) father, in particular in the Exodus narrative in which God liberates God's children from bondage to Pharaoh and forms a covenant relationship with them as a "kingdom of priests" (Exod. 19:6). In other words, their relationship with God is no longer primarily mediated through the patriarchal lineage begun by Abraham. See McClendon, *Doctrine*, 291–93.

holds, and public affairs. But others held up as icons the strange men who fled to the Egyptian and Syrian deserts and dedicated their lives to prayer and fasting. These men, sometimes called the Desert Fathers, provided an alternative iconic Christian masculinity that became institutionalized in medieval monasteries. Iconic monks in Europe proved their manhood in their constant wrestling with sin and their bodies' desires. Castration seems to have been an option for some in the early centuries—it was condemned at the Council of Nicaea in 325—and later on, some sought to transform or even renounce their masculinity by dressing as women.

Early Christian and medieval theologians shared Paul's strong preference for celibacy and virginity over marriage, and the extremely influential writings of Augustine (354–430), bishop of Hippo, suggested an indelible link between sex and sin. Augustine and most later theologians, however, tolerated sex among married lay persons when it was limited to procreative purposes. They typically judged all nonprocreative sexual activity, even between married partners, as far more grievous than potentially procreative acts including rape and incest. Thomas Aquinas's famous *Summa Theologica* (written 1265–74) grouped nonprocreative sex acts such as masturbation, bestiality, homosexuality, and anal and oral sex in the category "sins against nature." This category, too, has had an enduring impact on Western Christian cultures and the societies they have colonized.

Among the many shifts initiated by the sixteenth-century Protestant Reformation was, in Protestant lands, the destruction of iconic monastic masculinity. This symbolic destruction followed the actual destruction of monasteries and convents across Protestant Europe. Protestant pastors were expected to be married fathers, as were almost all other men. Martin Luther's teaching on marriage would scandalize many a Protestant today, but much of his reasoning is familiar.[11] He taught that, because men and women share an innate drive to procreate, almost everyone who can procreate should get married—and it didn't really matter to whom so long as they could help you procreate and were not your sibling, parent, child, grandchild, or aunt/uncle. If your partner turned out to be impotent, then you should consider "contracting a secret marriage" that will bear fruit. Luther's views may have been extreme, but they point to the birth of a Protestant Christian culture

---

11 Luther, "The Estate of Marriage."

whose embrace of marriage and procreation was unqualified by any monastic alternative.

The Reformation coincided with the beginnings of European colonization of other parts of the world. European Christians encountered ancient cultures—some of them Christian—in Africa, Asia, and the Americas that had their own understandings of gender and sexuality. In many indigenous cultures in the Americas, for instance, some men dress as women, fulfilling special ceremonial roles or taking husbands. (Women sometimes do the same but in fewer numbers.) These are known as "two-spirit" persons whose gender is neither simply male or female: they are considered to be a third gender. Similar cases, and even cases of fourth and fifth genders, are found in many parts of the world. European colonizers tended to regard these persons as sinful "sodomites" (or homosexuals, after that term was invented in the nineteenth century) and attempted to enforce conformity to European Christian norms for gender and sexuality. More recent theological work by two-spirit Christians, sometimes done in conversation with transgender Christians, is leading to a reevaluation of the earlier judgments.

Colonialism affected Europeans as well as colonized communities. In encounters with cultures that tolerated or promoted third genders, sex between men or between women, polygamy, premarital sex, and other practices they regarded as unchristian and unnatural, European Christians tried both to reform their colonized subjects and to strengthen their own commitments to "righteous" gender and sexual norms. Renewed attention to gender and sexuality occurred in and through the newly widespread use of the category of "race" to classify populations and individuals. This category was invariably organized with white bodies at the top, black bodies at the bottom, and other bodies somewhere in between.[12] While some—especially lower class—colonial men pursued stable sexual relations with colonized women, and *many* men raped or had short-term sexual relations with them, racial classification was used throughout the colonial world to control marriage and the coinciding inheritance of property. These developments have had an enormous impact on global politics and economics and also on sexual practices and conceptions of gender. For instance, for many colonizers and their male descendants, the sexual conquest of women of color has been a mark of manhood. For their part, colonized men have been viewed as sexually vora-

---

12 Jennings, *Christian Imagination.*

cious "beasts" or as asexual and effeminate; the portrayal varies according to the needs of the colonizers. Notions of femininity, too, have been shaped by conflicts between white women and colonized and enslaved women of color.

One colonial society that has developed a distinctive vision of Christian masculinity is the United States. Historically, white American men have pursued a vision of iconic masculinity sometimes called "the self-made man."[13] This vision emerged in the aftermath of the American Revolution, during the westward expansion and accompanying genocide of indigenous Americans, and later through business ventures, sports, men's groups and clubs, arts and entertainment, and consumer goods that seek to recapture an individualistic and adventuresome spirit of manly domination. A key aspect of the genesis of the American self-made man was the confinement of women to the "domestic sphere" of childrearing, cooking, and cleaning.

Religious pursuits have at times been identified with women and domesticity, but men have also sought to take back Christian faith as a manly endeavor. This is especially the case in the movement known as muscular Christianity, which near the end of the nineteenth century began to construe discipleship as requiring the manly virtues of strength and toughness in mind, body, and spirit. Recent exemplars of muscular Christianity include the Promise Keepers organization and popular books such as *Wild at Heart* and *Every Man's Battle*. Mennonite men in the United States (and Canada) have had to define themselves in relation to this muscular Christianity—an especially tricky task, given the common labeling of nonresistance and humility as effeminate.[14] Though I did not know it by name, muscular Christianity had an impact on me through the message I heard about men, faith, and sexuality: though we men are uniquely and constantly besieged by sexual temptation, we must resist—and can do so victoriously through Christ.

This brief historical review of Christian understandings of gender, sex, and sexuality suggests that many aspects of this message have deep roots in Christianity: there has long been a suspicion of sexual desire and intercourse, and masculinity has long been associated with sexual control and with domination of women

---

13 Kimmel, *Manhood in America*.
14 On General Conference Mennonites, masculinity, and militarism, see Hiebert, "Crisis of Masculinity." On the Mennonite Church (MC) shift from humility theology to a theology of strength, see Hurst, "Articulation of Mennonite Beliefs about Sexuality," chap. 1.

and other men. At the same time, many features of the message I was taught can be seen as novel or at least questionable in light of other Christian roots.

Some of these "strange roots" include the preferences for single celibacy over marriage and for exclusively procreative sex within marriage, which is rooted in the New Testament and ancient Catholic Christianity; a "one sex, two genders" understanding of bodies that was prevalent until recent centuries; Jesus's complex masculinity and the egalitarian impulses evident in his ministry and elsewhere in the Bible; theological reasons to doubt the equation of God and maleness; Luther's freewheeling theology of marriage; and the violent and disturbing legacy of European Christian gender and sexual norms of the colonial period. To this list could be added items such as periodic reversals in assumptions about whether men or women are more inclined to sexual desire and ancient and modern attempts to justify practices such as polygamy and same-gender sex and romance on Christian theological grounds. The message I received is not self-evidently the only or the "traditional" Christian teaching. The conception of Christian masculinity I and many Christians inherited need not be permanently binding.

Conclusion

At the beginning of this essay, I posed a series of questions about the nature of manhood, about what makes a man a man. How much closer are we to answering these questions? By offering a dynamic definition of masculinity that highlights its historical and cultural variability, I have suggested that there are no simple answers. Reflecting on my birth certificate, I showed how bodies are classified by powerful institutions such as the state. These classifications, including gender classifications, so thoroughly shape how we identify bodies that we do not have recourse to neutral biological descriptions to answer our questions about masculinity. Instead, we see that there are multiple, often conflicting perspectives on masculinity, organized in relation to a smaller set of iconic masculinities. However we answer questions about masculinity, we need to acknowledge the existence of multiple masculinities, and their relations to one another and to women. In my own case, masculine icons such as my father, athletes, and musicians offered me different possibilities for being a man, some of which I have needed to question in order to seek racial, gender, and sexual justice for and with marginalized persons and communities. The essays in part 2 of this volume give further evidence of the existence of multiple masculinities.

Our Christian faith ought to give us some guidance, although we have seen that there are multiple Christian masculinities, too. The message about men and sexuality I learned as a teenager can trace some of its roots to places deep in Christian history. Nevertheless, studying a broader range of Christian roots leads to the conclusion that there are diverse Christian perspectives on masculinity (and sexuality). Sorting through these to offer substantive theological arguments requires hard work, work I have not attempted to do in this essay. My hope is that the section on Christian history, together with the sections on the body and masculine icons, will serve the church in its ongoing discernment.

I have said that we cannot simply choose a new masculinity on a whim. But we can learn about masculinities in general and examine how we have been shaped by specific masculinities. Through that process of learning, we might come to see some masculinities as more harmful than others and initiate efforts to transform ourselves and our communities. If Mennonite and other men are going to become peaceful at heart, then we will need to engage this and other learning processes.

I submit that the goal of these processes should not be to carve out an ideal masculinity that, when embraced, will position purportedly peaceful men to dominate women and others. Rather, I propose that we focus our attention on the transformation of men by the Holy Spirit to be disciples of Jesus Christ in mutual partnership with others.

Bibliography

Brumberg, H. L. D. Dozor, and S. G. Golombek. "History of the Birth Certificate: From Inception to the Future of Electronic Data." *Journal of Perinatology* 32 (2012): 407–11, https://www.nature.com/articles/jp20123.

Butler, Judith. *Gender Trouble: Feminism and the Subversion of Identity*, 2nd ed. New York: Routledge, 1999.

Connell, R. W. *Masculinities*, 2nd. ed. Berkeley: University of California Press, 2005.

Edwards, Tim. "Femenism." In *Cultures of Masculinity*, 25–43. New York: Routledge, 2006.

Hiebert, Bruce. "A Crisis of Masculinity: North American Mennonites and World War I." PhD diss., Simon Fraser University, 2008.

Hurst, Brenda Martin. "The Articulation of Mennonite Beliefs about Sexuality, 1890–1930." PhD diss., Union Theological Seminary and Presbyterian School of Christian Education, 2003.

Jennings, Willie James. *The Christian Imagination: Theology and the Origins of Race.* New Haven: Yale University Press, 2010.

Kimmel, Michael. *Manhood in America: A Cultural History*, 3rd ed. New York: Oxford University Press, 2012.

Luther, Martin. "The Estate of Marriage," trans. Walther I. Brandt (1522). *Luther's Works*, vol. 45: *Christian in Society II.* Philadelphia: Fortress, 1962.

McClendon, James Wm. *Doctrine: Systematic Theology*, vol. 2. Nashville: Abingdon, 1994.

Messer, Neil. "Contributions from Biology." In *The Oxford Handbook of Theology, Sexuality, and Gender*, ed. Adrian Thatcher, 69–87. New York: Oxford University Press, 2015.

National Center for Health Statistics. "Section 4—Technical Appendix." In *Vital Statistics of the United States, 1980*, vol. 1, *Natality*, 4–6. Washington, DC: US Government Printing Office, 1984, https://www.cdc.gov/nchs/data/vsus/nat80_1acc.pdf.

Paoletti, Jo B. "Pink is for Boys." In *Pink and Blue: Telling the Boys from the Girls in America*, 85–99. Bloomington: Indiana University Press, 2012.

Thatcher, Adrian. *God, Sex, and Gender: An Introduction.* Malden, MA: Blackwell, 2011.

_____, ed. *The Oxford Handbook of Theology, Sexuality, and Gender.* New York: Oxford University Press, 2015.

Wiesner-Hanks, Merry E. *Gender in History: Global Perspectives*, 2nd ed. Malden, MA: Blackwell, 2011.

Yarrow, Simon. "Masculinity as a World Historical Category of Analysis." In *What is Masculinity? Historical Dynamics from Antiquity to the Contemporary World*, ed. John H. Arnold and Sean Brady, 114–38. New York: Palgrave Macmillan, 2011.

Tradition and Change in the Quest for a Healthy Masculinity

Kurt Horst

I pastor a congregation in Hesston, Kansas, a town of about 4,000 in an agrarian community in part of the United States known for its conservative political leanings. I serve as regional conference minister for South Central Conference of Mennonite Church USA, a conference on the conservative side of the denomination's continuum. I am in my mid-sixties, so I am in touch with a more traditional outlook characteristic of people of earlier generations.

I grew up in small-town mid-America, just a generation or two removed from the farm. In traditional Mennonite communities, the church was the central social organization, *the* alternative to social clubs, pool halls, lodges, and dance parties. The traditional family had two parents, a father and a mother, and their roles were complementary. Dads went to work, and moms worked part time outside the home only after the children reached school age. Divorce and single-parent families were the exception. In the words of Tevye in *Fiddler on the Roof*, "Because of our traditions . . . every one of us knows who he is and what God expects him to do."[1]

Since the mid-twentieth century, Mennonites have become more urban and wealthier, more educated and politically more liberal, as documented in a 2006 survey of Mennonite Church USA members.[2] With members' increased education and mobility, the impact of women's rights activism and changing ideas about gender has also increased. For some, these changes are welcome. For others, the loss of traditions has contributed to uncertainty, anxiety, and an erosion in personal and community identity. Now the church's divisions mirror those of the culture, and church attendance is in decline.

The training in Christian discipleship that I received as a child and youth did not explicitly address masculinity. For thirty years I have studied men's issues, yet I have rarely incorporated fruits of that study in my teaching and preaching. I have given a few semi-

---

1 Jewison, *Fiddler on the Roof.*
2 Kanagy, *Road Signs for the Journey.*

nars at church conventions and written a series of study guides for college men's groups, but otherwise I have encountered little desire to hear about men's issues. Perhaps our church's history of male dominance means that I should allow my voice to remain silent. Or perhaps I can see my silence as a way of identifying with Jesus, the suffering servant who did not open his mouth (Isa 53:7). But in the context of an apparent lack of interest in masculinity in the church, how am I as a man to lead a life that is spiritually healthy?

In what follows, I describe some of the complexities surrounding questions about masculinity, as seen from what we might call a traditional North American Mennonite viewpoint. These include cultural confusions that have arisen with the introduction of feminism and developments in broader intellectual culture and historical confusions arising from transformations in work and the home during the Industrial Revolution. At the conclusion of that analysis, I reflect briefly on work, gender, and sin in biblical and theological perspective. In the final part of the chapter I offer some thoughts about hope for getting beyond these confusions. After considering the question of why we need hope, I propose a "traditional" vision that moves beyond either the version of masculinity advocated by conservatives or the one supported by liberals; both of these make normative some aspect of the fallen gender order. I end by pointing to places where I see hope for a better way emerging.

Complexities in a quest
for spiritually healthy masculinity

My quest for spiritually healthy masculinity has been a varied exploration. As an athlete and a competitive oldest child of an oldest child, I found Muscular Christianity attractive for a time in my youth. Yet I turned down athletic scholarship offers in order to attend a denominational Christian college. I am biologically male, heterosexual, and sometimes unsure about whether I am masculine—or whether that should matter. I want my two sons to be secure in their maleness but not necessarily in their manliness. I want them to act honorably in their relationships with women and be respectful in their attitudes toward women. I observe gender patterns in the play of my seven grandchildren and wonder how they will sort out the mixed messages about gender that they receive from parents, media, church, culture, and friends.

I struggle to know what language to use in talking about men and masculinity. Gender theorists tell us that to varying degrees we are female or male, masculine or feminine, woman or man. Women's studies courses are popular; men's studies courses are hard to find. Feminism is affirmed, while masculinism seems like a bad word (although it is one that my dictionary doesn't recognize). Masculinity needs to be plural (masculinities), while femininity (singular) is for "girly girls" and is not seen as one viable option among an assortment of femininit*ies*. In popular culture, if a man is not masculine, he is feminine. In contrast, a woman may be seen as more feminine or less feminine, but if she is regarded as less feminine, she is not necessarily labeled masculine. Increasingly, to use "male" and "female" as binary categories is politically incorrect.

Even the question *Am I male?* has become a complex one. When a survey asks for one's sex, that is still generally understood as a biological question, although it is beginning to be understood as a gender question. In 2014, the social media site Facebook expanded to fifty-one the options for identifying one's sex. How are men to navigate the intersection of these cultural issues with our identity as man, male, masculine?

Minority and oppressed groups sometimes observe that those in privileged majority positions exhibit an unwillingness or inability to see or talk about themselves as an identified group. I have witnessed resistance to organizing an all-male consultation: it can be construed as a manifestation of male dominance, and it risks provoking opposition from women's rights advocates. But I wonder whether this resistance could be an expression of an avoidance or denial that perpetuates destructive attitudes among men who see themselves as progressive, sensitive, and even feminist.

Spiritual quests for healthy masculinity have a varied history. Beginning as early as the nineteenth century, men formed a variety of organizations in response to emerging women's movements. They include Muscular Christianity, which originated in England in the mid-nineteenth century. It equated exercise, athletic competition, and physical strength with spirituality. The mythopoetic men's movement in the 1980s and 90s invited men to join in coming-of-age rituals intended to call them back to themselves, separate from women. The movement took its cues from indigenous tribes' male initiation rites. Founded in 1990, Promise Keepers is an evangelical Christian organization that seeks to "ignite and unite men to become warriors who will change their world." Promise Keepers reports, "We have found that men tend to be more open to God's presence when they are with other men. There is something unique about the all-male environment that sets men free to drop the normal posturing and humble ourselves in Jesus Christ, committing to new beginnings."[3]

As part of my personal quest for answers, in 2005 I wandered into the campus bookstore at The College of William & Mary in Williamsburg, Virginia. I browsed in a large section labeled "Gender Studies," but I found nothing about heterosexual men. Two-thirds of the titles focused on women's issues, and the remaining third was on homosexuality. When I voiced my frustration, the clerk asked whether there was a title I would expect to find. When she had checked for *Healing the Masculine Soul* (1988) in the catalog, she told me that it could be ordered, but it would be shelved under "Self Help."

In my search of an online international listing of college undergraduate degree options, I found that of 406 listings under the heading "Gender and Sexuality Studies," 51 were "Women's Studies" programs, 39 were "Gender Studies" programs, 299 were degree programs that included "gender" in the title, 279 included "women," and 13 included "feminist." None had "men," "male," or "masculinity" in the title.[4] I found one college, not included in the previous list, that offers a minor in "Men's Studies."

A glance at Wikipedia, the ever-changing online encyclopedia, reveals that "men's studies" (often called "men and masculinities") is "an interdisciplinary academic field devoted to topics concerning men, masculinity, feminism, gender, and politics" that "draws upon feminist theory in order to analyze different ideologies having to do with masculinity."[5] On more than one occasion, my search for men's studies resources produced the suggestion that I look to criminology for research on men's behavior.

Where should men turn for answers to the questions *What is a man?* or *Am I a Man?* If it were a matter of anatomy, one could just "look in your jeans," as a Biology 101 classmate told me. Even arriving at a definition of masculinity is an adventure: it is a complex and evolving set of social constructs that take shape in different cultural, racial, ethnic, sociological, and even economic settings.

These and other observations have drawn me into exploring cultural changes and gender roles as they have developed over the last few centuries. Because of the rural social location of my Mennonite ancestors, these changes had only limited effect on my

3 "NXS: Blake Koch."
4 See the website Studyportals, www.studyportals.com.
5 Wikipedia, "Men's Studies," accessed May 17, 2018, https://en.wikipedia.org/wiki/Men%27s_studies.

grandparents, but their impact has been more significant for me and my family as we participate in mainstream North American—white, Protestant—culture.

My search for answers yielded some surprising results. What are often accepted as traditional North American assumptions about masculinity have close connections to (1) cultural patterns and roles that emerge when external threats cause work to be divided according to gender and to (2) family patterns that emerged out of the industrial revolution. Following is a summary of my discoveries. While I have given more focus to gender roles than to masculine identity, the two are intimately intertwined.

Cultural patterns and shared gender roles

In her book *My Brother's Keeper*, social psychologist Mary Stewart Van Leeuwen reports on two studies based on a large collection of independent cultural observations. When the data in this collection were cross-referenced with observed levels of gender differentiation, they revealed that societies characterized by relative peace and justice have less differentiation in the roles of men and women.[6]

In both studies, the variable most likely to predict greater equality between men and women is the early involvement of fathers in care of their children. The data showed that where fathers are involved in early childcare, women are devalued less, and both men and women are more likely to be active participants in community decision-making. Van Leeuwen concludes, "When young boys have primary caretakers of both sexes, they are less likely as adults to engage in woman-devaluing activities and in self-aggrandizing, cruel, or overly competitive male cults." The second most consistent predictor of greater gender equality is significant involvement of women in the control of family and community resources. All other factors are either not significant or only modestly significant.[7]

This research does not claim to establish cause and effect, but other observations also suggest that co-parenting and shared decision-making are associated with greater gender equality and harmony.[8] Early involvement by caretakers of both sexes correlates with less gender-role differentiation, reduced gender-identity anxiety, and increased likelihood that men, women, and children will experience greater happiness, peace, and purpose. Conversely, the

6 See Van Leeuwen, *My Brother's Keeper*, chapter 6.
7 Van Leeuwen, *My Brother's Keeper*, 121.
8 Van Leeuwen, *My Brother's Keeper*, 121–25.

less involved fathers are in early childcare, the greater the male insecurity that is displayed, and the more likely that men will devalue and abuse women and will develop competitive patterns with other men. The researchers haven't been able to do valid comparisons about results of the absence of women in early childcare because they haven't found an adequate cohort of subjects to study.

The researchers also note that cultures with more egalitarian gender roles are usually equatorial or tropical island cultures. In these settings, finding and gathering food is not risky: there are few aggressive neighbors or predatory animals to be defended against, so men do not need to be absent for prolonged periods to engage in war and hunting. Unlike less peaceful and less secure cultures, these cultures do not exhibit a precarious, elusive, or artificial construct of manhood that needs to be established against powerful odds. While the research does identify some peaceful cultures marked by clear gender differentiation, it finds no warring cultures without significant gender differentiation. In peaceful and secure settings, men and women share roles. Male involvement in the care and nurture of infants and children is common. The availability of enough food (justice) and a lack of natural and human enemies (peace) allows for greater male involvement in the lives of children, resulting in less gender differentiation. Followers of Jesus, the Prince of Peace, should not find the results of this research surprising.

Family patterns that emerged out of the industrial revolution

Separating the worlds of work and home

A family friend asked our four-year-old son, "Where does your daddy work?" Michael responded, "My daddy doesn't work. He just goes to meetings." I was pastor of a small suburban church, and my office was in our home. Michael's picture of the world of work was based on his observation that Grandpa and Uncle Rick "left for work" each weekday morning, and when they went to work, they wore "work clothes." The only time I put on such clothes was to do yard or garden work. Since I was often at home with him, and sometimes took him along on pastoral visits, my daily activities did not qualify as work.

But work hasn't always been done away from home, and it hasn't always been tied to making money. For most people, for much of human history, men, women, and children all worked.

Historically, there were two basic ways of organizing a society around the necessary work.

Hunting and gathering societies. Hunter-gatherers divided work between genders. Hunting, being riskier and requiring extended absences from home, was generally the work of men. The period from conception to weaning was about three years and kept women in and near camp. The high-risk work went to men because they were not essential to the care of infants. In many hunter-and-gatherer cultures, rituals developed for calling young men away from their mothers and into "manhood." (These patterns form the background for the mythopoetic men's movement.)

Settled societies. A second organizational pattern emerged in settled agricultural, merchant, and trade societies. Everyone—parents and children—worked together in the family occupation. Families took on names related to the family work: Miller, Weaver, Taylor, and so on. While there were divisions of labor, particularly when there was an infant in the home, the "business" was the family's and not something anyone went away to do. As children grew up, they were apprenticed in the family business. The expectation that everyone worked in the family business was also true of "middle marketing families" who ran stores (mercantiles) that were often extensions of the family living quarters. The exceptions were the soldiers and sailors who were often away for extended periods of time, as in hunting and warring cultures.

The industrial revolution. The practice of going to work and coming home to a place where you "don't work" is a relatively recent development, a product of the industrial revolution, mass production, capitalism, and the modern factory. Factories needed laborers who lived close to the work site. To attract workers, companies provided housing. Company housing, accompanied by wages, marked the beginning of a cultural change. For men, having a job replaced owning property as the mark of responsibility. The resulting association of work with wages had the unfortunate effect that women who stayed home did not "work." Advances in transportation, agricultural production, and food preservation (including refrigeration) made it possible for large populations to locate farther and farther away from the point of food production, which enabled the development of larger cities. The resulting mass migrations of people to cities disrupted childcare support systems traditionally provided by extended families. In many cases, aunts, uncles, grandparents, nieces, and nephews no longer lived near enough to assist with care and supervision of children in their extended family.

Separating the worlds of men and women

Before the industrial revolution, families worked together in caring for the land or the family business. With the industrial revolution, men began to spend many hours away from their families. The eight-hour workday and the five-day work week were things of the future. The care of infants required the presence of women, while men could be absent for hours and even days. Like soldiers and sailors who worked in all-male settings with dictatorial captains, working men spent many hours in predominantly male places of work, sometimes under the supervision of slave-driving bosses. Men no longer apprenticed their children and were less involved in daily training and discipline. Home was no longer a place of shared production but was idealized as a place of refuge from the rigors of work.

The church eventually found ways to bless these significant shifts in parenting roles. A review of clergy advice from the colonial era gives the impression that eighteenth-century men were considered morally and spiritually superior to women in matters of childrearing. By the end of the nineteenth century, women had come to be considered morally and spiritually superior. Motherhood had become a sacred calling, and care of children was seen as a vocation for which women were better suited than men. In effect, the industrial revolution made women the nurturers of children and men the economic providers. Churches supported this arrangement, declaring it natural and scriptural. Masculinity entailed rationality, competition, and profit in the marketplace, the academy, and politics; femininity was associated with domesticity, sacrifice, tender emotion, and piety.

Home, for men, was to be an emotional respite from the ruthless public world of work, competition, and profit. Family was to be a noble retreat from work, but men began to come home to places where they felt like strangers, even intruders. Children began to make their own choices about occupations and marriage partners. Men felt more important at work than at home. Tired from a day's work, they were expected to straighten out the problems that had emerged during the day. "When Daddy gets home" became a threat to unruly children, while decisions about family priorities were often made without the father's input because he was either at work or too tired to be burdened with them.

Historians James Juhnke and Carol Hunter point out patterns of gender conflict that emerged out of the industrial revolution.[9] As home became a woman's world, men found other places to go after work. In bars and clubs, men found camaraderie. By 1901, 5.5 million men—five times as many men as belonged to unions—belonged to all-male lodges such as the Odd Fellows, Moose, Eagles, and Knights of Columbus. Saloons, bars, and clubs were even more popular than lodges. According to historian Jon Kingsdale, "Many urban working-class districts had at least one saloon for every fifty adult males."[10] Bars became places to recover from a strenuous day of work. Saloons and clubs—like areas for "rest and relaxation" in port cities and near military installations—became spaces for male fellowship and free self-expression, where unattached women served the men. These patterns continue into the present, as demonstrated in a bit of dialog from the television drama NCIS: One character in the crime lab says, "This is a safe place for us to . . . voice our concerns." Another responds, "Huh. In my world we call that a bar."[11]

Women, who increasingly saw themselves as the guardians of morality and social decency, responded with the temperance movement. As they became aware of their political power, they set out to promote domestic and moral values through the political arena. In the United States, a constitutional amendment prohibiting the manufacture and sale of alcohol passed in 1919, with massive support from the Women's Christian Temperance Union. A year later, in 2020, the nineteenth amendment gave women the right to vote.

Along with these cultural changes, the nineteenth and early twentieth century saw a decrease in church attendance among men. Men still held most church offices, but the organizations that carried on the ministries of most churches depended on the volunteer "labor" of "non-working" women. Meanwhile, public places in the world of men were taking on religious names. They became "temples of commerce" and "cathedrals of learning." Some, notably banks and transportations centers, even took on the traditional architecture of churches.

Meanwhile, in the rural areas of North America, agrarian life continued patterns that required everyone's involvement in the

9 Juhnke and Hunter, "Gender Matters," 167.
10 Kingsdale, "'Poor Man's Club,'" 472–89; cited in Juhnke and Hunter, "*Gender Matters*," 167.
11 Sammie28, "Mile High City Affair."

family economy. Here, destructive patterns of gender differentiation were less prevalent.

Separating the worlds of labor and management

By the mid-twentith century, the workplace, like the ship or the army, became a place where many men served and a few ruled. Foremen and bosses ran factories, and owners were sometimes even referred to as captains of industry. Where owners and bosses were dictatorial, pay inadequate, and working conditions oppressive, workers organized to challenge the power of management. Strikes and violence entered the world created by the industrial revolution. One can easily draw parallels between the closed world of the ship headed by an autocratic captain and the closed world of the shop; between the mutiny of sailors and the protests, strikes, and revolts of angry laborers. These disputes, and the violence that accompanied them, created sharp divisions between labor and management.

In this context, a sense of community developed among workers. Laborers were "in it together," against a common enemy. They looked out for one another, and a fraternal community emerged in the shop. When "one of ours" had a crisis, others were quick to help. Nevertheless, while company loyalty among labor was often judged to be weak and became a management concern, management-level workers were more likely than common laborers to jump ship if a better job came along.

For management, economic power, authority, and job title determined status. In the shop, a man's persona away from the job established status. Recreation among management often involved one-on-one competitions (tennis, golf, gambling), while labor joined in group activities and team sports (softball, hunting, fishing). The culture of the shop was "man against nature" or "man against machine," while the culture of the office was "man against man."

Inner division: Sin and the curse

In biblical and theological terms, do men have a different relationship with, understanding of, and attitude about work than women? The Genesis creation story suggests that, because of the curses that result from sin, men and women do have differing attitudes toward work. As a result of sin, God decreed that women's burden would be in birthing children and men's burden would be in toiling to produce food (Gen 3:16–19). A further curse falls on Cain after he kills his brother Abel: the ground will no longer yield its strength for him, and he is driven away from the soil. Cain becomes a fugitive and a wanderer, until he establishes a place of commerce, a city, where a living could be made by barter rather than through direct dependence on the earth (Gen 4:11–17). This account of the fall and its aftermath suggests that under the curse, and with a connection to suffering, women find identity through children and men find identity in work. In addition, the curse of Cain suggests that violent men find their identity in an economy in which they profit from dealing in the fruits of other people's labor. The biblical texts do not assume that men will work and women will not. Both men and women will work, but the text suggests that men, because of sin and the curse, have a different relationship with and attitude to work.

We too often forget that according to Scripture, these differences are a result of sin and the curse and not part of God's original intention in creating humanity. Jesus came into the world to liberate humanity from these curses. Christians, knowing their liberation, are to demonstrate the values of the reign of God, not—as some Christian traditions seem to do—to proclaim the curse as normative, part of God's intended order.

Within this understanding, spirituality is not different for men and women, but the path to spiritual wholeness may be quite different because men and women begin their journey from different places. Because of the curse, men's love-hate attitude about work makes them more vulnerable to using work to authenticate their identity. A materialistic connection between income and sense of self-worth is a result of the curse, and in the realm of God's intention it is known to be false and idolatrous.

Work is good and necessary. Work must be available to all who are able to undertake it. It must be valued but not idolized, and it should be valued apart from any income it produces. People who care for children and maintain households remind us that the fact that their work does not generate income does not mean that they are idle and lazy. Good work is good work, regardless of whether it produces income. Statistician and economist E. F. Schumacher, in *Good Work*, tells us that much of what we call work, because it produces income, is far from good. He cites a provocative line from a *London Times* article: "Dante, when composing his visions of hell, might well have included the mindless, repetitive boredom of working on a factory assembly line."[12]

---

12 Schumacher, *Good Work*, 1.

Hope?

Traces of discouragement

The above discoveries and observations leave me with conflicting responses to some aims of some women's movements and also to the so-called family values of the evangelical Christian right. For its part, the Christian right proclaims a masculinity that is as much a product of the Industrial Revolution and the privileges of wealth as of biblical teaching. At the same time, where women seek an equal share in the "successful" men's world of coercion, power, and wealth, their "progress" may be not a step forward but only a step up the rungs of the broken ladder that takes us toward devaluing human capital.

Knowing that fear-based cultures manifest greater gender separation that produces attitudes that demean women, I cringe at the global increase in militancy and fear and the power-based political rhetoric of class, racial, and gender struggle. Unless we can find ways to reduce violence, tribal and nationalistic posturing, an obsession with maintaining borders, and ethnic and economic segregation, the political polarization that many lament will continue to produce polarization between the sexes.

With the increase in single-parent households and the changing patterns around marriage, divorce, and family, I wonder where future generations of young men will learn about healthy masculinity and shared gender roles. According to a 2013 article in *The Globe and Mail*, family incomes began to stagnate and family structures changed radically beginning in the 1970s.[13] It was also in the 1970s that North America made the turn from an industrial to post-industrial service economy. Divorce rates soared, marriage rates fell, and more women began to have children outside marriage. In the United States, 41 percent of babies are born out of wedlock, and in Canada, 25 percent. Among developed countries, the United States has the highest percentage of single-parent families, followed by Canada. The poverty rate among lone-parent families is four times that of two-parent families with children. Estimates are that 50 percent of children will spend some part of their childhood in a single-parent home. Massachusetts Institute of Technology economists David Autor and Melanie Wasserman report a direct link between the rising tide of fatherlessness and the growing failure of boys in school and the labor market. Boys without fathers are more likely to develop serious behavior problems at an early age.

---

13 Autor and Wasserman, "Wayward Sons"; cited in Wente, "Inequality."

They are more antisocial and aggressive; more disruptive; and more likely to drop out of school, get in trouble with the law, and become less employable. They are less inclined to get married but quite likely to produce children.

As households find it more and more difficult to get by with a single income, and both parents leave home in order to work, children have fewer opportunities to observe women and men working together cooperatively. Some have reported to me that the first time they observed a parent in a work environment they were surprised to discover that the person they thought they knew was quite different from the one they saw at home. A controlling mother became a willing servant, and an angry, uninvolved father was everybody's friend.

Geographic separation from extended family and the loss of available time for parenting and also take a toll on parents and children. Day care is a privilege of the rich but an economic necessity for poor and single-parent households. The load on government social service agencies (children and youth welfare systems, foster care, etc.) is threatening to expand beyond our ability to manage it, while caring for aging parents adds to the burden of already overburdened families and is a social concern and a drain on the economy.

Traditional perspectives on masculinity

I believe that when historians look back a couple hundred years from now, they will identify the ready availability of contraceptives as a development as socially and politically transformative as the invention of the printing press. Easy access to contraceptives (and the view that abortion is a contraceptive option) has changed sexual encounters into recreational pursuits rather than re-creational unions. Even within the church, marriage is not so much a holy ordinance as a legal arrangement. The level of premarital sexual activity and cohabitation among church members is much like that in wider society.

Before contraceptives, the risk of pregnancy created an imbalance of power between a man and woman involved in a sexual relationship. Feminism celebrates the introduction of contraceptives because it "levels the playing field," balancing the risks and burdens women and men face. But if contraception was supposed to nurture a healthier masculinity, it has failed. Instead of creating an environment where men are more responsible, the result has been a general irresponsibility (apart from concern about sexually transmitted diseases) and a degrading of intimacy. Jesus predicted that "because of the increase of wickedness, the love of many will grow cold" (Matt. 24:12). As making love becomes a recreational rather than re-creational activity, some emotional and spiritual intimacy is lost, and the act of becoming one is desecrated, its sanctity violated.

The Bible says, "The man knew his wife Eve, and she conceived" (Gen. 4:1). The injunction to humanity to be fruitful and multiply is given both at creation (Gen. 1:28) and again after the flood (Gen. 9:7). Jesus's prediction that love will grow cold foretells an increase in isolation and longing for intimacy. The cooling of love is not just a loss of romance but a spiritual loss. The biblical teaching on becoming one flesh—"For this reason a man shall leave his father and mother and be joined to his wife, and the two will become one flesh" (Mark 10:7–8)—is often read as if "become one flesh" refers simply to the sexual union. But I believe it includes the understanding that the two becoming one will result in a new human life, a new flesh. When Jesus adds the words "What God has joined together, let no one separate" (Mark 10:9), he is teaching not just that those who are married should never be separated but also that marriage should never be separated from its intended purpose, procreation.

This understanding of marriage has an impact on our view not only of marriage and family but also of singleness. I once heard of a Mennonite theologian who, after careful study, reported that the Bible teaches that marriage is good, but singleness is better. The church should give greater respect to unmarried people. Paul's teaching that "each person should remain in the situation they were in when God called them" (1 Cor 7:20 NIV) means that those who aren't married when they become Christians should remain single unless God calls them to marriage. (In contrast, the church's view has been that remaining single takes a special calling.) I counsel couples anticipating marriage that unless they are convinced that their ministry for the reign of God will be greater together than it would be without their partner, their marriage will not meet the biblical standard for a Christian marriage.

A final observation: having lived long in rural settings, I have seen roosters, stallions, and bulls strut their stuff. My acquaintance with animal sexuality makes it easy for me to see parallels between the alpha-male patterns of the barnyard and the problems that arise when masculinity turns toxic. The apostle Paul in the first chapter of Romans equates humans who adopt the ways of creatures (rather than exhibiting the image of God) with a cessation of proper worship. The toxic masculinity that takes on alpha-male patterns evident in the animal world is the spiritual result of self-worship. With the rejection of the Creator, a form of masculinity that mimics the animal world becomes the norm. The loving servant patterns of Jesus, who revealed the nature of God (Col. 1:19–20; Phil. 2:6–7), fail to become the norm for human interactions. These animal patterns are toxic for humans and form the root of what I sometimes call "male pattern irresponsibility."

Paul observes further that fallen humans take their perversion beyond what animals display. But for Paul, the ultimate perversion is not degraded sexual relationships:

> And since they did not see fit to acknowledge God, God gave them up to a debased mind and to things that should not be done. They were filled with every kind of wickedness, evil, covetousness, malice. Full of envy, murder, strife, deceit, craftiness, they are gossips, slanderers, God-haters, insolent, haughty, boastful, inventors of evil, rebellious toward parents, foolish, faithless, heartless, ruthless. They know God's decree, that those who practice such things deserve to die—yet they not only do them but even applaud others who practice them. (Rom. 1:28–32)

Clearly, for too much of modern history, the church has treated the fallen gender order as if it were God's intention in creation. Whether in the Crusades, Muscular Christianity, the Ku Klux Klan, Promise Keepers, or Wild at Heart, proponents have taken their cues from the behaviors of fallen humanity rather than from Jesus. As a result, the church has sometimes blessed destructive masculinity and abusive patriarchy. But I fear that, in the same way the conservative church has built its case on a fallen humanity, the liberal wing is susceptible to blessing behaviors that emerge from fallen reactions and godless anger rather than from the love and mercy of Jesus. I am ambivalent toward the Christian right and the left, and I don't see where I have a side in the fight. An Anabaptist understanding of the way of Jesus as a third way continues to inform my reticence about joining either side in these culture wars.

Glimpses of hope

I see glimpses of hope as North America moves further into post-industrialism. The shape of masculinity is changing for young families and for single adults. As manufacturing jobs drop below 10 percent of the workforce and service sector jobs make up over 50 percent of employment opportunities, men and women are more likely to be working together and forging new ways of defining themselves. Single adults (now half the adult population) are changing the assumption that marriage is necessary to fulfillment. I conclude with a number of places I see glimpses of hope.

I see glimpses of hope when I see peer interactions becoming more egalitarian, shared work and household roles becoming more varied, and regular inclusion of single-parent households in social interactions giving children chances to observe men and women working cooperatively.

I see glimpses of hope where work is understood in terms of its value in household and community, not just because of its monetary value.

I see glimpses of hope when men share the work of their households and where children are not just assigned chores but share work with their parents.

I see glimpses of hope where adults—men and women— include neighborhood children in neighborhood projects.

I see glimpses of hope where men, women, and children work together for peace and justice on local, national, and international levels.

I see glimpses of hope when husbands and wives make sure their children see them sharing economic information and decision-making and where they make charitable giving and service projects part of family life.

I see glimpses of hope where women and men are involved together in schools, community development, recreation programs, and churches.

I see glimpses of hope when I see men model healthy cooperative leadership as they work alongside women in programs for children, including those in sole-parent households.

Bibliography

Autor, David, and Melanie Wasserman. "Wayward Sons: The Emerging Gender Gap in Labor Markets and Education." *Third Way Fresh Next*, [2013], http://content.thirdway.org/publications/662/Third_Way_Report_-_NEXT_Wayward_Sons-The_Emerging_Gender_Gap_in_Labor_Markets_and_Education.pdf.

Jewison, Norman, dir. *Fiddler on the Roof*. Beverly Hills, CA: United Artists, 1971.

Juhnke, James C., and Carol M. Hunter. "Gender Matters: Peace Begins at Home." In *The Missing Peace: The Search for Nonviolent Alternatives in United States History*, 2nd ed. Kitchener, ON: Pandora Press, 2004.

Kanagy, Conrad L. *Road Signs for the Journey: A Profile of Mennonite Church USA*. Scottdale, PA: Herald Press, 2007.

Kingsdale, Jon M. "'The Poor Man's Club': Social Functions of the Urban Working Class Saloon." *American Quarterly* 25 (December 1973): 472–89

"NXS: Blake Koch will Pilot the No. 8 Promise Keepers Toyota Camry this Weekend at Richmond International Raceway." OnPitRoad.com, April 23, 2015, https://www.onpitroad.com/?p=15012.

Sammie28. "The Mile High City Affair," chapter 8, NCIS Fanfiction Archive, https://www.ncisfiction.com/viewstory.php?sid=5192&chapter=8.

Schumacher, E. F. *Good Work*. New York: Harper & Row, 1979.

Van Leeuwen, Mary Stewart. *My Brother's Keeper: What the Social Sciences Do (and Don't) Tell Us about Masculinity*. Downers Grove, IL: InterVarsity, 2002.

Wente, Margaret. "The Inequality We Don't Talk About." *The Globe and Mail*, November 2013; updated March 3, 2018, https://www.theglobeandmail.com/opinion/the-inequality-we-dont-talk-about/article15636708/.

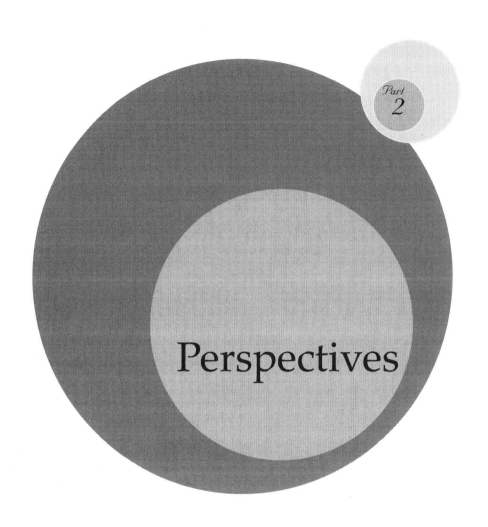

Part
2

Perspectives

An African American Man

Leonard Dow

"Now when they saw the boldness of Peter and John and realized that they were uneducated and ordinary men, they were amazed and recognized them as companions of Jesus." –Acts 4:13

It was a good day because all my homies were with me sitting on Mr. George's stoop at the corner of 18th and Glenwood in North Philadelphia: Little Earl, Stevie, Greg, and me. We often sat on Mr. George's stoop because he was like our local celebrity since he was the only white person still living in our otherwise all black community. We had just finished playing our Saturday morning stick ball game down the street in between passing cars, all the while utilizing the boarded-up factory across the street from our row homes. The abandoned four-story factory was a painful reminder of the golden age manufacturing but was also perfect for us to use the floors and windows as ways to mark our hits as singles, doubles, and so on. We did this all the while shouting out our favorite professional players.

"I'm Bob Gibson!" "I'm Dick Allen!" "I'm Hank Aaron!" And of course we all wanted to claim the great Willie Mays.

After the game sitting on Mr. George's stoop, our trash talk intensified into who won the game and as always led us into the conversation about who was the best, greatest, fastest, strongest baseball, basketball, or football player of the early 1970s. But on this day, for the first time, we also began to talk about and compare our dads: Who was the strongest? Who made the most money? Who was the coolest?

It was obvious to all of us that Stevie's dad was the strongest and baddest because he was a police officer, wore a blue uniform with boots, and carried a gun and billy club—all of which made him look like a giant to us. And of course Little Earl's dad made the most money because they had the nicest house on the block, and Greg's dad, who wasn't even around much, easily won the coolest because he drove a very cool big car. Even as we laughed about our dads, I was beginning to think to myself, *What about my dad?* Eventually, in the midst of the banter, Little Earl noticed and said something about the elephant in the room: "Leonard, what about your dad?"

Thankfully, my best friend Stevie spoke up for me and said something like, "Leonard, your dad is cool; he's always around working!"

He was right. My father was either pressing clothes at the factory, helping out at the family flower shop on 22nd St., hustling by selling flowers on the corner of 19th St. on Easter, Mother's Day, and in the cold winter months, or selling trees for Christmas. In an attempt to save face and lighten up the moment, I said out loud, "Great, my dad's only superpower is that he's always around."

We all looked at each other and broke out into laughter, promising one another that when we grew up to be men we were going to be even better than our dads and hopefully more like our favorite famous athletes. For me, though a child at the time, it was sobering day. That was the day that I came to realize that my dad was an ordinary man. And early on in my development, an ordinary man didn't fit at all my dreams of a father who was a hero, beat up the bad guys, accomplished daring feats, rescued the damsel in distress, and was still home in the evening to play catch with me. Instead, my father was an ordinary man—very ordinary, in fact. He was

- uneducated, forced to drop out of school in sixth or seventh grade because of undiagnosed dyslexia and a family facing the shame associated with an underperforming eldest son;
- unsophisticated in the arts and sciences and never traveled outside his military service, so he knew very little of the world or the complexity of international affairs;
- average height and build and nonathletic;
- far more comfortable behind the scenes serving others than being served and rarely spoke in public;
- an underpaid laborer his whole life forcing him to have to work all the time to try to support his family;
- an ordinary black man in a world that values whiteness.

When you're an ordinary black man in America, you're either seen as a problem or not seen at all. My ordinary experience as a black boy growing up in America meant being socialized to be invisible and silent, to know and obey the rules (even if unjust), and to be resolved to the fact that I would have to do twice as much and be twice as good as any white boy just to receive the same opportunities. Early on—and especially as I grew to be six feet, three inches tall and a formidable athlete—I was consistently told by my fearful father to recognize that in this country I would be viewed as a threat and was therefore a problem. He would tell me, "Son, it's not fair, but to make it in this world avoid eye contact with white folk, speak softly, don't draw attention to yourself, and always follow the rules."

The sad irony is that avoiding direct eye contact with whites, being invisible, following the rules, and smiling in the midst of tears have not been of benefit to me or any other black man in America. Author Marc LaMott Hill writes that to be African American is to be a nobody. To be a nobody is to be

- vulnerable to violence, illness, and premature death;
- subject to state sanctioned violence through police brutality and mass incarceration;
- abandoned by the state and left with underfunded public schools yet a revenue generating prison system;
- considered disposable and, as a result, able to be erased, abandoned, and even left to die.[1]

Juxtaposed to this reality is that, when ordinary African American men are seen, our mere presence becomes a problem and a threat in white America. Phrases such as *driving while black, walking while black*, and more recently *waiting (at Starbucks) while black* are representative of our lived experience and the effects of racism toward African Americans in our country. And because we are viewed as the problem, we constantly monitor our surroundings, adjust our clothes, hair, car speed, and speech—all in attempt to minimize our blackness and maintain the comfort of whites. This is why for many in black America the hoodie has become a symbol of defiance. At the root of the tragic events surrounding the murder of seventeen-year-old Trayvon Martin—an ordinary African American teenager—was that he was seen as a problem and a threat while wearing a hoodie. And because he was wrongly perceived as a problem and a threat, it cost him, his family, and his community his precious life. While it could be argued that Trayvon Martin's killing is the best-known tragedy, his was neither the first nor the last. Emmett Till was an ordinary fourteen-year-old African American who was lynched in Mississippi in 1955, after a white woman said she was offended by him in her family's grocery store. She

---

1 Hill, *Nobody*, xx–xxi.

would later recant her story as being false. The Central Park Five in 1989 was a group of ordinary teenage boys of color (four African American, one Hispanic) who were coerced into confessing to a crime, sentenced, and incarcerated by an unjust legal system but eventually cleared years later of all false allegations and charges in 2002. And in recent years many ordinary African American men—including Eric Garner (New York City), Michael Brown (Ferguson, Missouri), Tamir Rice (Cleveland, Ohio), and Eric Harris (Tulsa, Oklahoma)—have become victims of police brutality.

In her seminal work *The New Jim Crow*, Michelle Alexander rightly reminds us that the likelihood of ordinary black men being negatively impacted by the police, unjust legal system, or the prison industry is extremely high. For example, she writes, "The United States imprisons a larger percentage of its black population than South Africa did at the height of apartheid. In Washington D.C., our nation's capital, it is estimated that three out of four young black men (and nearly all those in the poorest neighborhoods) can expect to serve in prison."[2]

Despite this stark reality, my father—like most Americans of his day and still today—desperately wanted to believe in the American myth that everyone, even ordinary black men like him, would one day have equal access to the American dream. My father got his chance in 1975 when we moved from my grandmother's row home in North Philly into the promised land of East Oak Lane, Philadelphia. For my father, the iconic words of George Jefferson rang true because we had finally "moved on up." With a combination of construction expertise my father gained from a handful of white Christian men in his life, a lot of prayer, and everyone in the family helping to save, my parents purchased their first and only house for our intergenerational family of eight. Our move took us out of the heart of the city in North Philly onto the last street in the city, the most northern edge of the city before exiting Philadelphia and entering the suburbs of Montgomery County. When we moved in the mid 70s, East Oak Lane was still an exclusive all-white community of large, three story, six to eight bedroom homes and was considered one of the last bastions of purity from African American housing integration. To this day, I believe the only way we knew about the house, got an agreement of sale, and were approved for a mortgage was because so many white people helped my parents in the process. Because of this, my father saw this move as affirma-

2 Alexander, *New Jim Crow*, 6–7.

tion of all his prayers and a reward for being an ordinary African American who "behaved well within the white system." Then in his late forties, he felt he was finally going to be seen as a peer to his white mentors. Why not? Like them, he had accomplished homeownership of a large home in a white community, attended a white church, had a steady (albeit woefully underpaying) job, and was father of a respected nuclear family. By most measurements of success in America, he had finally made it—or so he thought.

Even as a twelve- to thirteen-year-old, I could tell that no one—and I mean no one—in our new East Oak Lane neighborhood wanted us there. And it wasn't because of lack of trying by the Dows. We smiled, waived, invited, and kept our music turned down. On top of that, my father's military background ensured that our house was kept in order: our trash was always put out on time, the house was always organized and neat, we swept up the front of the house every week, our grass and hedges were cut every weekend, our flower beds were colorful, and in the winter all snow was removed within hours after it fell. Nevertheless, without a word, within a year or so after our arrival all but one of our near neighbors moved out of the neighborhood. Our neighbors' white flight broke part of my fathers heart, though he rarely spoke about it. This brokenness that routinely weighed heavily on him impacted his ability to see himself as made in the *imago Dei* (image of God). Instead he struggled—as many ordinary African American men do today—seeing himself with the limiting lens of racism.

For most of my life I mistakenly measured my father's success on a flawed framework that demanded he fulfill my generation's yet unfulfilled desires and outcomes. I placed him in the negative light of ordinariness because he wasn't as relevant as I thought a black man should be in a country that treated grown men like him as a boy in front of his son. I often wondered why he didn't at least try to speak up for himself in public spaces when disrespected. Why didn't he try to draw greater attention to himself, his family, and the plight of our African American community? He was never a powerful or influential man in the classic sense of sitting on a board, leading men, writing a book, supervising employees, or having financial resources or political influence. As a result of what I wanted my father to be, I almost failed to notice and appreciate my father and his ordinary life, in the ways author Ta-Nehisi Coates talks about before acclaim eventually came his way as a journalist: "I learned to use this ordinariness to my advantage. There was something soft and unthreatening about me that made people want to talk. . . . I built myself around ordinary things—family, friends, and community. I was a good father, a good partner, a decent friend."[3]

Over the years, I have come to realize and appreciate that my dad resisted the temptations of trying to be what author Henri Nouwen identifies as the three temptations Jesus faced in the desert and throughout his ministry found in the Gospels: the temptations of being relevant, remarkable, and powerful. Instead my father passionately loved God and his neighbor while he fathered us "to do justice, and to love kindness, and to walk humbly with your God" (Micah 6:8). He was a nonanxious presence in an anxious world, and he served as a bedrock for my family, extended family, church, and friends. Over the years as I have begun to mature in my faith, I have started to see that what I thought were my father's biggest weaknesses were really strengths and daily signs of the presence of the fruits of the Spirit: love, joy, peace, patience, kindness, goodness, faithfulness, gentleness, and self-control. As a result, I've begun to rightly remember, take notice, honor, emulate, and more recently tell my father's story to other men—of how his life as an ordinary man is our call as well. God still desires to use ordinary men in extraordinary ways. This is our call as men of God.

Let us consider a few ways my dad exhibited to me how to strive toward acting with greater justice, growing in our love of kindness, and passionately walking together in humility with our God. First, my dad was consistent. He showed up every day to a thankless job involving cleaning floors and bathrooms and pressing suits that he could not afford for himself. He was consistent by daily being present at home, in the community, and at church. It has been said that 80 percent of the battle is won by simply showing up. I would echo this sentiment by saying that 80 percent or more of being faithful to God is being consistently available. Are you available? As my friend Stevie noted when we were growing up, my father was consistently available to his family, his community, his church, and his God. Unbeknownst to me, my father was daily debunking the myth of the absent black father.[4]

---

3 Coates, "I'm Not Black, I'm Kanye."
4 Author Josh Levs devotes a chapter in his book specifically to myths about African American fathers. Here are just a couple of the facts: (1) Most black fathers live with their children. There are about 2.5 million who live with their children, and 1.7 million who don't, according to the CDC. (2) Black dads who live with their children are actually the most involved fathers of all, on average, a CDC study found. See Levs, *All In*, 148–49.

Second, my dad sought to be compassionate. Despite rarely experiencing compassion as a black man in this country, my father, by God's grace, was passionate about compassion. He treated people the way he desired others to treat him. Amazingly, my father refused to be bitter about his lot in life and all the injustices he faced: with his inadequate schooling, limited military benefits, loss of manufacturing jobs to overseas workers, disrespect by neighbors, and the disinterest of the church in naming racism as a sin. Instead, I saw for myself how he compassionately took time to listen and even to invite the homeless into our home for a meal, conversation, and place to stay. I saw how he extended compassion to our extended family who were in hospice care and financially had nowhere else to go, allowing them to die with dignity in our own home. These acts of compassion also included being the primary caregiver for over a decade of my mom's mother, who battled the debilitating disease of Alzheimer's. His nonanxious presence and *agape* love allowed him to live with compassion without an expectation of receiving anything in return. My father was what we now call culturally compassionate. He was a lifelong learner, and because of his humble educational background, he never made the assumption that he had the right answer or idea; rather, he approached everyone with a posture of learning, listening, and sharing.

Third, my dad was courageous. Indeed, he was courageous in ways it took me a while to notice. When I thought my father was being complacent, it turns out he was acting behind the scenes on my and other African Americans' behalf. I have come to realize and learn for myself that just because we do not see change happening right in front of us, we should never assume it isn't happening. My parents challenged the wealthy white center-city commuter church they were attending in how viewing homeless African American men as nobodies to be ignored or as a problem and threat is inconsistent with loving our neighbor. Even when these homeless men would sleep and beg on the steps and block the entry to the church on Sunday, my father saw them as fellow brothers and therefore as image bearers of God who are worthy of compassion and hospitality. My parents demanded that the church help the men in their homelessness and not ignore them or give into fear. As a result, my parents helped begin a homeless ministry at the church that went beyond a soup kitchen to also include connecting men to their families and providing social, health, and legal professionals on site as a way to provide support to those who were often invisible. This ministry continues to grow and impact lives to this day—all because my ordinary father insisted that the church be a place that provides a pathway to dignity for the homeless by compassionately offering listening ears, warm meals, gently used clothing, soft skill job training, mental health/legal/social support, and an opportunity for the men to join the church and serve, thereby giving back. In other words, my dad helped the church provide them a pathway to dignity.

In the final months of my dad's unexpected three-year battle with cancer, I was humbled to witness more intimately than ever before how extraordinarily loved this ordinary man had become by both those in power and those in poverty. To my great surprise, during his few months of hospice care, this ordinary man had ranking city politicians, notable pastors from around the country, authors of books he couldn't read for himself, and executives of Fortune 500 companies he couldn't qualify for a job in all come into our home to sit with him for ten to fifteen minute visits. Likewise, there were numerous times individuals who were homeless called him. I knew they were homeless because whenever it would take me a minute or two to get my dad to the phone, I would hear a recorded request for a quarter to continue the call. Eventually when the volume of calls became so great for my weakening dad, I would take the calls and pray or talk with the men and women who simply wanted to say thank you to Deacon Dow for being available to them or to tell me their redemption story and how my dad led them to Christ or saved them from an addiction, divorce, or homelessness. More often than not, they found themselves so overcome with emotion that we would simply cry together over the phone.

I was humbled and blessed to be by my dad's bedside when he went home to the Lord. His last words to me were that he loved me and was proud of me and that I should be patient with my mother and keep serving the Lord. But what I'll cherish most are the words from the obituary of this ordinary black man still unable to fully grasp the how and why God had enabled him to be used in extraordinary ways:

> I am a man of few words, yet there is so much I want to say now. Mostly because God has shown exceptional grace to me, and I want each of you to know that the Scripture is true. His grace is sufficient. I am grateful to God for life, that I was able to experience a few things, loved a lot of people, and had only a little money to

spend (so my mind could stay on Jesus). In the end, it was all too short. Praise be to our eternal Father who grants us all peace and love.[5]

Amen.

Bibliography

Alexander, Michelle. *The New Jim Crow: Mass Incarceration in the Age of Colorblindness*. New York: New Press, 2012.

Coates, Ta-Nehisi. "I'm Not Black, I'm Kanye." *Atlantic*, May 7, 2018, https://www.theatlantic.com/entertainment/archive/2018/05/im-not-black-im-kanye/559763/.

Hill, Marc Lamont. *Nobody: Casualties of America's War on the Vulnerable, from Ferguson to Flint and Beyond*. New York: Atria, 2016.

Levs, Josh. *All In: How Our Work-First Culture Fails Dads, Families, and Businesses—And How We Can Fix It Together*. New York: HarperOne, 2015.

---

5 Excerpt from obituary of Lawrence Jacob Dow.

Chapter 5

A Latino Man

Hugo Saucedo

When I was asked to contribute to this book, I laughed out loud—first because of the title *Peaceful at Heart* (the thought of men being peaceful is foreign to me) and then because someone thought it was a good idea to ask me to write a chapter about experiencing masculinity from a Latino perspective. I say this not to be cute or funny but rather because in the not-so-distant past no one would have dared asked me to be part of a project like this. For the past decade or so, I have been battling with my masculinity and what I believe it means to be a man. I have been engaged in a dark battle for peace in my heart and soul. Although I can't say that I have arrived at a place of lasting peace, I can say that I am in a much better space. Perhaps my contribution to this body will be to give testimony to the fact that, yes, a macho Latino male can find peace in who he is and can help others take steps towards seeking that peace.

My path to manhood began not with the sage words of other men but with with the example set by the women in my life—in particular my mother, my mentor, and my daughter. I was born in Brownsville, Texas, in the 1970s. Growing up in this region of Texas (deep south Texas) during this time was challenging. I vividly remember going to Woolco's downtown and entering the building through the alley instead of the front door. When I asked my mom why we had to enter through the alley, she reminded me that Mexicans had their own "special" door in the alley and that we couldn't enter through the front door. That was just like my mom, always trying to soften the blow of reality for me. I still remember her trying to downplay that reality as well as so many other things we had to experience as minorities in our own community. This sort of experience sounds foreign to us now, but this was in the not-so-distant past.

My family was poor. We didn't have a lot of material belongings, but we had each other, and for a time that was enough. My father was a longshoreman, and he often worked in very dangerous conditions. It was hard work, but it paid well and was steeped in macho stereotypes of what a man had to do to provide for his family. This was all well and good until one inevitably got hurt or killed, which endangered the fine balance between poverty and indigence. This reality became all too real when the phone rang late one summer night.

I must have been ten or eleven years old, and I can remember my mom crying in the kitchen. I found out later that my father was in a work related accident and was seriously injured. The initial shock of the situation subsided, and after surgery and a lengthy hospital stay, my father was home. The problems, however, had just begun. Like most Mexican men, my father was accustomed to being the financial provider for the family. Now he was relegated to lying in bed most days trying to recover, which meant my mom would be the primary breadwinner. This did not sit well with my dad, but he figured it would only be temporary. Little did he know this would be a very long journey that would last over a decade. This would be a decade of searching for my dad because he had to take a back seat to my mom who would now be the primary financial provider. This was a difficult time for him, but it was a much more difficult time for me and my siblings. We were used to my mom caring for us daily. She would make us a complex breakfast to fill our bellies before sending us off to school with a delicious lunch, and she would cap that off with an "I love you" before sending us out the door. Now she had to find a job and try to keep us from falling into financial despair. As a young man of barely ten, I found these difficult changes complicated by the disdain my father was dealing with now that he was left to care for us while his wife went to work daily.

I never realized just how much machismo I grew up with. But this reality was magnified in a number of spaces, starting at home. I grew up with a healthy work ethic. As a ten-year-old I was up at six o'clock in the morning doing chores around the house, and in the summers I worked at a variety of odd jobs. These jobs were mainly manual labor, where I was surrounded by men. Rarely did I encounter a woman working the fields or mending fences on a ranch. My dad instilled in me that I had to work hard for everything and that if I wasn't sweating, I wasn't doing it right. To add to that dogma, I was constantly surrounded by macho men who were always trying to prove they were more manly than the other. After my dad was relegated to bed rest, leaving his wife to become the primary financial provider for the family, his self-esteem took a hit—and in many ways so did mine. This was not an easy time for any of us. My siblings and I missed our mom and how she cared for us, and my dad missed being the bread winner. I am often conflicted when I reflect on this time period. It should have been a time to connect with my dad, but it felt so unnatural that it was a burden at best. One particular memory of this time is what my dad would make us for breakfast. For some reason my dad thought that the kids loved chorizo and French fries. It was fun eating a beloved side dish for breakfast at first, but after years of the same breakfast it became disgusting—so disgusting that to this day I don't eat either French fries or chorizo. (My therapist and I are still working through that tragedy.)

However difficult this time period was for us, I realized that it was equally difficult for my mother who had to work all day and then come home to work just as long and hard. As a dutiful son, I tried to help as much as I could. As a ten-year-old this was not easy, but over the next ten years I grew to learn many lessons from my mother that today have contributed to the man I have become. Some of my fondest memories are of cooking with my mom, and it was during this time that I began to form my thoughts on gender and gender roles. As was often the custom, my family shared our table with family and extended friends. This usually meant more women helping to make meals. It was from these women that I learned not only to cook but also about the inequity they were enduring. The stories of survival and the tools used to navigate the expectations of stereotypical gender roles by these women are inspiring.

My mother in particular taught me that it was better to be right in secret than in practice. What this looked like varied by occasion, but one instance stands out. My mother had returned from work one night to find my father passed out on the couch. It was a Saturday, and it had been a particularly difficult day filled with pain for my father. It was the first time I saw him cry. He cried due to the immense pain he was in from his back injury, and it was difficult to watch. To alleviate the pain, he kept taking pain pills all day—so many that he fell into such a deep sleep that we couldn't get him to respond. When my mom made it home, the house was a mess and we were all hungry. My mom had just worked a twelve-hour overtime shift on a Saturday, but she didn't complain or miss a beat. She organized us kids, and together with a joyful spirit we cleaned the house and made dinner. As we were sitting at the dinner table, my father came to the dining room and asked how long he was asleep. Again without missing a beat my mother reassured him he had only taken a small nap and that he did a great job of caring for us and keeping the house in order. This memory stayed with me, and years later I asked my mom why she did that. Her response was that it was to keep the peace as my dad was injured enough already. This display of love and patience would be the foundation of how I would later attempt to structure my life. My mother's nurturing example eventually led me to consider a career in education, and many of the people who would become a positive influence on me were teachers. These teachers helped me come to a new realization of what it meant to be a young man and ensured that I would one day work at positive self-actualization.

In the world of public education women generally dominate the teacher ranks, but women still lag behind men in the area of administration. This is a byproduct of not only gender bias but also of expectation bias. For example, a man is expected to be a strong leader with command of the school, while a woman is supposed to fill the role of caregiver and soother. Thankfully my experience as an administrator has been mostly influenced by women. Again, my personal experience is that women have a much better command of school leadership than men and that they leave personal emotions such as anger and frustration out of their leadership style. Most male principals that I have worked were the exact opposite, often using anger, fear, and intimidation as tools to keep the rank and file in check.

One particular and profound influence in my professional life has been my mentor, Michelle (not her real name). Michelle taught me how to be organized, proactive, and compassionate, but most importantly she taught me how to be vulnerable. Michelle is not your typical administrator. Somehow she is always the first person at school in the morning, despite being a single mother of a young child and the primary caregiver for her two elderly parents. She more than holds her own when fathers come in to deal with their kids' discipline issues. I have seen many a dad looking silly and weak after he tried to belittle her just because she was a woman, yet she did not waiver. Likewise, when another male counterpart once tried to mansplain something she had already eloquently explained, her response was swift and piercing. Unfortunately, her piercing wit and to-the-point demeanor has limited her and has caused her to hit a ceiling in the administrative ranks. Michelle could be a great principal, but year after year she is passed over for less qualified (mostly male) applicants. She's been told over and over again that she doesn't look or act the part. Conventional thinking would say that it is fine for a man to have an ego when it comes to the workplace, but for a woman to have an opinion is dangerous and must be subverted.

I am aware of my privilege as a male over my female coworkers, and I hate it. I have had people at work come up to me and ask for explanations about something Michelle has already explained, but for whatever reason they want to hear it from me to be sure it's legitimate. It bothers me when people do that. I try to make a conscious effort not to feed that discrimination. Unfortunately, in the world of educational leadership, many people see women in one of two categories: slut or bitch. I have sat through many conversations where my male counterparts belittle their female administrative partners based on their fear that one day they likely will have to serve under these women's leadership. This fear often leads not only to bad words but also to the insidious and demeaning objectification of these women. I am ashamed to admit that at one point in my life I subscribed to this way of thinking, and had it not been for my friend and mentor, Michelle, I would likely still be deep into that mindset.

After applying to be a principal several times over the last three years, Michelle was finally offered the promotion last year. But then, while the excitement was still at its peak, she got word that the district would not be promoting her after all but instead would be giving the job to another applicant—a man. Not only was she passed over for a man; she was passed over for a man who had only one year of experience as an assistant principal, whereas she had ten years of experience. The reason she was given was that the community stakeholders wanted to hire this particular person over her because he was charismatic and possessed traits that would represent the school and those involved with the school in a manner that they felt was more appropriate than her personality traits. In essence they wanted a man who exuded machismo and perpetuated a certain status quo.

I was crushed for my friend. I was sure she would be devastated, and I tried to avoid speaking to her about the situation as much as possible. Then one day out of the blue I couldn't handle it, and I simply blurted out, "I'm so sorry, Michelle, for what they did to you."

Michelle stopped what she was doing and asked me rather sharply what I was talking about. I expressed my sorrow for her being passed up again and in such a horrible way. She calmly looked at me and said something I will never forget: "Hugo, I don't need anyone to tell me how good I am at my job, nor do I need anyone to validate me. I am here, and I continue to stay here in this position not because I don't have options. I stay here because I love working with people like you. A man didn't beat me out of a job; I work with the real men like you."

Michelle was being kind. We often talked about how patriarchy has contributed to her lack of leadership opportunities. She simply wanted me to understand that not all men were bad, and I was one of the good ones. Even as I grieve what happened to Michelle, she continues to show me what it means to be a man. A man takes no joy in the demise of others, and he doesn't dwell on what could have been. This lesson has stuck with me as a reminder of what my mindset should be, especially when things begin to fall apart around me. It has been a valuable tool for me as I navigate being a father and consider how I raise my own children.

One of the most difficult experiences of my life was losing my job. In many ways my identity as a man is tied directly to being able to provide financially for my family. When that was taken away during the economic downturn in the mid-2000s, I was suddenly faced with a similar dilemma my own father experienced many years before. To add to the despair was the fact that I had placed much of my personal identity into my job. In many ways my job was a calling, and therefore much of what I believed in was directly tied to that job. When it was gone, much of who I understood myself to be was gone too. In my experience, men in particular suffer from this identity coupling too often. We are so concerned with showing our love by providing materially for our families that when we lose the ability to express our love in this way we often lose ourselves all together. After this happened to me, I had to face a double dilemma: I couldn't provide financially for my family and I no longer knew who I was. I never experienced such a deep resentment for life as I did in those dark days. I couldn't sleep, eat, or even imagine living.

My wife and kids watched from the sidelines as I slowly entered a dark cocoon and shut myself off from the world. I spent days in our garage simply sitting and stewing in anger. How could this be? How could I lose myself? And how could I let myself stay in this state of despair? It was a long summer of spending hours on end asking myself these questions while sitting in the garage. Then one day I began to formulate a plan. Instead of a comeback plan in which I could go back to school or find a job in my old field of education, my plan was focused on one thing: how I could end my life. I felt that in many ways my life was already over, and I was just going through the motions. I showed no goodwill towards anyone and couldn't show any love to my family because I had no love for myself.

With my plan set, I now just needed to implement it. On a hot day in late July, I sat by myself in the garage. I had spent the better part of the morning pumping myself up to do this. I would call 9-1-1 and let them know to come to my home before my wife and kids returned from swim lessons. I waited patiently for the hour of their departure. When they left, I couldn't even give them a hug and kiss as I was in such a dark place. As I sat on a chair ready to end it all, the door flung open and in ran my little girl. Her loving eyes were fixed on me with such intensity that they frightened me. It was as if she knew I was up to no good. Instead of death, my daughter brought with her love. She ran up to me and gave me a hug that engulfed me so profoundly that I felt like someone had pumped the room full of laughing gas. My reaction was to hug her back and start laughing. I laughed so hard my ribs hurt.

Then I began to sob uncontrollably. My daughter stopped me and asked why I was crying. I told her that for the first time in a long time I was happy. For the first time in a long time I felt alive. I found out later that my family turned around because my daughter forgot to tell me she loved me, and she insisted that it was her last chance. Little did she and my family know just how true that could have been. That day and every day since my daughter has set the example of how I should deal with my emotions. She made me realize that I don't need to have the answers in every situation. I can simply be a dad, and dads don't have to be in control all the time. She taught me that my identity was tied not to a job but rather to the most important title I could hold—daddy.

Today I identify as a father above all else. I chose this identifier primarily because, for many of my friends, fathers are absent and a great cause of pain. Identifying myself as a father above all else is an empowering label because it helps me focus on what is most important to me. Additionally, this identifier has helped guide me through some very difficult realities. I am again facing professional and financial uncertainty, but for the first time ever I feel ready to take on the challenge. For the first time I am not afraid, and I do not feel like I must be in charge of every situation. I am comforted by Jesus teaching in the Sermon on the Mount: "Can any one of you by worrying add a single hour to your span of life? And why do you worry about clothing? Consider the lilies of the field, how they grow; they neither toil nor spin, yet I tell you, even Solomon in all his glory was not clothed like one of these" (Matt. 6:27–29). Likewise, I am thankful that I do not need to have all the answers. Instead I revel in my son who is an avid reader and my daughter who loves playing dress up.

The culture that machismo is built on—the need to be in control and to maintain a certain facade—clouds everything. This therefore makes it difficult to express emotions of insecurity and to grow out of those emotions. I have seen too many of my Latino brothers trapped in this prison of insecurity and fear, which becomes a cycle that spirals down the paternal line for generations. As an educator, I too often encounter young men who are lost because of a sense of abandonment from their fathers. Those who have active fathers in their lives often report that their fathers expect them to "act like a man" when faced with adversity. When asked what this means, these young men often answer that it means they should act aloof or generally show emotions of anger to respond to any given situation.

Then there are those young Latino men who are fatherless. They have never known their father and often live either with their single mom or with their grandmother. In my community, it is not unheard of for upwards of 50 percent of children to never know their biological father. This also has a chilling effect on how our boys grow to understand what masculinity is. Too often they are lead astray by the images of our culture that objectify their female counterparts, and without proper mentoring the cycle continues.

This cycle of toxic masculinity is pervasive in our culture, but it seems uniquely rooted in Latino machismo in ways that create a prison for Latino boys and men. I have been trapped in this prison where I need to be in control, and it has created in me a dangerous relationship with anger. This anger has guided my choices and in the past alienated those I love.

Thankfully I have learned a new way. The women I high-lighted in this essay have paved the road for me. This road is not influenced or controlled by anger; rather, it is guided by love. A mother's love sustained me, a colleague's love inspired me, and a daughter's love saved me. These women have molded the man I am today, and I couldn't be more thankful. I often look back at the day my daughter saved my life. I have never been in such a dark space, but I realize now that I was trapped in a way of thinking that could only be exited by extreme means. I don't believe I will ever fully overcome the influence of toxic masculinity. The best I can do is to become aware of its influence and pervasiveness in my life and, once aware, to then takes steps to mitigate its effects. Only then can I choose to model the kindness and peace I so desperately wish for my life and for the world.

An Indigenous Man

Harry Lafond

Nâpêw (man) and kîsâpêwin (on becoming a man)

My wife, Germaine, and I have entered and are living in the final quadrant of the circle of life here on Mother Earth. How do we know that? The house is quiet, and there are no young people to wake up in the morning for the trip to the local school. Then at Christmas time, the house comes awake bursting at the seams with small bodies and noise. These are the grandchildren (nôsisiminanak) who have come to find love, good food, and connections.

I am a commuter; everyday I travel to work and back for two hours. More often than not, I am travelling alone with the radio off and reflecting on the dynamic relationships that come from a family of five children, as many partners, and thirteen grandchildren.

As I experience with my children and older grandchildren their struggles to become nêhiyawak (Cree men and women) in a high-pressure world that has been pushing sameness for all of us, many reflective miles have passed under my van tires. I reflect on the man I have become and the man I could have been. It is not easy to admit major blunders. There are those moments I have wanted to pull back the words said, the actions taken. Regardless, the high points are celebrated and the low points are regretted. Understood in the context of spirituality, ceremony, humility, and love, the moments of blunder become formative. In the Cree world, every mistake is an opportunity to learn to move closer to miyo wâhkôtowin (having good relations).

My journey has been about understanding my family histories, especially the men, and the impact those families have on how I see myself as a man, as a father, and now as a grandfather. Where did âniskotâpânak (great grandparents) come from? What was their world like? What kind of colonial and cultural pressures did they experience as men of their families and communities? Finding these stories becomes important to understanding the lived legacies to my generation and the generations that follow us. To pursue this storyline, the first challenge is discovering who to talk to. Oral tradition has suffered traumatic damage in our communities from the pressures of colonial practices implemented by governments, churches, and institutions.

For me, it has been a hit and miss journey. During the period from 1885 to the 1950s, there were varying degrees of oppressive practices to suppress the cycle of ceremonies. The threat of imprisonment drove the ceremonial keepers into the bushes away from their central place in the family and community. The trust relationship between the ceremonial keepers and the public world was damaged to the extent that knowledge was not being transmitted to the next generation. In my community, the normal ceremonies like the sun dance, sweat ceremonies, and feast were not openly practiced until the 1990s when the people felt safe from the criticism of the church.[1]

The normal flow of the educational process was further interrupted by the imposition of the residential school regime.[2] In many cases, the natural tie between the knowledge keepers and the children became almost nonexistent. Two generations of grandparents were prevented from passing on important knowledge. None of my grandmother's children were trained in the medicinal knowledge she had to give to them. Her expertise went to the grave with her. The consequences continue today with several generations not having the educational contact with their grandparents to ensure the health of the oral tradition and its intended purposes.

---

1 From the earliest arrival of Europeans on the North American continent, Christian churches—propelled by evangelistic impulses and bolstered by the endorsements of the Doctrine of Discovery (1493) and often colluding directly with federal governments in Canada and the United States—imposed a strict reign of "Christian" values on indigenous people, decimating their cultural practices and dividing communities as some "converted" to Christianity while others refused to follow this foreign worldview. Today increasing numbers of indigenous people are rediscovering their spiritual heritage, either abandoning Christian practices completely or finding a blend of the various beliefs and practices.

2 The Indian residential school system in Canada was instituted soon after the Treaties were signed. There is documented evidence of the deliberate purposes set forth initially by government bureaucrats. The schools were to eradicate the indigenous culture from the being of the child and make the child in the image of the colonizer. Both the official and unofficial policies evolved, continuing their destructive processes from generation to generation until 1951. In that year, major amendments were made to the Indian Act to soften the colonizing process. The schools continued for another forty years. The destruction of social structures and family structures by the implementation of these policies over a number of generations continues today to be the major challenge by Indigenous individuals and families in the struggle to put meaning into personal and family reconciliation.

Sometimes I am fortunate to meet and receive learning from passionate Elders who understand the importance of knowing the Cree Creation story and how it explains the place men have in that process. Recently, a particularly passionate Cree Elder couple from the neighboring community taught us about the meaning of sâkihitowin (love).[3] It is a process of building a lasting relationship that defines the responsibilities of the partnership. He told us that, in the case of his relationship to his wife of many tears and many years, it is the simple things that make a difference. Bringing home a pack of gum for her from a trip to Prince Albert tells her that she holds a special place in his heart as he goes about his business. This resonates for me, and since then I never come home without some token of my awareness for Germaine's important place in my life.

For these Elders, life begins before conception and flows into the birth process to enter into a circular cycle. Oskawâsis (young child) is the first stage. During these early years, okâwîmâw (mother/mom)—with support from the grandparents and extended family, teachers, mentors, and ceremony—helps oskawâsis transition to nâpêsis (boy, little man) and oskinîkis (young man), the second stage. This is the time for the young man to explore his identity through learning and ceremony about the gifts and talents given by the Creator to help him define his identity and find his place in the family and community. Usually this is the time roles are determined and nurtured. Many oskâpêwisak (ceremonial helpers/trainees) begin at this time and eventually become the ceremony keepers.

There is no set age or time when nâpêsis transitions into the third stage, nâpêw (man). It is more a determinant of the circumstances in the family and community. In some families, the transition occurs gradually over a period of time characterized by the assuming of responsibilities like taking a spouse and having the first child. In other families, nâpêsis is mentored and encouraged early in his maturing years to make decisions and assume responsibilities of becoming an independent person. In today's context, very often the mentoring is about going to school, graduating, and obtaining employment. Very often the Elders caution nâpêsis not to forget their cultural roots. Elders have shown me through their

---

3 A. J. and Patricia Felix. Cree Law 2. Sturgeon Lake First Nation, Saskatchewan. May 9, 2018.

teachings that classroom education is meant to complement Cree education and not to be a replacement.[4]

Then comes my favourite stage, even if it is full of arthritic joints, failing ears, thick glasses, and stomachs fit only for moose broth and bannock: omosômimâw time, or more commonly, mosôm (grandfather). It is a time of grandchildren who replace their parents as number one visitors in mosom's house. Countless times I have listened to testimonials from grandchildren speaking about the formative impact their grandparents have had in their lives and the special relationships nurtured between them. Very often the stories are about the gift of spirituality nurtured and mentored by the grandparents.

Mosom becomes âniskotâpânak (great-grandparent and great-grandchild), which names both great-grandparent and great-grandchild. One Elder explains how the circle closes and opens where the great grandparent exits into the Spirit World and the child, a gift of the Creator, enters to be born to parents. Âniskotâpânak are charged each with a new role, one to be in the Spirit world and the other to enter Mother Earth. Each enters into a new understanding of wâhkôtowin (making relations). And so the cycle progresses as it has for thousands of generations.

For me, this is the foundation. It may be damaged by time and circumstance, but it holds the truths of nêhiyawak (Cree) and nâpêwak (men). My generation and more so my children's generation are challenged to piece back the picture and massage their relationships toward healing for our families and communities.

For many, the challenge is too great and too painful. A walk through the Muskeg Lake graveyard is a walk of frustration, of anger, of a deep sense of loss for what could have been. I have felt the pain of the families as I helped them prepare to bring their youth to a premature grave. The symptoms of trauma generated by cultural confusion and identity loss end up in alcohol abuse and, more recently, in drugs, gangs, HIV, sexual violence, and suicide.

For me, the journey has been long; it has pain; it has loss; it has grown love; it has brought some understanding of our family history; it has brought hope for my grandchildren. I have been gifted with a strong partner and some key friends who have directed my journey. Whether it is through Marriage Encounter, ceremony, or the gift to speak well publicly, I have been able to

---

4 Kevin Lewis, Ph.D. Indigenous Language Instructor Program. University of Saskatchewan. 2016–17.

slowly, like an archaeologist, brush away the dust to reveal the foundation so necessary for healing. Sometimes the discovery has been as simple as discovering a new relative and experiencing that emotional moment of connecting with a growing family. (We have many relatives! My second son is fond of asking, "Is there anyone you aren't related to?")

Here is where I come from and where I hope to engage my whole family and gift them with a refurbished nêhiyawak foundation.

Nohtâwiy and ohtâwimâw

"Astam nimis, ahciyaw ta mikoskâcitin" (come, my older sister, let me bother you for a short time); a faint smile from her wise brown eyes tells me that it is quite okay to ask questions when tobacco is not readily available. She has been my teacher for the past thirty years and has added depth to my understanding of who I am and what my ancestors meant for me to be. Later, after the life lesson, we will recess to the outdoors to share her Players cigarette. For me the smoke is about giving thanks to the Creator for the gift I have just received from one given to be a knowledge keeper in our community.[5]

Back to my office, the big question for me: "When I say 'nohtâwiy,' what does that mean? What does it teach about relationships?"

She looks down to those gentle hands that have seen and loved many grandchildren. I wait like I have done many times before. Slowly the words come in a mixture of nehiyawewin and English. She begins to unravel the culture from within the simple word that holds generations of meaning:

> "Ohtâwimâw" is the word that tells us about the man in the family; "nohtâwiy" means my dad. "Nôtokêw" [old woman] is the teepee, and she wraps her arms around all her relatives. She tries to hold them where they are safe and are loved. Sometimes, there are too many relatives, and the teepee widens as it gets to the earth. Nôtokêw watches over the children. She will make sure they have food and what they need to become happy,

healthy people. She teaches about love and sharing. Ohtâwimâw [father] is the support for nôtokêw. He is a partner who brings along the child. The word refers to leading and bringing along. That is what the man is given to do. He protects the child by bringing them to the safe place of the family. This he does by teaching, by leading, by mentoring."

The lesson is short but vibrating with currents of meaning far beyond the simple nêhiyawewin and English sharing of knowledge. Put into the context of the nêhiyaw worldview, the lesson is about a people who see themselves in a circular world with four distinct realities that merge together in a dynamic reconciliation of self and family. Ohtâwimâw (father) becomes a complex process of movements that work to balance the four realities. It is a process of leading and bringing along the child to be a physically healthy being, to grow emotionally strong, to be strong in the ways of knowing, and to recognize the source of all life. All this is ground-ed in the creation stories that root nehiyaw awasis (Cree child) to Mother Earth through teachings of relationships (wâhkôhtowin).

Disconnect

What happened? Why didn't I know this Cree teaching when my oldest boy was born? Why did it take me five children moving out of the house before I began to feel that I was finally beginning to get it right?

Many years ago while on a retreat at Anderson Lake Ahnis-nabe Centre, I wrote a short poem about unpacking wâhkôhtowin.

ni papa

the road past Old Jake Turner's . . .
you never picked that patch of ice
you never wanted to fall
as chance would have it
or as God would plan it
you fell in that swirling snow . . .
opening my eyes to you . . .

I drew my fingers through your warm hair
Your eyes reached my heart . . . to us
In that moment—I loved you
as God would want me to love.

I found love staring into my eyes from the cold, hard surface of a gravel road in the middle of a typical Saskatchewan January blizzard. My drunk dad had slipped on ice and was now lying on the ground with the prospect of freezing to death if I wasn't able to help him back to his feet. I found a bit of myself at that moment even though I didn't recognize it for what it was until many years later. It was a moment when a metamorphosis was set into motion for me. Until that moment, I didn't think I loved my dad; his addictions pushed me away, and I felt only resentment for his inability to hug and express his feelings. One Saskatchewan blizzard changed all that, and over the next thirty years we learned to hug, we learned to talk, we learned to argue, we learned about love. I realized I needed the full story of the men in my family and to gift that to my sons.

Maybe this is a good time to shake out the stories and try to make sense of ohtâwimâw (father) for me, for my sons, and for my grandsons in 2018. The Truth and Reconciliation 94 Calls to Action[6] direct our energies to seek out the truth of our histories (79.2: "integrate Indigenous history, heritage values, and memory practices into Canada's national heritage and history").

Kayâs (in earlier times)

J. B. Lafond sat in council with kytowehow, pihtikwakew, mista-wasis, and ahtahkakoop through the winter and summer of 1876. On August 23, 1876, he signed onto the promises of Treaty 6 as a headman to kytowehow, chief of Muskeg Lake Cree. He was a Metis who chose to sign with the Crees. The remainder of his father's family chose to remain Metis. His wife, Josette Mustakumack (probably mistihkomân "big knife"), came from the Crees from the Green Lake, Saskatchewan, area.

Both J. B.'s Metis relatives and his adopted Cree relatives were experiencing the pain of disease and hunger. Prior to this, Muskeg Lake's oral history tells about a group of families working together to keep Fort Carlton on the North Saskatchewan supplied

---

6 Truth and Reconciliation Commission: Calls to Action. 2 June 2015. This Commission crossed Canada and held major gatherings in numerous places. At those gatherings, survivors of the residential school era in Canada were given the opportunity to tell their story of their experiences while at those schools. It brought to all Canadians the story of this sad part of Canada's legacy for the first time. From these stories, ceremonies and displays, Commissioners Sinclair, Littlechild and Wilson presented Canadians with 94 Calls to Action. These are meant to help Canadians come terms with their history and to actively become engaged in setting a new direction for the relationship building processes between they and their Indigenous partners. For more information visit www.trc.ca.

with game, primarily buffalo. The spirit of the buffalo was under attack and consequently disappearing from our land during the later part of 1860s and into the 1870s, making the local economy weak with few viable alternatives for the Metis and Cree hunters. This was the conversation around the home fires and again during the men and women council sessions. Both the Metis and the Cree had a fluid sense of the present and future using their governing practices to problem solve into change and adaptation. Their conversations were about survival and change, assessing their options and seeking new ideas. Some opted to small-scale farming; others tried selling products found on the land like medicine and fruit. In this way the Cree of Muskeg Lake pulled together and kept the community growing.

Sometimes colonist history portrays the people of these times as victims, with little mention of Indigenous perspective. What I heard, saw, and experienced in the 1950s before government welfare took over was about men and women creatively eking out a living on small farms, gardens, haying, cutting pickets, and the like. I heard about the people in the 1930s and 1940s bucking government policy and leaving the security of the home reserve to work on farms, in lumbermills in British Columbia, and in mines in Ontario and even joining the army (men and women). Many of these were J. B. and Josette's grandchildren and great-grandchildren. Inside this story is another thread, one that threatens to weaken and destroy the legacy of the Metis and Cree people, especially the men of the community.

In 1880, Andre was born to Josette and J. B. Six years later, right after the battles of Batoche, Andre found himself on his way to the Dumbo Residential School[7] just outside of Calgary and High River, Alberta. It is hard to imagine the emotional trauma he experienced during that long trip from Muskeg Lake to Calgary by horse and

---

7 The Indian Act was passed through the Canadian Parliament in 1876. Inside the act, one clause references compulsory education for Indian children ages six to sixteen. From this act, the government of Canada in cooperation with church organizations, Indian agents, and the Northwest Mounted Police (Royal Canadian Mounted Police), began to forcibly take children from their families and enrol them in residential schools. In numerous accounts, parents and grandparents were arrested for resisting the measures being taken. This practice of sending children to residential schools lasted until the 1990s. After 1952, if parents wanted their children to have an education, the options were limited to one-room day schools or residential schools. For many communities, the day school was not an option. In 1959, my community leaders negotiated an agreement with the local school board to allow the Muskeg Lake children to attend the town school with "white" kids. This was not easily accomplished; it was an unheard-of proposal in our area of Saskatchewan.

walking (about 750 km). He had to leave his mom, dad, little sister Rosalie, and the land he played on. Family oral history does not name the priest who took him.

For the next thirteen years, Andre lived completely apart from his dad, mom, and community of Muskeg Lake. During those formative years when, as a young man (nâpêsis) he should have been learning to become a Cree and Metis man, instead he was spending those years in a residential school without even the respite of summer months at home. Ohtâwimâw (fatherhood) was under attack in our family. We are in the fourth generation of this post treaty family. In each family, each father has had to struggle mightily to find his way back to wâhkôhtowin.

When Andre found his way back to Muskeg Lake, the Lafond family had grown. There were new brothers and sisters to meet and parents who had become strangers through the thirteen years. He was expected to find a wife. Madeline Greyeyes had just come home from St. Michael's Residential School after spending six years there. On June 23, 1900, Andre and Madeline were married. True to the sharing of Metis and Cree culture, the log home shook to the red river jig, drops of brandy and waltz. Some danced the night away, everyone ate, there were stories told, and laughter was shared. There were some smuggled spirits in the bush behind the house (Indian Agent was not invited). If the fiddle players could have been coaxed, there would have been a second night of the same.

July 19, 1903 (nohkom said she gave birth on July 16, but the priest was always right), a baby's cry broke through the hushed murmur of the midwife's instructions. This was Auguste's announcement to the world. I wonder how Andre felt that day. I wonder what he felt when Auguste was given to him—or perhaps he shied away from holding him. He had no experience to draw on and scant knowledge from his family on what to do with a new son. He had only just returned from residential school after a thirteen-year absence. The curriculum of the residential school did not cover fatherhood, taking care of babies, or the role of the ceremonies at the time of a birth. From his mother's family, there would have been prayers to be invoked by the father of the new child. Andre's maternal grandfather would have offered tobacco and gifts to the kehtaya (Elders of the community) to give the new son a name of a spirit helper. Andre did not have this knowledge; instead his son was taken to the priest to be baptized with the name Auguste.

I remember when Sarain was born: even though I had been around babies most of my life and even babysat some nephews and nieces, it was a powerful emotional moment followed by days of feeling overwhelmed at the responsibility this gift from the Creator brought into our home.

For Andre and Madeline, during those early years, babies arrived about every two years until there were sixteen births registered in nohkom's journal. It could not have been easy, only five of the sixteen survived to become adults. Auguste was the only male child to become an adult.

Andre had learned about ranching and farming; this knowledge served him well, and he began to establish a modest mixed farming operation. In 1912, he and Madeline built a log house near the creek on the south side of Muskeg Lake. His brother-in-law lived across the creek where he also raised a large family and established a mixed farm with a substantive orchard of apples, plums, currents, saskatoons, and chokecherries. During those early years, Auguste learned from his parents about farming—about ploughing the land and raising horses and cattle. Then, like Andre and Madeline, it came time for him to leave for St. Michael's Residential School, alone.

He had no siblings with him—perhaps some cousins from across the creek like Stanley Greyeyes, who was the same age as him. I don't remember nohtâwiy ever talking about his experiences at that school. During the second year, he was sent home because he had developed epilepsy. My mother told us that Auguste became epileptic from the abuse he had experienced from the big boys. For the rest of his life, his epilepsy became part of our lives, and we knew that whenever he experienced stress and sudden fright, he would have an epileptic seizure. Fortunately, as Auguste reached his grandfather years, the seizures became less frequent and his grandchildren were spared seeing him in the throes of a seizure. For us, there was always the niggling anxiety for that sound he made before falling into a seizure.

We can get a sense of his relationship with Andre during those formative years—from the time Auguste came home to his marriage in 1924—from the stories our mother told us. Ni mamanan (as we called her), Rose Moreau, was raised by her Metis grandfather. Jonas had fought at Batoche and hunted buffalo in southern Manitoba and northern states. Rose did not have access to schooling and lived her whole life without writing or speaking English. She had learned from her grandparents the value of memory and became an oral historian and storyteller. It was from these supper conversations and Sunday afternoon story sessions that we began to get a sense of who our dad was and who his dad was and the type of relationship they shared.

Andre was able to teach his son the necessities of being a farmer and to build a sense of honor in treating people fairly at all times. Did they have father/son conversations about fatherhood? Not likely, as Andre could not teach his son what he had not been taught. Ni mamanan told us that Andre was a man with a warm and gentle nature who loved to go to church and sing off key. She told us that Auguste became a "spoiled child" who was allowed by his parents to go his own way. During these years, Auguste began to experiment with liquor, which impacted the rest of his and our lives.

Jonas and Andre struck a marriage deal. February 12, 1924, Rose Moreau (age 15) was married to Auguste (age 20). Albert arrived eleven months later and for the next two decades and some, eleven children followed. I was number eleven. Seven of these are sons and five are daughers. Like Andre and Auguste, five of these seven sons and all five daughters attended St. Michael's Residential School in Duck Lake, Saskatchewan.

In retrospect, Auguste and I did not have a very strong Cree relationship. During my formative years we fought. It was hardly a time to learn about manhood.

The Cree worldview is about achieving and living in balance to our total being. This means the teaching and mentoring must incorporate the physical, the emotional, the mental, and the spiritual. Auguste and I connected most strongly in the physical and mental level.

Muskeg Lake people strengthened their entrepreneurial mindset after the signing of Treaty 6 as a way of ensuring survival in the new world. The stories of those early years are full of accounts of the men working at anything and everything to bring food and clothing into the family. Some men tried small farms; others worked in the neighboring communities as farm hands and as labourers cutting brush and picking stones. Some joined the armed forces during the First World War and again in subsequent conflicts. During these times, there are those who were damaged by the trauma of residential schools and could not live their lives without addictions to alcohol and violence. There are those who returned home from the

Armed Forces suffering from the experiences of war and carrying that into the lives of their families.[8]

It was during these times that Auguste taught us to work on our farm. As soon as I was strong enough to harness the horses, I was out in the hay flats by the creek mowing, raking, and hauling the hay for the winter feed. There were pigs to be fed and milking to be done. In the summer, the garden had to be weeded and potatoes had to be harvested (by the bushel, as they had to last us for the winter and spring). For Auguste, his most important role in the family was to help Rose feed and cloth us. Working to take of ourselves (pimâcihowin) became an ordinary part of who we are as a family.

If Auguste was not suffering from the drink from the Saturday trip to town, he would accompany the family to the Catholic church in Muskeg Lake. We knew he prayed, but it was a solitary experience, and we were seldom invited to participated in that prayerful time.

Êkwa (and now)

We learned about our dad's emotional frustration that erupted into violence during his drinking days; most often it took the form of shouting, angry comments, and self pity. As the next generation father, this has been the skeleton in my closet. This is where I have had to draw on my investigative prowess to find the thread that connects me to the âniskotâpânak, to a time before the trauma of residential school. Rose, our mother, helped to find that thread through her storytelling and her ability to bring to life the personalities of those old people. She helped me to understand that we have choices to make and alternative ways of building a healthy relationship with our children. In that struggle to change the patterns of fatherhood behaviour that Andre and Auguste mentored, it has been necessary to let go of feelings and beliefs in favor of retrieved knowledge that teaches that being a man (nâpêw) and being a father (ohtâwimâw) are precious gifts and responsibilities from the Creator to ensure the well-being of generations to follow.

September 1, 1964, I boarded the train and moved to North Battleford to attend high school (a Catholic boys' high school).

---

8 The balance between the men and the women tilted during these times. The family stories of Muskeg Lake from these times are full of marriage break ups, partner violence, and child neglect. For the past twenty years, the community has worked to rediscover its story, dust away to the foundation, and begin the process of reconciling the wâhkôtowin (relationship) between men and women.

This was my first big decision, supported fully by a mother who understood that leaving home at this time was the best decision for me. My generation can be characterized as the first generation with the sense of freedom to leave the reserve and seek a place in cities, high schools, and universities. We tried many things, we dreamed big, we fell many times, we picked ourselves up, and we tried again and again. In this new world, we tried to find our manhood among a myriad of unfamiliar influences. First came the hippies, and we grew our hair long—which became braids of activism during the days of Wounded Knee. Then we found culture and learned to drum, sing, and dance. Then some of us found partners and learned to mellow out our rhetoric into careers.

During all of this willow bush of directional confusion, we had an advantage to our Canadian counterparts: wâhkôtowin was still running through our veins, and it brought us home to touch base with our relatives. True, we came home and challenged the old order with different ideas and values. This generation was becoming adept at using the resources not only to discover their own Indigenous roots but also to incorporate values and ways from other cultures. This has become evident with my children's generation. Afro-American culture has many converts with low hanging jeans, hip hop moves, and creative word expressions about their own reality.

The fast-paced lifestyles of 2018 have complicated the reconciliation of Cree manhood. Jails in Saskatchewan are fast replacing the residential school experience, and once again our families are struggling to find the meaning of Cree manhood amid the pressures of gang recruitment. Recently, Red Earth First Nation and Muskeg Lake met to do some archaeology on the foundations of Cree Law. At the heart of the discussions were manhood and how communities can bring balance back to allow men the freedom to be good men (as the Cree define it).

Elders like Gladys Wapass Greyeyes and A. J. Felix speak about the strength of the family rising out of the type of partnership the man and woman forge within their home fires. The man serves the family and the community by leading the way forward and providing the security for the family as they grow through the stages of life. The woman gives life and nurtures the children that come from the partnership with man. This, they say, is a combination of spiritual and natural law. This law, the ceremonies, and the knowledge of creation provide the framework by which the partnership is to be molded by the man and the woman9.

I will end by sharing another precious moment and lesson from my oldest grandson (nosisê):

On Being an Adult at Bedtime

I lie in bed
Trying to stay awake.
There must be a better way!
Should I be doing something
more worthwhile, more adult?

A tiny voice rises from the dark
"moshom, I love you."
That moment becomes a
life time – the Spirit of
love reaches out to
etch my soul of adult things

---

9 A. J. Felix. Cree Law 2. Muskeg Lake Cree Nation. May 9, 2018.

An Asian Man

Hyung Jin Kim Sun

"To become a man, you need to do military service." "Asian men are too effeminate." "If you can't handle this in a manly manner, you should cut off your penis." "Go back to your country, slant eyes!" "But where are you from *originally*?" "I like to hire Koreans, because they work hard and don't complain like other immigrants do." "Do you know martial arts? Hai-ya!"

I grew up hearing comments like these. While they may sound harmless to others, these statements deeply affect Asian North Americans' understanding of masculinity. Given these stereotypes, writing about an Asian North American (ANA) perspective on masculinity is a daunting task. Asia encompasses more than fifty nations, and in each country there are numerous ethnic groups. Because of differences in education, culture, history, socioeconomic status, and experiences of North American culture, ANA men have different perspectives on masculinity. Given this complexity, I do not presume to write comprehensively about Asian North American masculinity. Instead, what I hope to offer is a limited yet valid perspective on the subject.

Let me start by situating myself. I am writing as a second-generation Korean Paraguayan and first-generation Korean North American who has lived in North America for more than ten years. This means that I write about Asian American masculinity predominantly as a Korean. Because Asian people living here have certain experiences in common, what I write is relevant to ANA men in general, but at the outset I give more attention to the Korean North American experience of masculinity. As the chapter develops, I turn to the broader experience of ANA masculinity.

This chapter is mostly a critical analysis of ANA masculinity. I examine how masculinity is influenced and shaped by Asian and North American cultures. Broadly speaking, ANAs are bicultural people, which means that they live between two cultures—Asian and North American. Because they have access to both cultures, they are different from those who grew up and lived mostly in one culture. An ANA man may feel more comfort with one culture, but the other culture does not cease to exist for him, and he has to constantly negotiate where he will situate himself on the spectrum spanning the two cultures.

A group of psychologists has identified four ways a bicultural person can respond to the two cultures of exposure: assimilation, separation, marginalization, and integration.[1] Assimilation is the choice to adopt the dominant culture of one's present location and relinquish one's previous culture or cultural heritage. Separation is the opposite of assimilation: one rejects the surrounding culture and maintains one's cultural heritage. Marginalization is a reaction against both cultures, a rejection of both. Integration finds a balance between the dominant culture and one's cultural heritage.[2] Using this framework for ANAs, to assimilate is to adopt North American culture; to separate is to reject North American culture and hold on to Asian culture; to marginalize is to reject both cultures; and to integrate is to balance the two cultures.

These categories, although helpful in naming different overall responses of bicultural people, are of limited utility because they treat a culture as a monolith and are too rigid to encompass diverse responses one has toward different aspects of a culture. For example, an ANA can reject the individualistic lifestyle prized in North American culture but accept the values of freedom and liberty espoused by the culture. Alternatively, an ANA can reject the work ethic of both cultures but embrace the value placed on family in both. In rejecting one aspect of a culture, one does not necessarily reject the whole culture, and in embracing part of a culture, one is not necessarily embracing the whole.

To reiterate and refine, then, ANAs are bicultural people who constantly negotiate their place between two cultures that they experience at every level of life, consciously or unconsciously. They choose to assimilate, separate from, marginalize, or integrate each of the cultural norms to which they are exposed. A man's decisions depend significantly on his experience with the people around him, his education, his socioeconomic status, his personality, and when he or his ancestors arrived in North America. For this reason, there are general differences among first-generation, 1.5 generation,[3]

---

1 See Berry, "Acculturation as Varieties of Adaptation"; Bourhis et al., "Interactive Acculturation Model."

2 Tadmor, Tetlock, and Peng, "Acculturation Strategies and Integrative Complexity," 106.

3 Here this designation refers to people who arrived in their current country as children and adolescents.

and second-generation ANAs. There are also differences between Asian Americans who began their immigrant life in North America as international students and those who came as refugees. These varieties of background and response make identifying a single ANA understanding of masculinity almost impossible.

Finally, as we turn our attention to identifying some factors from Asian culture that influence ANA masculinity, it is worth noticing that each culture has its own particularity, which creates, sustains, and reinforces certain values and norms that then influence understandings of masculinity. Even so, certain values and norms are widely shared among Asian countries, which are distinct from the values and norms of European, Latin American, and North American cultures.

In the next section, I examine one significant aspect of the culture of one Asian country—South Korea—and consider how it influences South Koreans and Korean men living in North America. This example illustrates how a feature of one Asian country affects the masculinity of that ethnic group living in North America. Then I analyze a Pan-Asian understanding of masculinity—"soft masculinity"—and observe how it affects Asian men living in Asia and in North America.

Asian culture

Military culture in South Korea

South Korea is a militaristic society, and military culture shapes South Korean understandings of masculinity. Not long after the Japanese colonization of Korea (1910–45) ended, the struggle between North and South Korea escalated to the point where each side began to use armed force, which led to the beginning of the Korean War in 1950. In that year, the government introduced universal male conscription with no alternative (nonmilitary) service option. The large-scale armed conflict ceased in 1953, when the two countries signed the Korean Armistice Agreement, but it was only a ceasefire and not an official end of the war. Technically the two nations remain at war, and their borders are heavily fortified.

The Korean War not only took many lives but also created animosity between North Koreans and South Koreans. From the time of the agreement through the late 1900s, South Korea adopted anticommunist nationalism as its ruling ideology.[4] This ideology permeated every aspect of society, from elementary school text-

---

4 Kang, "Disciplinary Politics of Antagonistic Nationalism," 690.

books to soap operas. Although it was propagated by the South Korean government, people were receptive to it because of their hatred of North Koreans. It united the people and justified the nation in maintaining its militarism. For this reason, the majority of South Koreans did not question the policy of mandatory military service,[5] and they came to believe that one only became a *real man* when he served in the military.[6] Those who question military service are generally seen as antisocial or antinational. The anticommunist nationalist ideology that fueled the transformation of Korean society into a militaristic society started to lessen as the nation began to mature toward democracy. Nevertheless, South Korea still exists as a strict militaristic-nationalistic country, and the National Security Act continues to punish political objection to military service and resistance to the authority of the military.[7]

The influence of the military in South Korean society is ubiquitous, and militaristic culture is deeply embedded in people's lives. The system of compulsory military service that requires all able-bodied men to serve functions to define manhood in South Korea. Since military service is mandatory, conscientious objection is illegal and no alternative service is provided for conscientious objectors. Men who evade military service are imprisoned.[8] The society is structured in a way that gives preference to those who have done military service, and evaders have difficulty finding jobs and a sense of belonging after they have served out their sentences. All these factors—historical, structural, legal, ideological, practical, psychological—come together in a Korean maxim: "A man must go through military service in order to take charge as a man."

---

5 Kang, "Disciplinary Politics of Antagonistic Nationalism," 694.

6 A widely viewed television program in South Korea is called Real Men, in which celebrities spend several days in military service and are transformed by it.

7 Kim, *Unending Korean*, 223.

8 There are a few exceptions where conscientious objectors were not imprisoned, but conscientious objection is still considered illegal. However, recently, a change is occurring. On June 28, 2018, the Constitutional Court of Korea ruled that not offering alternative services to COs is not consistent with the Constitution of the Republic of Korea. Therefore, the court requested to revise the Military Service Act by December 31, 2019, and now it is the responsibility of the National Assembly to make the revision. So far the members of the National Assembly are working toward the goal, but there are different views on what types of alternative service should be provided. While some members are suggesting service such as working in homeless shelters and hospitals, the members of the second largest political party, Liberty Korea Party, are arguing that more severe tasks should be given, such as mine clearance. Observing the current discussion in the Assembly, one can see that some proposals have punitive intention because they are requesting arduous works that require much a longer period of service than compusory military service requires.

One consequence of the defining role of military culture in South Korea is its impact on how Koreans understand what is normal for men. The military has been mandatory for all able-bodied men, but beginning in the mid-1990s, some were excluded as delinquents, orphans, transsexuals, and men who have difficulty sustaining their dependents.[9] There are legitimate reasons for the government's exemption (or better, exclusion) of these groups of people from the service, but according to sociologist Seungsook Moon, men in these groups are excluded because the government views them as untrustworthy, undesirable, or unsuitable for service.[10] In other words, men with a disability and those who are categorized as belonging to one of these groups are not viewed as normal men who function well. Not only that, but those who choose to be conscientious objectors, for religious or nonreligious reasons, are also considered unmanly. Military values and norms affect profoundly how the society sees those who for whatever reason do not do military service. These men are permanently stigmatized, and their stigma impedes them at every turn, hampering their ability to find a job and belong to a community. This burden is especially difficult to bear in South Korea, because the society is communal and therefore less tolerant than Westerners are of those who do not conform to communal standards and expectations.

The military culture also reinforces patriarchy and ageism. Since South Korea is a militarized society with near-universal male conscription, it is centered on men. Men are given more privileges and seen as more important than women. Although the society is becoming more democratic and is trying to provide women with equal opportunities, the culture and the social system are still patriarchal and still favor men, and women experience less economic participation and opportunity and political empowerment.[11] Moreover, military culture creates a hierarchy among men. Confucianism had already promoted a hierarchy among men, and military culture reinforces and intensifies that hierarchy. Hence, South Korea is a patriarchal society that supports ageism.[12] The

---

9 Military Manpower Administration of the Republic of Korea, "Byeongyeok-gam-myeon [Military Service Exemption]."

10 Moon, *Militarized Modernity*, 127.

11 See World Economic Forum data on Korea, Rep., 2016 Global Gender Gap Index, accessed October 1, 2017, http://reports.weforum.org/global-gender-gap-report-2016/economies/#economy=KOR.

12 Older people experience some ageism in hiring processes, and this is an important issue to be dealt with, but younger people also experience various types of discrimination in the society, which is generally overlooked.

hierarchy in the military is mirrored in hierarchies in the office, in school, in the family, and even in relationships among friends.[13] For this reason, as Koreans strive for greater equality and justice between men and women, they face the equally important task of seeking equality and justice among men.

What impact does this military culture have on Korean North American men? Even though they do not face compulsory military service, these men often have fathers who did service, and militarism influences Korean organizations that they are involved in, including churches and social groups. Korean North American men are intrinsically connected with Korean culture. Thus, the military culture affects their identity and their understanding of masculinity. Although they live in a society that favors egalitarian relationships and individualistic lifestyles, they are affected by a communal lifestyle, patriarchal mindset, and ageism from Korean culture. Between Korean culture and North American culture, they need to decide where they stand and what to embrace within each.

Soft masculinity projected through South Korean media

For North American readers, the concept that most appropriately describes Pan-Asian masculinity, or at least Northeast Asian masculinity, is soft masculinity.[14] Some scholars argue persuasively that the root of soft masculinity in an Asian context can be found in Confucianism. But as South Koreans accept capitalist consumption culture, as the country undergoes a transition to postindustrial democratic society, and as South Korean media are viewed extensively in Asian countries, a newly transformed soft masculinity has emerged. Cultural studies researcher Sun Jung has done a thorough study of the soft masculinity in Northeast Asian countries and explained why many Asian women idolize Korean actors such as Yonsama and Rain, who embody this soft masculinity, as well as why Asian men are striving to imitate the actors. She also describes how soft masculinity profoundly shapes Asian understandings of masculinity.

East Asian countries are heavily influenced by Confucianism, and soft masculinity can be found in the teachings of Confucius.

---

13 In Korean, the word for friend is generally used only among those of the same age. Age differences change the relationship from friendship to that of big brother and little brother, though there are some exceptions to this.

14 The masculinity found in Northeast Asia is described as soft masculinity to differentiate with North American masculinity. In Asian context, it is simply viewed as masculinity, but because the chapter is written for North American readers, I describe it as soft masculinity.

His depiction of an ideal man he called *junzi* (literally, son of lord/ruler). This term should be understood as referring to an exemplary man, a role model. Of course, Confucius's masculine ideal is exclusively for an elite and well-educated social group. According to him, a junzi has to have nine virtues, but the five most fundamental ones are genuine care, righteousness, respect for others in an appropriate manner, willingness to learn, and trustworthiness. How one should pursue becoming a junzi is then expressed differently in each country shaped by Confucianism. In premodern China, the people who sought to be a junzi chose wen masculinity (seeking mental attainment) rather than wu masculinity (seeking physical attainment). In Korea during the Chosen dynasty, the last dynasty before Japanese colonization of Korea (1910), people who followed the teachings of Confucius were called seonbi, and they were scholars who served the public, whether as officials or not. They abstained from manual labor, housework such as cooking and cleaning, and economic activity; they thought these activities would degrade them and prevent them from being a junzi.

Readers can readily see differences between Western settlers' masculinity and Confucius's masculinity. Rather than aspiring to be pioneers who know how to explore new territory, do the manual labor of building a house and barn, hunt animals, raise crops, and protect the community from invasion, seonbi focused on mental attainment, learned how to maintain order and peace and harmony in their community, and taught people wisdom. In short, people who strived to be a junzi preferred soft masculinity. Instead of seeking outer, physical strength, they sought inner strength. They embraced *oeyunaegang,* a concept well-known in East Asian culture: "a tender exterior and a strong inner will."[15]

This soft masculinity rooted in Confucianism is embedded in Asian understandings of masculinity, and it is one reason why men are encouraged to pursue academically rigorous careers. Nonetheless, the modern soft masculinity that is projected through South Korean media and which Asian women generally find attractive is quite different from the soft masculinity that can be found in wen and seonbi masculinity. This soft masculinity is a new trend for young Asian men, motivating them to invest time and money in their physical appearance. The goal is not to give an impression of male toughness but rather to appear as clean and well-groomed. Men use expensive skin-care products to beautify their faces, and

---

15 Jung, *Korean Masculinities*, 48.

a growing number of Asian men, especially Korean men, undergo cosmetic surgery. They pursue this form of masculinity not only to attract women but also to be the type of man who is widely accepted and viewed as sexy in Asian context.

Another stark difference from previous soft masculinity is seen in new attention to becoming empathic, showing sensitivity to others, learning how to communicate, and acting chivalrously. Men are becoming careful about what they eat and are increasingly aware of maintaining their health through regular exercise. They learn to cook and try to be supportive lovers. Sun Jung's observation about this soft masculinity, reflected in Korean media and Asian countries, is that it "is a hybrid product constructed through the transcultural amalgamation of South Korea's traditional *seonbi* masculinity (which is heavily influenced by Chinese Confucian wen masculinity), Japan's *bishonen* (pretty boy) masculinity, and global metrosexual masculinity."[16] From a Western perspective, this soft masculinity can be viewed as androgyny or even as feminine, but actually another type of masculinity is being lived out. This masculinity could be considered the ideal masculinity that Terry Colling, author of *Beyond Mateship: Understanding Australian Men*, describes: "Strong without hardness; soft without fear; powerful without oppression; gentle without shame; knowledgeable without arrogance; nurturing; led with humility and themselves with joy."[17]

The soft masculinity that is being embraced in South Korea and other Asian countries is to be celebrated in that it deconstructs an earlier understanding of masculinity that was oppressive of women. Besides, this masculinity lessens the difference between what it means to be a man and what it means to be a woman and therefore creates more common ground and closeness. However, this masculinity can be oppressive and exclusive of other Asian men, especially those who are not fortunate enough to pursue formal education, who do not have money for cosmetic surgery and expensive cosmetic products and clothes, who do not live in urban areas, or who have disabilities, either visible or invisible. Capitalistic consumer culture uses the appeal of this soft masculinity to encourage investment in products and treatments recommended for health and wellness, slowly shifting them from the category of "wants" to that of "needs," a move that exerts a strong pull in a community-centered society driven by honor and shame.

---

16 Jung, *Korean Masculinities*, 39.
17 Colling, *Beyond Mateship*, ii.

Furthermore, soft masculinity encourages chivalry; men are to protect and serve "fragile and powerless" women. Asian women who are fans of Korean actors welcome and long for this conduct from men. Yet this masculinity reinforces the message that women are in need of men's protection and help, and this message disempowers women. Thus, soft masculinity has some characteristics that align with feminists' views, but it retains elements of patriarchy. For these reasons, soft masculinity needs to be further transformed in ways that develop each man's particularities and that treat men and women equally instead of urging them to conform to media-generated images.

Given our earlier analysis of South Korea's military culture and our description of this soft masculinity, one might wonder how these two can coexist when they seem to be mutually exclusive. But in the current dynamics of Korean society, they are mutually constitutive and are key factors that shape and reshape South Korean masculinity.

In a globalized society in which Korean media are consumed throughout Asia and beyond, ANA men are affected by the soft masculinity projected there. They are not affected as much as Asian men, and they can reject this soft masculinity. Nonetheless, as ANA men they are exposed to several types of masculinity, and this soft masculinity is one of them. They can choose this soft masculinity, but in a North American context they may risk being perceived as too feminine. They can embrace Westerners' masculinity, but they may feel unfit. Because neither type is fully satisfying, ANA men may opt to live as hybrids, which leaves them with ongoing uncertainty about what an appropriate masculinity is.

North American culture

The portrayal of ANA men in Hollywood movies

We observed that South Korean mass media influence ANA men. Now let us see how the media produced in North America, especially Hollywood movies, affect them. In a digital era, it is not news that mass media influence people of all ages. Media are used for various reasons, from education to entertainment, and they are also used for specific propaganda and to distort information. Among several influential kinds of media are Hollywood movies. These films, which are consumed by people all over the world, profoundly influence perceptions and values, and they contribute to creating new trends in fashion and lifestyle. Movies can help us imagine our future, bring new social awareness, and challenge conventional thinking, but at the same time they can foster stereotypes of people and cultures. They perpetuate stereotypes of ANA men in particular.

Some of the most stereotypical images of ANA men are of martial arts experts and asexual, effeminate, nerdy, unromantic men.[18] In essence, apart from ANA actors who are skilled in martial arts, the movies portray ANA men as not manly enough, and these portrayals deeply affect ANA men emotionally, psychologically, spiritually, and socially. This recurrent stereotyping in cinema influences how society views ANA men, and as a result some ANA men are not recognized as fully masculine. This lack of recognition can have harmful results, as is explained in Don Neufeld's chapter in this volume.[19]

According to critical theorist Homi Bhabha, a stereotype is not simply a false representation of someone but rather an "arrested, fixated form of representation that, in denying the play of difference . . ., constitutes a problem for the *representation* of the subject in significations of psychic and social relations."[20] This stereotyping negatively affects ANA men in various ways, but I identify two main results here. First, it causes microaggression toward men. Microaggression is derogatory comments and behavior that, whether intentionally or unintentionally, are demeaning. Everyone experiences some microaggression, but people of some groups experience much more microaggression than others. The microaggression that ANA men experience disempowers them, and they need to work harder to prove that they are manly enough, in order to obtain recognition. Another negative influence of the stereotyping is that some ANA men shy away from their Asian culture and choose to embrace the "manly" image characteristic of Western masculinity. Integrating Western culture's masculinity is a process that is natural for ANA men, but rejecting Asian-ness and embracing Western masculinity means cutting off an important aspect of their life. And to do so because of stereotyping is particularly unfortunate.

---

18 Studies done on how Hollywood movies stereotype Asian American men include these two particularly helpful ones: Adachi, *Slanted Screen*; Shimizu, *Straitjacket Sexualities*. The recent movie *Crazy Rich Asians* does not reinforce these stereotypes, yet compared to all the movies that came out from Hollywood, this may be the exception that proves the rule, though hopefully it is a sign of changes to come.

19 See Don Neufeld, "Masculinity and Human Need" (chap. 1 above).

20 Bhabha, *Location of Culture*, 107.

In this context, we need to ask some crucial questions. Do ANA men need to assimilate the Western definition and view of masculinity, or should that perception of masculinity be challenged and changed? Is learning martial arts the only way for ANA men to be recognized as masculine in North America? Who defines masculinity in North America anyway?

Further stereotyping: Model minority and perpetual foreigner

The model minority stereotype is interrelated with the stereotype described above. If Hollywood movies portray ANA men as unmanly, the general cultural view of ANA people, whether men or women, is that we are a model minority. In North America, Asians are viewed as hard-working people who do not complain, who follow the rules and educate their children well, and who work tirelessly; as a result, they succeed economically. Politicians and people who do public policy work refer to Asians as a model to be emulated by other ethnic and racial groups: Asians succeed by working hard, and they don't complain about the social system.

Scholars disagree about the origins of the myth of Asians as model minority, but most agree that it was used by US politicians in the mid-1960s, when a militant black power movement was on the rise. Conservative politicians contrasted "rebellious" African Americans with quiet and submissive Asian Americans. These politicians deemed improvements in the social welfare system unnecessary because some minority groups—notably Asian Americans—were succeeding in the existing system. To these political leaders, the problem was African Americans who, unlike Asian Americans, complained and did not work hard enough.

Although this model minority image may appeal to some ANAs, the 1992 report by the US Commission on Civil Rights identifies four ways that it is harmful to Asian Americans:

> First, it leads people to ignore the very real social and economic problems faced by many segments of the Asian American population and may result in the needs of poorer, less successful Asian Americans being overlooked. Second, emphasis on the model minority stereotype may also divert public attention from the existence of discrimination even against more successful Asian Americans. . . . Third, the model minority stereotype may result in undue pressure being put on young Asian Americans to succeed in school, particu-

larly in mathematics and science classes, and in their careers. Too much pressure to succeed on young Asian Americans has been linked to mental health problems and even teen suicide. Finally, the origin of this stereotype was an effort to discredit other minorities by arguing that if Asian Americans can succeed, so can blacks and Hispanics, and many Asian Americans resent being used in this fashion.[21]

To connect the model minority with ANA masculinity, ANA men are seen as submissive people who should not be in leadership positions, as people needing to obey and to assimilate into the mainstream. This stereotype pressures ANA men to conform and not speak critically about the injustice they experience. The message is that by following the stereotype, they can have a better reputation than other racial-ethnic groups. But they will still not be seen as being as good as Caucasians. This stereotype shapes ANA men's understanding of masculinity.

Another stereotype that influences ANAs is that they are seen as perpetual foreigners. Regardless of when their parents migrated to North America, and no matter how fluently they speak English (even when English is the only language they speak), ANAs are seen as people who are here temporarily or who have moved here recently. This stereotype is in evidence when people ask ANAs where they are from. Many Caucasians will keep asking a person of Asian descent where he is from *originally*, even when he was born in Toronto or New York or Los Angeles or Kansas City. Stereotyping leads to microaggression, and constant microaggression sends a message that one may be welcome here but does not really belong. For many second-generation ANAs, the United States or Canada is their only country, but constantly getting the message that they do not fit in has severe effects on their sense of identity and belonging. It also affects how ANA men form their masculine identity. ANA men are portrayed as unmanly, so some choose to embrace a Western style of masculinity. But they continue to receive the message that they cannot be *true* Americans, no matter how long they (or their ancestors) have lived here. And the struggle around belonging and identity continues.

All these stereotypes, these "arrested representations," shape ANA masculinity, and they blind others from seeing diverse as-

---

21 U.S. Commission on Civil Rights, *Civil Rights Issues Facing Asian Americans in the 1990s*, 19.

pects of ANA men. Because of these arrested representations, the social roles to which ANA men have access are limited. In order to become "liberated representations," to resist the stereotypes, and to work for transformation, inner strength, resilience, and positive self-esteem are indispensable. But where can ANA men find these resources? Can the Anabaptist Christian tradition contribute something to these men?

Outlook

I have described the complexities of life for one who is bicultural, where one has to constantly negotiate cultural difference and choose where to situate oneself between Asian and North American cultures. I then explored some prominent influences from Asian and North American cultures that affect ANA men. As Asian men are influenced by these forces, they have to constantly consider which parts they will choose to assimilate, separate from, marginalize, and integrate. In general, the first immigrant generation tends to hold on to Asian culture and the second generation assimilates more to American culture, but this pattern is not universal.

As ANA men, we are aware of the emergence of soft masculinity in Northeast Asia, and we are aware of the stereotyping that exists in Hollywood movies and in North American society in general. As bicultural people, we are constantly moving between these cultures, seeking an appropriate form of masculinity. Nonetheless, the reality is that we will never find one right understanding of masculinity for ourselves: each culture puts forward a masculinity that fits their culture, and because we are bicultural, we will not be satisfied with a masculinity that comes from one or the other. Hence, a more appropriate understanding of masculinity for us is a hybrid that combines elements of both cultures. But there is no one-type-fits-all hybrid masculinity either; we have to choose what blend of elements is a good fit for ourselves.

As a Christian, I believe that one's masculine identity starts not from exterior factors but from something much deeper. It has to come from the perspective of our Creator. As an Anabaptist, I am convinced that the manifestation of full human masculinity as intended by our Creator is Jesus. In Jesus's life, teaching, and death, we can see what *real* masculinity is.[22]

---

22 In the third section of this volume, contributors take on the theological work of examining Jesus's masculinity and considering how we can live it out in our concrete context.

Although theological work and biblical exegesis can provide key insights about masculinity, they are not enough to offer a full understanding of what it means to be healthy ANA men. It is our task to live out those key insights and figure out what it means to be ANA Christian men while we move between cultures. Each culture has a perception of masculinity that contains elements that are oppressive and elements that are life-giving. Holding on to the key insights and continuing to ask what is just and what makes peace, we can assimilate, separate from, marginalize, or integrate any particular aspect of these cultures' views of masculinity. Through this endeavor, we can come up with a variety of healthy ANA masculinities and empower young ANA men to live well, challenge stereotypes, and bring change.

Although each ANA Christian man will need to discern the shape of masculinity that is suited to him, I want to end this chapter by recommending several general ways ANA Christian men can move toward greater health.

First, I propose that we engage more in physical activity. In part because of the influence of Confucianism, ANA culture values intellectual work over physical work. In biblical perspective, physical activity and manual labor are blessed by God; viewing them as unimportant is not a healthy perspective. We need to develop a more positive view of physical work and learn to enjoy the fruits of our physical labor.

Second, I recommend that we engage more in critical thinking. As a group of people who experience exclusion and microaggression in various ways, ANA men have to think more critically about our communities and societies. Christian feminists have begun to use critical theory to name several types of oppression. Through this endeavor, they have unmasked injustices, inequities, and imbalances of power that exist in society. We can benefit from the analysis these feminists have done, and it can guide us in reexamining our lives and the social systems that we depend on to see whether and how—consciously or unconsciously—we are oppressing women. Furthermore, in addition to being attentive to the voices of feminists and becoming more self-critical, ANA men need to examine how our community and our society silence and distort our identity and our understanding of masculinity. Many of us have been trained to do well in standardized exams, and now we have to develop critical thinking skills in order to identify how we are mistreating others and name the injustices that we are experiencing.

Finally, it is not enough to think critically. We also need to be actively involved in working for peace and justice. While showing self-control and being gentle and patient are vital virtues, ANA men have been well-schooled in them. We have not been taught enough about being assertive, disruptive, and resistant toward people in authority who misuse power. Since these values are lacking in ANA masculinity, I encourage ANA men to be more actively involved in the work of peace and justice as they think more critically. If in the process we discover that civil disobedience is called for, we should be disobedient in nonviolent ways. If we need to be disruptive because our society is maintaining a false peace that excludes our stories, then we should disturb this false ethos. If society demands that we assimilate into a way of life that is unhealthy and unjust, we should be bold enough to resist. My hope is that, through our actions we will inspire our non-Asian sisters and brothers in North America to stand in solidarity with us as we seek transformation in our lives and in society.

Bibliography

Adachi, Jeff. *The Slanted Screen: Discover the History of Asian Men in Hollywood*. San Francisco: AAMM Productions, 2006.

Berry, J. W. "Acculturation as Varieties of Adaptation." In *Acculturation: Theory, Models and Some New Findings*, ed. Amado M. Padilla. Boulder, CO: Westview, 1983.

Bhabha, Homi. *The Location of Culture*. New York: Routledge, 1994.

Bourhis, Richard Y., Léna Céline Moise, Stéphane Perreault, and Sacha Senécal. "Towards an Interactive Acculturation Model: A Social Psychological Approach." *International Journal of Psychology* 32 no. 6 (December 1997): 369–86.

Colling, Terry. *Beyond Mateship: Understanding Australian Men*. New York: Paramount, 1992.

Jung, Sun. *Korean Masculinities and Transcultural Consumption: Yonsama, Rain, Oldboy, K-Pop Idols*. Hong Kong: Hong Kong University Press, 2011.

Kang, Jin Woong. "The Disciplinary Politics of Antagonistic Nationalism in Militarized South and North Korea." *Nations and Nationalism* 18, no. 4 (Oct 2012): 684–700.

Kim, Dong-Choon. *The Unending Korean War: A Social History*, trans. Kim Sung-ok. Larkspur, CA: Tamal Vista, 2009.

Military Manpower Administration of the Republic of Korea. "Byeongyeokgam-myeon [Military Service Exemption],"

accessed October 1, 2017, http://www.mma.go.kr/contents.
do?mc=usr0000209.

Moon, Seungsook. *Militarized Modernity and Gendered Citizenship in
South Korea*. Durham: Duke University Press, 2005.

Shimizu, Celine Parreñas. *Straitjacket Sexualities: Unbinding Asian
American Manhoods in the Movies*. Stanford: Stanford University Press, 2012.

Tadmor, Carmit T., Philip E. Tetlock and Kaiping Peng. "Acculturation Strategies and Integrative Complexity: The Cognitive
Implications of Biculturalism." *Journal of Cross-Cultural Psychology* 40, no. 1 (January 2009): 105–39.

U.S. Commission on Civil Rights. *Civil Rights Issues Facing Asian
Americans in the 1990s*. Washington, DC: U.S. Government
Printing Office, 1992.

A Gay Man

Pieter Niemeyer

Held by Love

God is love is one of the deepest core convictions of faith that holds me. I believe that Jesus is the heart of God's revelation of love toward humanity. I believe the Holy Spirit is God's pervasive and wooing presence that calls us ever deeper into that transformative power called Love. I believe through faith that Love will reconcile all things to God through Christ and that this reconciliation, through both means and end, is shaped by Love. It is a substantive love that has the power to overcome enmity. It is through this spiritual understanding that I approach the complicated interplay between Christian faith, masculinity, and being gay.

I understand masculinity as mostly a socially constructed term, subjected to linguistic, cultural, and biological factors. My terms of reference are nondualistic, meaning that I navigate this discussion not from a perspective of strict categories of masculine or feminine but rather within an interplay of biology, culture, language, sexual orientation, and gender identity. Most people, especially people within religious communities, tend to think gender matters in rather straightforward biological terms. You're either male or you're female—end of discussion. However, there are minority populations who don't fit so neatly into such categories, such as transgender people and intersex people. Their stories shine a light on the complexity of gender and gender identity for us as a larger society. There are approximately 1 in 2,000 children born with ambiguous genitalia and approximately 1 in 100 whose bodies differ from standard maleness and femaleness. This means that the intersex population—persons born with a reproductive or sexual anatomy or biological identity that do not fit typical definitions of male or female—is as common as the variant of red-haired people in the world; and in North America we all know someone who's a red head.

The Problem

Any serious conversation of masculinity should take into consideration the abuse that has taken place under the historical framework of patriarchal masculinity within Western societies. Masculinity has been rooted in the will to power at the expense of others, derived from the belief that male dominance is ordained by God. People of color, women, children, and LGBTQ+ persons have all experienced deep societal prejudice and institutionalized legal discrimination as part of this patriarchal framework rooted in a particular hermeneutical lens of reading Sscripture. In her book *Daring Greatly*, Brené Brown writes, "When looking at the traits associated with masculinity in the US, the researchers identified the following: winning, emotional control, risk-taking, violence, dominance, playboy, self-reliance, primacy of work, power over women, disdain for homosexuality, and pursuit of status." Brown continues, "There's a cultural message that promotes homophobic cruelty. If you want to be masculine in our culture, it's not enough to be straight—you must also show an outward disgust for the gay community."[1] The violence that has been perpetrated against the LGBTQ+ community, in the name of asserting masculinity, is why the "closet" exists for many LGTBQ+ persons. A friend of mine shared that his father once sat him and his brothers down and said that if anyone of them were to come out gay, he would kill them. I asked my friend if he really believed his father would do such a thing, to which he responded that he absolutely had no doubt and that he therefore was in the closet for survival. Although this was not my reality, there was more than enough hostility in my life to realize the safety of the closet.

Observe the goat—lessons from the barn

It is a journey of courage to come out from behind fear and discover an authentic way of being a man who is gay. God brought this home to me one day as I was doing barn chores. One of my tasks for the last several years, along with pastoring, is doing chores at an educational farm, which is located where I live. On one particular morning, I opened the door to the barn, and as if on cue, the barn erupted with braying, squealing, and clucking in anticipation of breaking the night's fast. However, within the cacophony I could hear one holler in particular that indicated a potential problem.

---

1 Brown, *Daring Greatly*, 108.

When I investigated, I found a kid goat whose head was thorough-ly stuck in the hay feeder. Its horns prevented it from backing its head out of the square frame, which is designed to hold in the hay. I climbed into the pen and inspected how I might maneuver its head out and set it free. The goat, however, was not in tune with my good intentions. As I moved its chin up, it forced its head down. As I tried to move its body backward, it moved with all its might forward. Fear made it blind to my good intention to set it free. The struggle was immense and needed to be precise. If not careful, I could easily pinch the goat's ears between its horns and the slats. Another delicate aspect to the maneuver was avoiding choking the goat. I had to hold the goat's body firmly between my knees while lifting its chin, holding its ears out of the way, and then backing its head out of the tight square frame, all the while preventing it from choking. Fear and panic blinded the goat and complicated everything immensely.

As I wrestled to free the goat I was struck at how powerful an illustration this was for my life. As a gay man in the church, I had tried to live according to the traditional rules of masculinity and its intrinsic homophobia, thinking this was the right thing to do. Yet, to do this required living into both a profoundly discordant way of being and an ever-present sense of fear. If you are a straight cisgender (identify with the gender assigned to you at birth) person, imagine being told that you have to be in intimate relationship with someone of the same gender as you. I can well imagine it is a discordant way of imagining yourself. I can imagine that for many it is too much to ask. Closeted LGBTQ+ people navigate this way of living all the time within a predominant society that assumes heteronormativity. It is a physically, mentally, emotionally, and spiritually exhausting way of living. Fear is not sustainable for living.

In my own life, my deeper conviction of love was winning out, but the final struggle to ultimately surrender felt epic. There was a great deal of fear in coming out, and the consequences were enormous to come out publicly and to live into an alternative understanding of what being male is and isn't about—though the consequences of not coming out would have been enormous as well.

As I observed the goat, I observed myself. God intended my sexuality for my good, and here was I, like the goat, working at odds against God's good intentions for me. As in the hymn, this odd barn scenario became "my Ebenezer" to raise. Desist the struggle and let go. It was a call to deep trust and to learn anew. And so I let go, even though there was no guarantee that others would respond in love. Safety is a significant consideration when coming out, and someone once said that "courage is fear that has said its prayers." I moved with courage and faith that love would see me through to the place of wholeness and well-being in who I am as a man, a gay man, and a person of Christian faith.

I have described my coming out as something akin to taking a leap of faith. The mind says this is unreasonable in every way, yet faith says do it. I did it and discovered that God provided a series of safety nets—none more significant than my wife, Susie. She was to me the incarnation of Christ's love. Right from when the words "I'm gay" left my mouth and through our journey of sorting out all of what that means together, she has been an incredible person of profound faith, hope, and love. Right from the beginning, even if she didn't know exactly how to articulate it, she understood the systemic aspect of what I was—and therefore what we were—dealing with. What I mean by the systemic aspect is the metanarrative of church and society that pathologized and even criminalized LGBTQ+ persons, relationships, and identity. However, understanding the larger systemic aspect didn't minimize the pain or confusion we both uniquely felt; it only helped us to navigate it by trying to not do more harm to each other. This became a real way to put into practice our commitment to our peace theology.

Our LGBTQ+ Christian family and allies became an incredible resource of emotional and spiritual community, of being church, for us. For the most part, the institutional church was ill-equipped and unprepared to know how to journey along with us in redemptive or hopeful ways. Thankfully the institutional church in our context gave us enough space to figure things out without complicating the journey through overtly punitive measures, as has been the experience of many other LGBTQ+ persons.

Together Susie and I wrestled with the lack of language to help us work through what we needed to because, in theory, mixed orientation marriages were not supposed to exist, and therefore there wasn't even language to navigate it. The scripts that did exist were either of divorce or of continuing a charade of a heteronormative marriage—and neither of those options was acceptable to us. As we discerned what honoring reconciling love, moving toward wholeness, and holding covenant could look like in our context, we began to use the language of being queerly covenanted. This meant going through a process of releasing what's not true about our relationship and embracing what is true. This journey of releasing and embracing led us to hold a new way of being in covenant relationship that reconciled things according to what is as opposed to what others want it to be.[2]

The lesson for me was to not be like the goat. I learned to allow love to do its work and to bring me to where I needed to be and trust that Love has plans not to harm me but to give me hope and a future (Jer. 29:11). I am not suggesting that all LGBTQ+ persons need to come out or that remaining in the closet is a sign of cowardice. All too often, remaining in the closet is exactly what needs to happen because lack of safety makes it so. Moreover, the context for many mixed orientation couples varies greatly, and so the path we have taken is not meant to be prescriptive but is rather descriptive of how we navigated the journey.

Rupturing binaries for Love's sake

My journey of faith and life took me through profound shifts that took me deeper into understanding the complexity of Scripture, layered within the complexities of hermeneutical communities and the path of lived discipleship. I began to grow in appreciation for other hermeneutical lenses through which to understand Scripture and Christian faith and to move beyond the stagnant polarity, or binaries, of conservative and liberal thinking. These new understandings became a lifeline for me.

The unique Christian doctrine of the Trinity, as a primary lens through which to understand God, resonates deeply with me. God as holy community, one in three, three in one, underscores God's love as deeply relational and not solitary. It isn't surprising that in Genesis 2, the only thing declared *not good* was the aloneness of *ha'adam*. The one created in the image of the Community of Love cannot be alone and needs to be in relationship. The creation story within Genesis underscores a significant human truth: we were meant to belong and be connected not only with God but also with one another. In my deepest place of faith, God is Love; that love is fundamentally relational; and as a relational being, God—according to the Christian confession of faith—is non-binary.

All language for God is symbolic and limited in its capacity to capture the essence of God. God supersedes categories of male

---

2 A copy of our "release and embrace" ceremony can be found at the website for Generous Space ministries: https://www.generousspace.ca/blog/from-mixed-orientation-marriage-to-queer-covenant-a-ceremony-of-release-and-embrace/.

and female. God is neither male as "Father" might suggest (Matt. 6:9–13) nor female as "child of her womb" might suggest (Isa. 49:15); similarly, God is neither animal as "Lion of the tribe of Judah" might suggest (Rev. 5:5) nor mineral as "Rock" might suggest (Deut. 32:18). The Bible uses all these metaphors to describe God, and for one metaphor to be dominant at the expense of all others is a harmful form of idolatry. When the only acceptable way of imaging God is as a male, then we diminish the witness of Scripture regarding God and make God less than who God is. There are rich metaphors that speak of God with ideas of maleness and femaleness in human, animal, and spiritual or noncorporal terms (e.g., Sophia). There are environmental metaphors such as rock, water, light, darkness, wind, soil, and plants, all of which convey meanings of God's good care and love for us.[3]

Although the descriptive language of the creation story employs binary language of night and day, water and dry land, sky and earth, we know that the rich diversity of creation inhabits not only those spaces but the spaces between as well. Entire species that owe their being to in between spaces such as dawn and dusk, marsh lands and estuaries, ocean depths and floors, and mountain heights and skies. So too with male and female, creation bears witness to the rich diversity, adaptations, and manifestations of maleness and femaleness within many living things. There is no singular definition of masculinity or femininity, although the realities of these concepts have existed from time immemorial and have been expressed and valued in multiple and at times contradictory ways.

In the story of the Patriarchs, Esau, who epitomized Ancient near eastern masculinity and power and was favored accordingly, was usurped by Jacob, who the Bible describes in more feminine terms. The biblical narrative describes God as favoring this usurpation and inversion of power dynamic—an inversion of power that various biblical accounts consistently play with in their storytelling. It is often in these places of role reversals and upsets that God's salvific purposes move and unfold. The apostle Paul bears witness to this trajectory of undoing power dynamics and divisions when he writes that in Christ "there is no longer Jew or Greek, there is no longer slave or free, there is no longer male and female" (Gal. 3:28). Dividing walls are broken down.

The Christian faith is in its very essence about rupturing binary concepts, which isn't surprising when one considers the Christian

3 Johnson, *Quest for the Living God*, 96–106.

understanding of God as trinitarian. The incarnation ruptures the binary order between the God of creation and creation itself. The Christian confession is that Jesus is both fully God and fully human. The resurrection ruptures the binary between life and death. In the cross, we witness that God dies. In the resurrection, a human body returns from the dead, and death no longer has the last word. Finally, the Christian life of discipleship continually crosses boundaries of power imbalances in tribal or ethnic affiliation, disparate social status, and gender power dynamics.[1] Love is at the heart of this rupturing of binaries.

The example of Jesus

There is a scene in the movie *The Shape of Water* wherein the character Richard Strickland, an archetype of the patriarchal-white-Christian-male, gives Zelda—his antithesis, a black woman who cleans the toilets—a "talking to" regarding the "creature" being held in captivity. Strickland states, "You may think that thing looks human—stands on two legs—but we're created in the Lord's image, and you don't think that's what the Lord looks like, do you?" Zelda replies, "I wouldn't know, sir, what the Lord looks like." Strickland responds, "Well, human, Zelda. He looks like a human. Just like me—or even you. A little more like me, I guess."[5] This exchange between Strickland and Zelda reveals in its simplicity the power dynamics of patriarchal masculinity rooted in religion through a particular reading of Scripture.

Strickland stands in stark contrast to the incarnation of Jesus, who in his masculinity models something very different. Jesus's encounter with the Samaritan woman subverts patriarchal masculinity and redresses its negative impact by crossing boundaries—religious, ethnic, and gender. She is a marginalized woman within a marginalized community, and he, a man, a teacher of Israel. The two were never supposed to cross paths, let alone encounter one another in such a profound way. It's a story that illustrates Jesus's abandonment of power, moving beyond binaries for the purposes of love. We are called to imitate such love as in the early church's liturgy, as so beautifully expressed in Philippians 2:5–8:

> Let the same mind be in you that was in Christ Jesus,
> who, though he was in the form of God,
> did not regard equality with God

---

4 Edman, *Queer Virtue*, 17–24.
5 Eltoro, *Shape of Water*.

as something to be exploited,
but emptied himself,
taking the form of a slave,
being born in human likeness.
And being found in human form,
he humbled himself
and became obedient to the point of death—
even on a cross.

A man's man

In December 2017, my father died. He died at the age of ninety-one. I loved my father dearly. When I came out to him several years ago, his response to me was, "I love you more now than I did before." My father, in his senior years, was far more gentle, loving, and demonstrative of his love than when he was younger.

At my dad's memorial service, a relative of mine who hadn't seen my dad for several decades came to the mic and described his memories of my dad as "a man's man." That choice of wording landed awkwardly on my ear because that was not how I had come to understand my dad. It took me some time to realize that this reflection emerged not from whom my father had become but from a rather different time, a different man. My father's last thirty years were very much a gift. At the age of sixty, my dad was diagnosed with advanced stages of cancer that required removal of significant portions of his bowel, the entirety of his bladder and prostate gland. In the last thirty years of his life, my father, with significant help from my mother, managed a new life that navigated the realities of life with a colostomy and ileostomy and without a prostate. It was the latter that affected my father significantly. He felt emasculated. Like many men, his sexual capacity was intrinsically woven into his self-perception of maleness and masculinity. My father—a former Dutch Marine, a fiercely independent man, a strong, tall, and physically imposing man, a man who inhabited virtually all the traditional concepts of masculinity one could imagine (so much so as to be called "a man's man")—had to relearn what being a man was about. What he knew about masculinity had been handed down to him for generations in ways that he wasn't even conscious of, ways that shunned emotional intelligence, vulnerability, or interdependency. For the next thirty-one years, my father learned to become a different man, one not so defined by traditional masculinity but one who owned his emotions more, learned to express love, and was not afraid to hug. My father often used the phrase "the fullness of your love" in his prayers to God, and I feel that God answered his prayers by showing some of what that meant over the last years of my father's life. It was an important journey for me to witness because I too had to wrestle with what was passed down to me.

Schoolyard politics

When I came out as gay to my family of origin, a number of my siblings and some cousins said they suspected as much. I looked at them puzzled because I thought I had done a fairly good job of acting within the accepted stereotypical male gender norms. When I asked how they knew, their response caught me off guard. They suspected I was gay because as a child I was "kind and gentle." Kind and gentle were the telling signs of being gay? What a stinging indictment of masculinity in our culture. As I think back to my childhood, I remember clearly how important it was to navigate "masculine" norms because if one didn't, the price to pay was high. I thought of other children who couldn't navigate those norms, and they suffered much more at the hands of those who took it upon themselves to be the enforcers. I remember a kid from my school — on my bus route actually — who could not fit into those norms no matter how hard he tried. From an adult perspective, I now understand that this kid was transgender. If the traditional definition of being masculine is being non-feminine and eschewing anything in a man that might be considered feminine traits — however those are imagined — then transgender female children suffered mercilessly. In the face of their torment, I remembered feeling powerless, guilty, and very afraid. I felt that if I spoke up I would be "guilty by association" and subjected to the same treatment but, more than that, would be exposed. The school yard was the arena in which many of us LGBTQ+ children learned why it was essential to move into the closet. The closet is not something of our creation for the purposes of deception but is rather for our safety.

When I came out to my family of origin, it was also interesting to me that family members suspected I was gay long before I reached an age of sexual awareness. Like many other gay men, I realized that there was something different about me in my childhood, yet I would not have been able to put it into words or to conceptualize what it was. "Faggot" was the schoolyard term, but I didn't know what that was, nor how such a term, spoken with such vile, could relate to me. Yet, somehow, I knew that term was referencing me and something about me. Even though I didn't get it, or understand what it was about, it was nevertheless apparent to me, and apparently to others, that I was different. My masculinity was not in the tradition of being a man's man, but it was a masculinity being formed and shaped by God's love.

As a child I was artistically inclined, and creativity was something that came naturally to me. I enjoyed picking up crayons—or whatever medium was at hand—and drawing. I enjoyed reading and learning and was not so good on the sports field, whether it was soccer, baseball, or football. Being good at drawing and bad at sports singled me out for "special" attention. I learned to make myself invisible as best I could. Other boys who were gay and good at sports navigated the closet differently but with the same fears of being exposed. To be considered an "effeminate" male was to endure shame upon shame.

Whenever I am together with other gay men and we discuss our childhoods, the storytelling is almost universal as it relates to policing or censoring oneself. How was I sitting? Did I have my legs crossed? How much was I talking with my hands? If one lost oneself in too much enjoyment and one's guard came down just a little too much, then the worries would set in: Did I betray anything? Did my voice sound too gay? If I said what TV shows or music I liked, did it out me? To enjoy skipping games in the schoolyard or to hang around with female friends too much was part of deciphering how to manage the closet. Where did my eyes wander to and upon whom? Best to just keep one's head down and not give anything away. Anything that would elicit a comment from someone—"Only girls do that" or "You're such a sissy" or "What a fag"—could bring the whole thing crumbling down and mark one for the rest of one's school life. Life in the closet had to be measured and monitored so as not to betray oneself to the homophobic vitriol that was the schoolyard politics shaped by traditional masculinity. The good news was that I encountered God in this stage in my life, and that encounter was felt even in the closet. I knew God knew me at the deepest part of my being, and in God's love I never felt rejected—confused, yes, but never rejected. It was God's people that I worried more about.

At peace and unafraid

In my life journey, honoring faithfulness, loyalty, and fidelity are important to me. Claiming my voice as a gay person is an integral expression of that faithfulness. When I first came out to my counsellor, he said, "I'm glad that you are gay!" I thought to myself, "Well, that makes one of us." Regardless, God used those words to bring healing into my life. I'm good with who I am now, and what's more, I see who I am as a gift. This journey of struggle and hope has shaped me, or marked me, in ways that have allowed me to be sensitive to the struggle of others within my pastoral ministry. To borrow from Joan D. Chittister, I am scarred by struggle and transformed by hope: "It is struggle that is the foundation of hope, not hope that is a hedge against struggle."[6] Christian spirituality recognizes the importance of struggle, vulnerability, courage, and hope. Growth in faith and love takes deeper root and produces better fruit when we have faced our fears and allowed courage to be born anew.

Every human has elements of what has been described as masculine and feminine characteristics within them, however that is culturally determined and expressed. So much of our Western culture has historically favored characteristics described as masculine. Feminine attributes have often been used by men to denigrate other men, particularly boys: "You're throwing like a girl" or "Stop crying like a little girl" or, conversely, "Be a man and take some leadership." Negative messaging regarding gender roles has been used to reinforce certain ideals of masculinity at the expense of embracing characteristics traditionally ascribed as feminine. This has negatively impacted both men and women, whether they be straight or LGBTQ+. All have suffered under generations of men who have believed, and tried to live into, masculine ideals that have left them ill-equipped to understand and navigate emotional intelligence, vulnerability, interdependence, and relational health and well-being. As feminist writer bell hooks writes,

> Until we are willing to question many of the specifics of the male sex role, including most of the seven norms and stereotypes that psychologist Robert Levant names in a listing of its chief constituents—"avoiding femininity, restrictive emotionality, seeking achievement and status, self-reliance, aggression, homophobia, and non-relational attitudes toward sexuality"—we are going to deny men their full humanity. Feminist masculinity would have as its chief constituents integrity, self-love, emotional awareness, assertiveness, and relational skill,

---

6 Chittister, *Scarred by Struggle*, 96.

including the capacity to be empathic, autonomous, and connected. The core of feminist masculinity is a commitment to gender equality and mutuality. . . . Such a commitment always privileges non-violent action over violence, peace over war, life over death.[7]

A vision of masculinity that allows men to live into their full humanity is a masculinity that is no longer defined by domination, or the will to power, as patriarchal masculinity has been. It is a vision of being human that is rooted in non-binary love; Trinitarian love; an incarnational love that nurtures a deep sense of connection to others in the strength of mutuality, the courage of vulnerability, and the wisdom of emotional awareness; a love rooted in Jesus's call to peace and peacemaking—with Jesus as the ethic that calls all, regardless of gender, gender expression, or sexual orientation, into a way of peace that breaks down dividing walls (Eph. 2:14).

What's at the heart for Jesus is that the community of Jesus is one that inhabits mutuality rather than domination, peace rather than violence. It is the recognition that Jesus's peace is what holds us together in spite of our differences. It is a love that does not require masculinity to define itself over and against women, nor does it need hatred against LGBTQ+ persons to assert and validate itself. It is a substantive love that has the power to overcome enmity and bring healing, as Ephesians reminds us. To this end I pray,

that Christ may dwell in your hearts through faith, as you are being rooted and grounded in love. I pray that you may have the power to comprehend, with all the saints, what is the breadth and length and height and depth, and to know the love of Christ that surpasses knowledge, so that you may be filled with all the fullness of God. Now to [God] who by the power at work within us is able to accomplish abundantly far more than all we can ask or imagine, to [God] be glory in the church and in Christ Jesus to all generations, forever and ever. Amen. (Eph. 3:17–21)

---

7 hooks, *Will to Change*, 118.

Bibliography

Brown, C. Brené. *Daring Greatly: How the Courage to Be Vulnerable Transforms the Way We Live, Love, Parent, and Lead*. New York: Gotham, 2012.

Chittister, Joan. *Scarred by Struggle, Transformed by Hope*. Grand Rapids: Eerdmans, 2005.

Edman, Elizabeth M. *Queer Virtue: What LGBTQ People Know about Life and Love and How It Can Revitalize Christianity*. Boston: Beacon, 2017.

Eltoro, Guillermo, dir. *The Shape of Water*. Century City, CA: Fox Searchlight, 2017.

hooks, bell. *The Will to Change: Men, Masculinity, and Love*. New York: Atria, 2004.

Johnson, Elizabeth A. *Quest for the Living God: Mapping Frontiers in the Theology of God*. New York: Continuum, 2007.

Part
3

Theology

Men Reading the Bible

Thomas R. Yoder Neufeld

*T*he Bible is by men, for men. That familiar cliché is sometimes used to discredit the Bible as hopelessly out of touch with contemporary values. When its depictions of God as the ultimate "male" dominator, of heroic but deeply flawed men, and of salvation premised on placating the wrath of an angry "father" are given the normative force of revelation, the Bible is then often seen as valorizing a toxic masculinity.

In this chapter I wish to emphatically affirm that the Bible is *for us*—good news for men and those to whom they relate. But that affirmation is not without its complexities, as we will explore in this chapter. Christians know well that the Bible belongs to the church as a whole and not just to men. But for now we might benefit from asking what it has to say to men in particular.

The Bible and men

Bible

Every part of the statement that *the Bible is by men, for men* is deceptively simple. This is certainly true, first of all, for the Bible. People view and experience the Bible in vastly different ways. How do we read it? As the revelatory Word of God? As human words? As both? Is patriarchy the old packaging in which the Bible comes to us, which we carefully open and then put aside? Or is patriarchy at the core of the message itself? Should it therefore continue to shape Christian thinking about what it means to be a man?

For some, Scripture's authority demands that we embrace male "headship" and that we speak of God using male pronouns. God is, after all, Lord, King, Warrior, Judge, and Savior or Liberator, who has a "Son" sitting at "His" right hand. These scriptural themes all reflect masculine strength and prerogative. Others read the Bible as expressing much the same perspective of male privilege, and for that very reason wish to carefully manage or even quarantine it. Still others assert the Bible's authority as divine revelation but insist that it needs to be interpreted in a way that questions male power and privilege. Ironically, they derive the basis of such an approach from the Bible itself. Within the Anabaptist community, we will find men taking positions across this whole spectrum. The debates around the role of women in family and church, around the bearing of arms and the use of violence in defending the vulnerable, and, most recently, around sexual orientation—all amply illustrate this range of views.

What complicates matters is that the Bible is not a one-author book, even if believers confess God to be the "author and finisher," as it were. It is a book of books, an archive of writings spanning centuries and of traditions much older yet. The Bible contains a diversity of literary genres, from story to song and poem, from law to prophecy, from Gospels to letters, from wisdom to visions and dreams. An archive like this does not easily lend itself to being used as a recipe book or manual on what it means to be a man. Nor, for that reason, should it be disparaged or ignored.

Men

If there is nothing simple about the Bible, neither is there anything simple about men. Men vary in physical vigor and ability, race, ethnicity, economic status, marital status, intelligence, education, social location, sexual orientation, spirituality, and so on. Some exercise power and responsibility; others struggle to survive. Some run society; others find themselves on the barely visible margins, if they are noticed at all. Men are socialized in vastly different ways. They vary in behaviors, attitudes, and ways of relating to others, especially women, children, and other men who don't fit their norms of masculinity. This diversity is found within the body of Christ, often within the circle of men's own congregations, where they live out their membership in the body of Christ most immediately. All this is critically important for how and from where the Bible is read. Different men listen with different ears, and they respond to what they hear out of a diversity of experience, culture, and character.

By men?

To claim that the Bible was written by men is to state the obvious. Historically, few could read and write. Given the patriarchal nature of society, those who could—scribes—were more than likely men associated with or educated in centers of power and privilege, whether palace or temple. To be sure, some men—as in the case of prophets and their scribes, like Jeremiah and his scribe Baruch, or of most if not all of the New Testament authors—wrote from the margins against the centers of power. But it was men who wrote, and it was disproportionately men whose words, actions, and perspectives were recorded. The voices of the powerless and marginalized men are at best found between the lines or through the voices of those such as Amos or James who were sensitive to their plight. To read the Bible from cover to cover with an eye to men's experience presents us with a great variety of men, from slaves to warriors, from shepherds to kings, from priests to prophets, from fisher folk to world-traveling apostles. The Bible thus both reflects and emerges from the hugely diverse experience of men.

And the voice of women? Are men's the only voices we hear in the Bible? Men, after all, live in relationship. Perhaps oftentimes women's voices were simply not heard, listened to, or recorded. We might expect that in patriarchal settings. It is also likely, however, that behind and within the written documents of men are traditions and tales women played a significant role in forming and transmitting, whether we think of the traditions of Israel or the oral traditions that underlie the Gospels. We might mention here the "war songs" of Miriam the sister of Moses (Exod. 15:20, 21) and Miriam the mother of Jesus (Luke 1:46–55). Through the work of feminist biblical scholars, men have been alerted to listen more carefully for the presence of women in these often male-centered texts so as to be able to read them against the grain of male privilege.[1]

To recognize this full humanity of the Bible does not diminish it. To the contrary, we see that God has spoken into a male-dominated world in need of transformation. "Incarnation," the Word becoming flesh, includes "inscripturation," the Word becoming words—*Logos* becoming *logia*, Word and words, first scrolls and then book (which is what "Bible" means). That puts before men the challenge of "correctly interpreting"[2] (2 Tim. 2:15) the often male-shaped Scriptures in a way that leads to the transformation of masculinity, to what Paul calls "new creation" (Gal. 6:15) or the "new human" (Eph. 2:15).

For men?

What about the assertion that the Bible is for men? Clearly it is relevant to men and is intended to be so. As we said earlier, biblical writers often assumed their audience to be male, an assumption for which Proverbs would be a clear example. But is it *for* men—that

---

1 See, most famously, Schüssler Fiorenza, *In Memory of Her*.
2 The venerable King James puts it as "rightly dividing" the word of truth. The term *orthotomeō* means "to cut straight," a pretty good term for good solid analysis and interpretation.

is, is it good news for men and, importantly, for those with whom they are in relationship? The answer may not always be about the Bible itself so much as about how men have experienced its use. Have they experienced it as supporting them in their own particular masculinity, as challenging them in a helpful and constructive—even if sometimes painful—way to become better men? Or has the experience of the Bible marginalized or even delegitimized them? Have they had a say in what the Bible means, or is the Bible interpreted for them and perhaps even against them?

What follows grows out of a deep conviction that the Bible is more than an archive of men's stories, reflections, teachings, songs, and visions. It is words becoming God's Word to us, as I've claimed earlier. There is a phrase in Ephesians about the "multi-varied wisdom" of God (3:10). God's word comes to us in and through the multi-varied wisdom and voices of countless men. Because this is so, the Bible both reflects and addresses the multi-varied community of men reading the Bible. Here are some suggested reading strategies that can aid in hearing the Word, and in finding a place in the community of listening, interpreting, and witnessing.

Reading the Bible as *for us*

Reading with humble openness

Let me state at the outset that I believe it is crucial that we receive the Bible as "Word of God."[3] Yes, the Bible emerges in and reflects particular times and places, and it reflects the particularity of those whose witness it contains. But the believing community has heard in its pages the living word of God that engages and transforms the world, specifically also the world of men. To be Christian means to believe that in this fully human and historical archive we hear God speak to us and for us (as in "if God be for us")—that is, for our benefit and blessing. It matters a great deal whether we come to the Bible with arrogant superiority or cool disdain, or with a disposition of trust—trust not in the words of the Bible or in our ability to interpret so much as in the God whose Spirit has pervaded the lives of the men who experienced God and wrote the Scriptures, the God whose breath has given life to the remembering, writing, and collecting of the words that make up the Bible, and who is with us in our reading.[4] It means that we let the Bible have the first word,

---

3 "Scripture," article 4 in *Confession of Faith*.
4 See the important article by Hays, "Salvation by Trust?"

that we read with a disposition of listening for God's word before we take issue with the Bible, before we argue with it.

Reading as wrestling

Holding such a high view of the Bible while recognizing its full humanity as an archive of human experience—of *men's* experience—will make wrestling with the Bible inescapable. The patriarch Jacob can be a kind of role model—not in his theft of the blessing from his brother Esau ("Jacob" is a play on the word for "supplanter"; cf. Gen. 27:36) but rather in his willingness to struggle fiercely (he is given the name "Israel," which means "God wrestler"; cf. Gen. 32:28). Before facing the brother he has wronged so grievously, and who has therefore taken a vow to kill him, Jacob has an all-night wrestling match with "a man" (Gen. 32:24). It is a brutal struggle, with Jacob refusing to let up until he has wrested a blessing from his opponent. The severity of the contest leaves him with a permanent limp. But in the morning Jacob names the place Peniel, the "face of God" (Gen. 32:30). Then he meets his brother, his sworn enemy, and Esau unexpectedly falls on Jacob's neck in reconciliation. Jacob responds, "To see your face is like seeing the face of God" (Gen. 33:10). Men will sometimes need to read the Bible with a fierce faith that will not let up until they have extracted a blessing, the blessing of hearing the voice of God in biblical texts that feel like the enemy. And while the encounter may leave them limping, they will name it "Word of God."

Sometimes this struggle will be a solitary one. Men abused by the powerful will struggle mightily with the injunctions in the Sermon on the Mount to turn the cheek and to love the enemy (Matt. 5:38–48) or with Jesus's demand to forgive (Matt. 18). Men who have themselves abused vulnerable persons will struggle with Jesus's brutal suggestion that amputation of the offending organ would be preferable to facing judgment intact (Matt. 18). Men who exercise power and responsibility will wrestle with the image of the slave as template of faithfulness (Isa. 40–55; John 13; Phil. 2:1–11). Gay men will wrestle with critical characterizations of same-sex attraction (Rom. 1:18–32). Successful businessmen will wrestle with the denigration of wealth (James 5:1–6).

Often the struggle will be communal. Men of faith read the Bible in community, together with men (and women) with diverse experiences, personalities, and cultures. They do so with the conviction that it is in community that the Spirit is present in the communal act of interpretation. We often call it the "hermeneutics of community," a core feature of Anabaptist tradition. As every church body knows from experience, the nature of the Bible and the diversity of persons in the circle of discernment will more than likely ensure not an easy consensus but divisive quarreling. That experience does not disqualify such wrestling. It might just be the exercise of our common bond within the body of Christ, not its failure, let alone betrayal. We are challenged, sometimes painfully, but also enriched by how others see things. At the same time, we become aware of both special insights and limitations we ourselves bring to the reading of the Bible. We are open not only to the diversity within the Bible but also to the questions, perspectives, and convictions of our brothers as we listen, interpret, and decide what to do about it. This encounter can prevent us from being enclosed in our own echo chambers (however Anabaptist they may be) in which our preferences and prejudices are simply confirmed. This is why a *shared* commitment to listen for *God's* word when we read the Bible, even amid deep difference and disagreement, and a commitment to each other as *brothers* in the family of God are essential in order to give our wrestling integrity and promise.

Men of the Bible — role models or caution signals?

The Bible provides men with both role models and cautionary characters.[5] Often they are the same person, as in the case of Jacob/Israel. They reveal both God's ways and the strengths and weaknesses of men. These characters are persons men can identify with, both in their vulnerabilities and in their worth in the unfolding story from creation to new creation.

It is remarkable, for example, that Jacob would be remembered by his descendants as having stolen the blessing, and thus the inheritance, from his brother, Esau. Who puts that into their family history? Perhaps he can be so remembered because he is also remembered as one who was obstinate in his insistence on a blessing and courageous in facing both his sin and his fear of his aggrieved brother.[6] I wonder whether Jesus might be deliberately referring to Jacob in his parable of the prodigal son, who, like Jacob, is finally ready to face up to his treachery vis-à-vis his father, only to be surprised by the gift of reconciliation (Luke 15:11–32).

---

5 Writing within and for the men's movement, Patrick M. Arnold treats biblical characters within masculine models or archetypes, in *Wildmen, Warriors, and Kings*. I have not attempted to "type" the men of the Bible, but rather to treat their stories as highly instructive, both positively and negatively.

6 See John Paul Lederach's profound exploration of Jacob and Esau's interaction in *Reconcile*.

The cloud of such flawed witnesses is large. Perhaps we should call it a rogues' gallery. Or is it a gallery of saints? For example, the liar Abraham (Gen. 12:10–20) becomes the epitome of faith (Gen. 15:6; Gal. 3:6; Rom. 4:3; Heb. 6:15; 11:8, 17; James 2:21, 23). The murderer Moses becomes the law-giving leader of his people. David, adulterous warlord and flawed king, is the peerless composer of psalms, a model of honest remorse and loyalty to God, an ideal king/messiah. His womanizing son Solomon becomes the sage par excellence. The impetuous and unreliable Peter becomes the "rock" of the church. The violent persecutor Paul becomes the wildly successful emissary of the crucified and risen Messiah. God works with and through men who have all the strengths and weaknesses that typically mark men's lives. The good news for men is that every man can see himself in these heroes, both in their failures and in their successes. To paraphrase Paul, in God's creative hands, weakness become strength (2 Cor. 12:7–10).

The Bible's ideal of masculinity

In this cloud of role models, there are also biblical characters whose bios carry little negative baggage and who represent determined courage, brutal frankness, resolute obedience, and unbroken loyalty to God: Nathan fearlessly confronts David about his murderous adultery; the "weeping prophet" Jeremiah can hardly bear the painful message he has been summoned to bring to his own people; Hosea dramatizes the passionate love of God for his unfaithful people by marrying a prostitute; and Daniel, at the top of the civil service of the Babylonian empire that has taken his people captive, refuses to bend the knee in worship of the oppressor. These men are profoundly worthy of emulation as pointers to moral and spiritual "perfection" in difficult and potentially compromising circumstances.

Today the Bible is often deployed to reinforce conservative social structures and relationships: men are to be heads of their families, good providers for spouse and children, and strong and wise disciplinarians. To be sure, the Bible values the propagation of the species—"Be fruitful and multiply" (Gen. 1:28)!—although the harms resulting from overpopulation were nowhere on the horizon for biblical writers. And also stressed in the Bible are care for families, rearing and education of offspring, and the cohesiveness of families and the bonds that keep them whole. (See, e.g., Eph. 6:4; 1 Tim. 3:1–13). Men can own such roles and tasks as God-given responsibilities, privileges, and gifts.

It is all the more important, therefore, to notice that the Bible also presents men who decidedly do not conform to a normal or ideal template of masculinity. For example, to be "fruitful" is part of God's design for creation. Eunuchs, men whose testicles had been damaged or who had been castrated, were thus to be barred from the temple (Deut. 23:1). It is thus all the more surprising that, as Isaiah 56:3–5 indicates, a future is anticipated in which eunuchs will be accorded special honor and status in that very home of God. Thus Luke's account of the beginnings of that future, the birth of the church, contains the story of a eunuch from Ethiopia, an outsider twice over to Israel's worshiping community, who asks tellingly, "What prevents *me* from being baptized?" (Acts 8:26–40).

Perhaps we should not be surprised that the most prominent of Jesus's emissaries, Paul, was apparently unmarried and childless (note how he compares himself in 1 Cor 9:5 with fellow apostles, such as Peter and Jesus's brothers, who travel with wives). The irony should not be lost on us. The very same Paul who is invoked in support of so-called family values—often used to marginalize men who don't fit the template of normal—might well be one of those "eunuchs for the sake of the kingdom" that Jesus speaks of (Matt. 19:12). To complicate matters even more, Paul is not reluctant to choose womanly imagery to describe his relationship with his beloved congregations: he gives birth with all the pain of labor (Gal 4:19), and gently nurses his congregations like an attentive mother (1 Thes 2:7, 8).[7]

Jesus as the perfect man

If we are startled by the figure Paul cuts as a man, the case of Jesus is even more startling. Jesus doesn't have a wife, he doesn't have children, he doesn't have a proper home—"nowhere to lay his head" (Luke 9:58)—and his relationship with his biological family seems strained (Mark 3:21, 31–35). For a righteous person, he hangs out with the wrong crowd. Precisely as a master, Jesus behaves like a slave by putting on a towel and washing his students' feet (John 13). He falls victim to religious hostility and imperial brutality without fighting back or defending himself. He is clearly both an outsider and an outlier. Might Jesus too be a kind of "eunuch for the kingdom"? How does one emulate such "perfect" masculinity?

For Christian men, to emulate Jesus is not optional. They do not emulate Jesus because he makes sense. In terms of the wisdom of this world, he often decidedly does not make sense, especially

---

7 Gaventa, *Our Mother Saint Paul.*

when it comes to being a so-called "real man." Jesus's resurrection revealed to his cowed followers that he was indeed not a loser but the very agent of God, the Messiah, the Son of God—indeed, the Wisdom of God behind and within the created world.[8] He is the Word made flesh (John 1), Emmanuel, "God-with-us" (Matt. 2). As Paul's great christological hymn in Philippians 2:6–11 puts it, he bears the "name that is above every name," the name that belongs to God alone. To confess that means that Christian men have no alternative but to follow him, to emulate him—as a man.

But Jesus is not only God-with-us, the second person of the Trinity, as theologians came to put it. He is *the* teacher and model for human behavior. Jesus is the "pioneer and perfecter of our faith" (Heb. 2:10, 12:2) as men experience it, able to identify with them in every way (Heb. 4:14–16). He is, to use the language of Ephesians 4:13, the "perfect man."[9] If men (and women) are created in the image of God, then in Jesus God appears in the image of men, even the most vulnerable and powerless.

In Jesus's teachings and in the way he is portrayed, we see that strength and power are found in what looks like weakness and sometimes even passivity. To turn the cheek, to walk the second mile, to give the last bit of one's clothing, to open one's wallet to those who ask—these are examples not of embarrassing passivity and docile acquiescence to injustice but of *deliberate* vulnerability. To forgive seventy times seven (Matt. 18:22) is not to be an enabling push-over but to *deliberately* forego closure or payback. More, it is a terribly risky and therefore always courageous way of forcing the door of the future to remain open for repentance, change, and reconciliation. Finally, to give one's life for others, even for enemies, is to manifest the power of God over death and estrangement (Eph. 2:14–16). To take up one's own cross is not to choose suffering, or to put up with it, but with utter selflessness to be engaged for the salvation and liberation of others. Jesus embodies his own teaching on what it means to love enemies and thus to be perfect as the Father in heaven is perfect (Matt. 5:43–48).

None of this characterization of Jesus denigrates the responsibility to guide, lead, teach, and protect—endeavors men "get" and are often socialized for. Jesus embodies these in his teaching, his care for the hungry, and his profound respect for the "little ones"

---

8 For a fuller discussion of both the creativity and complexity of Christological development, see Yoder Neufeld, *Recovering Jesus*, 291–328.

9 My translation. While this phrase is sometimes softened in translations so as to be gender inclusive and to refer to maturity more generally, I take it to refer to Christ.

(Matt. 18:1–5). Of particular relevance to the violence of men toward the vulnerable, notably children and women, we should note Jesus's white-hot rage at abuse (Matt. 18:6–9).[10] But lest these virtues of power and strength morph into the "lording it over others" that Jesus abhors (Matt. 20:25–28), they must not be separated from the Jesus who wears the apron, washes, and then dies for his disciples, his "bride" (John 13; Eph. 5:25–27). Service happens from strength. Just so, life-giving strength emerges from the heart of servanthood. Mutual subordination is empowered servanthood (Eph. 5:21).[11]

To insist that Jesus is the template for what it means to be a man is not to ask for slavish imitation of a first-century Galilean wandering teacher, healer, and exorcist. But seeing Jesus as model does mean loving God and others, including enemies, like he did; caring for others, rich and poor alike, like he did; being hungry for justice, like he was; loving and making peace, like he did; serving others, like he did; being truthful, like he was; taking up the cross, as he did; trusting God with one's life, like he did. In short, it means learning from him to be "perfect."

It will seldom if ever be easy to live out this volatile but essential mix of lordship and servanthood in the actual circumstances of life with others. Men will struggle interpersonally in their work and family relationships. At the communal level, given the inherently unstable relationship between power and weakness, churches and their institutional organization will vary in how Jesus's way is incorporated in structures and procedures and how that impinges on men's participation. That accounts not only for the diversity of church polities but also for the struggles and tensions around authority and leadership that afflict them all. That was true from the very beginning. Learning from Jesus, Paul's favorite term for a leader in the church was *diakonos*—literally, "table waiter." It would not take long for "deacon" to become a term of honor and status, much as "minister" is in our day in church and in government. And so the battle has been joined.

Imitating God

The central character of the Bible is God. Ephesians 5:1 asks readers to imitate God. To ask men to imitate God is to play with fire. If it is a problem to have a messiah complex, to have a God complex is to compound the problem. Certainly, one reason to sound the

---

10 For a fuller exploration of Matthew 18, see Yoder Neufeld, *Killing Enmity*, 36–56.
11 I have explored the highly contentious, even dangerous, household code tradition in Yoder Neufeld, *Ephesians*, 253–89 and 97–108.

alarm is that, without question, a great deal of ancient domination language is used for God. "Lord" (*adonai, kyrios*) becomes the most prevalent way of referring to God. We can add to that creator, judge, warrior, and liberator.

We might counter that, by confessing Jesus as Lord, we acknowledge him not only as our boss but also as God-with-us, Emmanuel. Jesus thus reveals God to us. In Trinitarian terms, the Son reveals the Father. Thus, we imitate God by following Jesus. However, as we see everywhere in the New Testament, much of the terminology we usually associate with God as he is introduced to us in the Old Testament is employed to honor and worship Jesus as Creator, Lord, Savior, and Judge. Like father, like son, we might say. Pointing to Jesus as model might not be the firewall we are looking for, if we wish for men not to learn domination from God.

There are a few features of the way the Bible speaks of God that point to a way that men can truly imitate God without reinforcing what we have come to recognize as deeply flawed and dangerous ways of being men.

First, as much as men are created in the image of God—and as much as God is "with us" and "like us" in Jesus—men are not God, nor should we create God in our image. God is before and beyond us in ways that defy our understanding. Our first response must thus always be what the Bible calls "fear"—awe, respect, and requisite humility. Such fear is the beginning of understanding (Ps. 111:10; Prov. 1:7; 9:10). A patriarchal imagination will find patriarchal language with which to express such awe. While such language might grate in contemporary settings, it remains a poignant reminder that God is God and we are not.

But, second, "we do see Jesus," the writer of the letter to the Hebrews asserts (2:9), reminding us that that infinitely other deity has graced us with his presence in one like us. In Jesus's way of being and relating to the world, we thus glimpse God in ways he does wish us to imitate him. As we have seen, Jesus reveals God to us in a way that cautions us not to see the "Father" as the super-male. Tellingly, the call to imitate God in Ephesians 5:1 is paralleled by the self-giving of Jesus in 5:2 and sums up the exhortation in 4:31–32 in which readers are asked to do away with "bitterness and wrath and anger and wrangling and slander, together with all malice, and be kind to one another, tenderhearted, forgiving [literally, gracing] one another, as God in Christ has forgiven [graced] you."

Third, God as gracious, kind, and forgiving is not new in the New Testament. God is father to the fatherless, husband to the widows (Ps. 68:5), king of stateless slaves (Exod. 15:18), covenant partner to those who have nothing but their love and loyalty to bring to the table. Should we be surprised that God is spoken of as *goel*, usually translated "redeemer" (ransom payer) but most literally rendered as "next-of-kin," the one the family can count on especially to look after those who are vulnerable? While that designation resonates with the "manly" experience of offering protection and care for the vulnerable, it also points to what is often perceived to be the "maternal" side of God. God is not only uncle but also mother. To illustrate, the Hebrew term for mercy, *rechem*, derives from "womb" (cf. Isa. 49:15). The motif is expanded in 1 Peter, where the merciful God (a father with a womb, as it were) gives birth to us (1:3, 23) and nurses us with the milk of kindness (2:2). In short, the imitation of God in "her" mercy and grace can put us in touch with our inner mother, as it did for Paul (as noted above).

Fourth, God's mercy is part of God's righteousness or justice. With God, mercy and justice are not alternatives but aspects of the same drive to reconciliation. Paul insists that it is the justice or righteousness of God that is revealed in putting forth Jesus as the "mercy seat" (Rom. 3:21–26). In Romans 5:6, 8, and 10, Paul reminds us that God loved us while we were still weak, sinful, enemies. We recall that in the Sermon on the Mount, Jesus insists that if we wish to be sons of our "Father in heaven," we need to love our enemies. Jesus summons us to "be perfect" as our "heavenly Father is perfect" (Matt. 5:44–48). It turns out that the destabilization of male stereotypes we see in Jesus is found with respect to God more generally.

Lastly, one of the highly creative ways men who wrote the Bible spoke of God's engagement with creation was through a personification of wisdom as a woman. Every Jew knew that God is the creator, but they spoke of Woman Wisdom (*Hochma* in Hebrew or *Sophia* in Greek) as God's architect and agent of creation (Prov. 8). Moreover, every Jew knew that God had given Torah to Israel, but the Jewish people identified Torah as Woman Wisdom having come to live with Israel (Sir. 24). Notably, the deepest well from which New Testament writers drew their language with which to talk about Jesus was from Wisdom. Jesus identifies himself explicitly as Wisdom in Matthew 11:19; Paul refers to Christ as the Wisdom of God (1 Cor 1:24); the great christological hymns of John 1, Colossians 1, and Philippians 2 are all wisdom poems. (Compare them, for example, with the poem in Wisdom of Solomon 7:22–30). We speak of Jesus as God's "Son," sometimes forgetting that New

Testament writers want us to make an intense connection between the "perfect man" and God's "daughter."

The call to men to imitate God is a call to see the whole array of metaphors, titles, images, and narratives, from the masculine to the feminine. Men are summoned, as in Ephesians 6, to put on God's armor (cf., 1 Thess. 5, Isa. 59). They are to put on the breastplate of justice and the helmet of liberation, which means that they participate in the liberating activity of God in the world. Such imagery fits male fantasies well, even if we too often miss the subversive potential of the armor consisting of truth, justice, peace, liberation, and the spirited word of God. But the biblical imagery for God also presents us with the challenge to imitate the loving and caring creator who like a mother gives birth (Deut. 32:18), who cares for the fruit of her womb (Isa. 49:15; Hos. 11:3–4), who like a mother hen gathers her chicks (Matt. 23:37; Luke 13:34), who like an older sister delights in hanging out with the human race (Prov. 8:31), ready to throw a party of bread and wine (Prov. 9:1–6). This is the father in Jesus's parable of the prodigal, who, unlike a shamed and angry patriarch, rushes out—mother-like—to welcome home a long-lost son. No wonder Rembrandt needed both a male and a female model to get just right the hands in the embrace of the prodigal son.[12]

This imagery reminds us forcefully that men are in no better position to imitate God than are daughters, sisters, wives, and mothers. Put positively, men can be faithful imitators of God in their masculinity, but only together with their daughters, sisters, wives, and mothers. Men are imitators of God, followers of Christ, also together with those men who are outliers from common cultural norms. To paraphrase Galatians 3:28, "In Christ there is no longer one kind of man."

How then do we read the Bible—as men?

I conclude with seven proposals for how men in particular might read the Bible:

- We read the Bible as the Word of God—word from and about God—in human words, images, and metaphors. For these reasons, reading the Bible as Scripture is always an act of courageous faith.

---

12 Henri J. Nouwen, *Return of the Prodigal Son*, 94.

- We read with receptivity and humility—that is, with a readiness to be instructed, corrected, inspired, renewed in mind and body, and thus renewed in our relationships (Rom. 12). Anabaptists could characterize this as a defenseless or nonresistant reading.
- We read the Bible for the direction in which it points, for the narrative arc, one that leads us to Jesus and then allows us to read the story and stories from there. This is not the kind of "progressive revelation" that denigrates everything that comes before Jesus. Nor does it boil the Bible down to one story. If it is *a* story, it is one that contains countless substories, some of which are not easily fit into a coherent, smooth account.
- We read the Bible cautiously, aware of its great potential to buttress the kinds of masculinity that are anything but peaceable. As necessary as they both are to a life-giving reading of the Bible, caution and defenselessness will never enjoy an easy relationship.
- We read with critical honesty. The very nature of the Bible as an archive, a witness to a lively relationship between God and God's people, demands it. Reading critically means recognizing that the Bible reflects both the highs and lows of men's experience, and thus also of perceptions of God born within those contexts. Reading critically also means being self-critical about our own reading and being open to the criticisms of others that grow out of their experiences of faith and of disappointment. These are aspects of a defenseless reading.
- We thus read the Bible together with others—both men and women. Just as the Bible is shared memory, so we listen for and to God's voice together with others, most especially those unlike us, whose experiences and perspectives, whose culture, race, and class are different from our own. Such listening might come via reading with the insights of others, however challenging it is to our cherished convictions. We read the Bible with those who delight at what they find but also with those for whom the Bible has become a stone of stumbling.
- We read the Bible contritely, with a humble acknowledgment that we are heirs to and often practitioners of reading it against others. We confess how easy it is to read an

authoritative and revelatory text in a way that serves our interests and cements our privileges.

In summary, we read the Bible with courageous faith and trust in God, with humble openness to the Spirit that gives it life, inspiring not only the Bible but also us in our reading of it. We read the Bible with a readiness to be molded and shaped into the "new human" by the perfect man, Jesus (Eph. 2:15, 14; 4:13). We become peaceful at heart and peaceful in our relationships—family, church, work—by following Jesus in our everyday lives. We do not—and cannot(!)—do so alone, but we do so in community, as members together of the diverse, often broken, but always renewing and transforming body of Christ.

Bibliography

Arnold, Patrick M. *Wildmen, Warriors, and Kings: Masculine Spirituality and the Bible*. New York: Crossroad, 1992.

Confession of Faith in a Mennonite Perspective. Waterloo, ON: Herald, 1995. http://mennoniteusa.org/confession-of-faith/scripture/

Gaventa, Beverly Roberts. *Our Mother Saint Paul*. Louisville: Westminster/John Knox, 2007.

Hays, Richard B. "Salvation by Trust? Reading the Bible Faithfully." *Christian Century*, February 26, 1997, 218–223.

Lederach, John Paul. *Reconcile: Conflict Transformation for Ordinary Christians*. Harrisonburg, VA: Herald, 2014.

Nouwen, Henri J. *The Return of the Prodigal Son: A Story of Homecoming*. New York: Doubleday, 1992.

Schüssler Fiorenza, Elisabeth. *In Memory of Her: A Feminist Theological Reconstruction of Christian Origins*. New York: Crossroad, 1983.

Yoder Neufeld, Thomas R. *Ephesians*. Believers Church Bible Commentary. Waterloo, ON: Herald, 2002.

_____. *Killing Enmity: Violence and the New Testament*. Grand Rapids: Baker Academic, 2011; published simultaneously as *Jesus and the Subversion of Violence: Wrestling with the New Testament Evidence*. London: SPCK, 2011.

_____. *Recovering Jesus: The Witness of the New Testament*. Grand Rapids: Brazos, 2007.

Men, Masculinity, and Discipleship

David Augsburger

At the outset, it must be clearly said before anything else: in speaking of male identity and masculinity, one must pause to recognize the culturally substantiated traditions of gender inequality, the false claims to privilege and rights assumed by males that have abused women, oppressed minorities, excused exploitive acts and attitudes, distorted relationships, and empowered social rules. All of these violate the central tenets of discipleship. Everything in this chapter stands in radical opposition to any assumptions of male dominance, privilege, right to power and initiative.

In light of these realities, this chapter proposes (1) that a man, to be truly hu-man, must examine, redefine, and redirect the core concepts of masculinity learned from family, community, faith, and culture to make them authentically his own, and (2) that he does this by apprenticing himself to a guide. It argues (3) that most popular guides are superficial, many are untrustworthy, and only a limited number have proven to be enduring and worthy of a life. In particular, it explores (4) the radical and revolutionary potential of discipleship to the most original model and cotraveler, Jesus.

A story of level relationships

We pull up at the White Lane exit from the 99 in Bakersfield. A sunburned young man, thirtyish, is holding a cardboard sign. I dig for my wallet as the light holds back the rush. I toss it to Leann. She fishes out paper. We pull up to him, and he looks up, more surprised by our red smart car than by the gift. We grin. He grins. We buzz off.

"Did you do that in memory of Hal?" Leann asks.

Consciously, no.

Unconsciously, yes.

It has been little more than a week since Hal met us at Phoenix Sky Harbor Airport, then after a quick stop at Starbucks, hurried us to Trinity Mennonite Church to prepare for the morning service.

At an interchange enroute, a man stood waving a cardboard sign. Hal pulls over, reaches to a ready kitty, and hands the man some cash saying, "Here you go, buddy."

Warm, equal, like passing grub at a camp-out, no condescension of charitable giving, no strings in moral or religious attachment—it is the tone of passing the food down a breadline. I recall that he spent years working on the streets; I admire his modeling a flattened playing field.

A week later Hal is gone. His life is dashed in a motorcycle crash. And we are in Phoenix for Hal again, this time for the memorial service. The obituary reads, "Hal Leigh Shrader. 1967–2015."

It is hard—hard like Hal defined hard times. (Once when helping his daughters do math homework, he answered the complaint, "But Daddy, it's hard," with one of his classic one-liners: "Hard things are hard.")

As we drive to the church, the man is still waiting by the exit lane. Same man? We cannot tell. We hand him the bill with Hal's words, "Here you go, buddy," and he replies, "Gotcha."

Gotcha? We will think about that. What did he get? A tone of voice that breathed level respect, and he gave it back. Gotcha.

At the service there are dozens of little reminders of why we loved Hal so much, but for the thousand people gathered, the opening line said what needed to be said.

"Welcome to this service of remembrance. . . . You are all here because Hal welcomed you, welcomed you into his life, into the circle of loving acceptance."

In his life as a theologian, pastor, prophet, agitator, peacemaker, reconciler, father, spouse, friend, disciple, Hal said a lot of insightful and wise things.

But perhaps none was better than the level words, "Here you go, buddy."

Finding a story worth dying for

Each of us finds a story with the power to shape life. The size, the depth, the width of the story determines the dimensions of the life that follows. If one, like Hal Shrader, chooses a story of solidarity with *human*kind rather than just *man*kind, a story of level relationships in a world of hierarchy and ranked order, a story of mutuality in a world of egocentricity, then one chooses a compassionate story that explodes primal masculinity to become authentic humanity.

Jesus-followers call such a self-forgetful story that urges one onward "the way of discipleship."

Coming to be a disciple is a matter of finding a centering story outside of one's self-story that captures the deep imagination of the soul. It is living out a personal drama that promises much more than self-fulfillment. It is joining a social drama that offers a community of cotravelers who find a *reason for being* in a shared story.

As story-telling creatures, we live not by those stories that we possess but by the stories that possess us. It is not so much that I choose a story to live by but rather that a story captures my deeper loyalty and compels me to invest all in its pursuit. It is more like falling in love with a person than like adopting a life narrative. It is out of response to the discovery that we live in a friendly and not hostile universe, on a visited and not an isolated planet, with a God-given destiny and not a self-driven success drama.

Family and community are primary story sources. We may choose a story contiguous and consistent with our family's values, or we may break away and embrace a script from peers or the opinion leaders around us.

We may not know the source of our story—or when we adopted it or first obeyed its guidance. We may have absorbed it unaware from family of origin or communal context of childhood and youth. We may follow its commands and prohibitions without questioning their authority or authenticity. Then as identity forms, a conscious story may come to replace the unconscious narrative that we absorbed and obeyed.

One's story identifies who a man is (selfhood), what masculinity should be (gender and role), how one should live (ethics and morals), and what it means (faith and conviction).

If a man comes from a military family where generations of males have found identity and life purpose by joining a Marine or Navy or Air Force story, then the discipline provided by the narrative of location and loyalty in the violent tradition of a nation-state "makes a man of you," it is said. "It was my destiny," a student tells me. "I knew from childhood that I would win those stripes."

If a man comes from an agricultural family where the farm has provided a grounded story for grandfather, father, and now self, the story of harvesting the earth, reaping its produce, nurturing the soil, living by the seasons, and moving from seedtime to harvest shapes vision, thought, values. Standing between rows of grapes, a man declares to me, "I don't know when I began to love the soil; it is in our blood."

If a man comes from generations of factory workers or bankers, miners or military, builders or wreckers, salesmen or educators, healers or legal gatekeepers, each provides a story with its model characters, life-plot, and life-long progress toward a denouement. "I admired what my dad did."

The narrow range of stories that once guided men within pre-destined traditions of family, tribe, and community have opened wide possibilities as social change, education, and mobility offered alternatives to simply "mapping the past onto the future" and enabled constructive selection of life directions. But the skeletal structures of character and principle—pursuing justice, living out compassion, living out co-humanity—remain unchanged although ambition, self-service, greed, and dominance regularly replace them as prime motivators. *Success* (the rags to riches myths), *conquest* (the return of the hero myth), *greed* (the gain the world myth), *immortality* (the star, idol, record book myths), *fame* (the "I'm gonna live forever, they'll remember my name" myth) and all other strategies for safety and security substitute for faith, character, and moral conviction.

The basic story of human existence undergirding and moti-vating all of the above, argues ethicist Stanley Hauerwas, is the ancient tale of "humankind's quest for certainty (permanence) in a world of contingency (impermanence.)." Hauerwas explains, "This mythic pattern is told in the various dominant modern narratives. . . . Ironically, the function of . . . all accounts, is to tell a story that shows why we no longer need stories, to decree that stories are pre-scientific, according to the story legitimizing the age which calls itself scientific."[1]

We have not outlived and cannot outgrow our need for sto-ries to explain our lives to ourselves and to others. In our deeper self-understanding, we do not give up the quest for a story that is worth dying for. Atheists affirm a story of a random universe; believers a story of purposive creation and creatures; hedonists a story of seizing pleasure as it flies; nihilists a story of destroying useless structures; Machiavellians a story of claiming dominance and control as ultimately satisfying.

Arguably the most compelling male story combines power, dominance, pleasure, and sensuality in the sacralization of sex—the pursuit of cyclical satisfaction of conquest, interpenetration of bodily warmth, the explosion of temporary fusion with the attractive other—that is sacralized in becoming the most precious

---

1 Hauerwas, *Peaceable Kingdom*, 25.

possibility, possession, potential in masculinity. Men worship the omnipresent sacred symbols of sexuality, such as fashion, form, style, posture, figure, carriage, and gesture. In the male mind, the thought of sexual union is never far from reverie and fantasy. The attractive other becomes the desired object and the pursued dream of conquest. Gender dominance has been the fatal flaw of the human species. Imagine a male whose essential story is one of lasting compassion rather than fleeting passion, of consistent respect for all others rather than constant rating of others' sexual desirability. What kind of man would this be? What sort of story would shape such a life of masculinity as true humanity?

A discipleship story is a matter of companionship, of coming to trust, prize, value, and love the central figure of the story, the Master, and choosing to join oneself with him and his agenda. For followers of Jesus it begins with a discovery that we are irreducibly valuable and undeniably loved by God, and in response to that love, we get up and follow. It is not an employer-employee relationship where one earns the benefits; it is discovering that true loving relationship is grace, is gift, is grounded in trust and in response to a greater love. The masculine tendency to measure all things by what is accomplished, to value what is gained through achievement, must be laid aside as one becomes a disciple of Jesus.

Which human story is worthy of a life? Can one find an enduring story, a to-be-continued account that does not end arbitrarily or vacuously? Theologian James McClendon ends his masterful volume *Ethics* with his splendid words on the essential nature of fitting one's life into a mega-story:

> Two essential Christian convictions must round out the account. One is the conviction (call it the doctrine of the Israel of God) that my own story is inadequate, taken alone, and is hungry for a wider story to complete it. That gives us the communitarian element in Christian ethics: My story must be linked with the story of a people. The other is the conviction (call it the doctrine of salvation) that *our* story is inadequate a well: The story of each and all is itself hungry for a greater story that overcomes our persistent self-deceit, redeems our common life, and provides a way for us to be a people among all earth's peoples without subtracting from the significance of others' peoplehood, their own stories, their lives. Christian ethics, because its truth entails character,

must find that truth in a community that is of necessity story-shaped. Christian morality involves us, *necessarily* involves us, in the story of God.[2]

In search of a life-story, postmodern minds find a dismaying array of popular models and mentors. Many traditional models have lost their appeal, many no longer offer hope and get tossed into the dustbins of history. Christianity has lost its promise for many. Jesus remains cogent and compelling, although the contradictory versions and the self-serving practices of many claiming to be followers of Jesus are dismaying. Jesus has been sentimentalized, infantilized, co-opted, distorted, profaned, commercialized, and reconstructed into the image of movement upon movement. Which Jesus? one must ask to identify any reference. Who is he? Person or persona? Peace of Mind panacea or disturbing prod to the conscience? Irrelevant ideal or unquenchable revolutionary?

What is his call to discipleship? What does discipleship mean when he calls us to follow? As the linking voice between Hebrew prophets and the Jesus core group, the ascetic John the Baptist quoted Isaiah. The Galilean, he promised, would upset the world's perspective on all values and virtues. If men, *males*, were to follow Him, he would level the mountains of patriarchy, straighten the crooked paths of male entitlement, smooth the rough places of blatant inequality, raise the valleys of oppression and exploitation, and, as the prophet envisioned, create a level playing field for all humankind. Disciples of the coming Galilean would join him in calling for justice and refusing all unjust advantage and edge, step away from the foot up privilege to join in a new dance of mutuality where justice work begins. To be a disciple is to learn the discipline of relinquishment, to surrender special privilege, to give up entitlement. All these come with traditional gender rights. Jesus in no way supports such male presumption and systemic violence.

Giving up your agenda and trusting Jesus with his

The parallel stories told by Mark and Matthew open with the signal announcement that Jesus appeared saying, "Repent, and believe in the good news" (Mark 1:15; cf. Matt. 4:17). "Repent" may be an old word, but its meaning in contemporary language is to give up one's agendas. And the invitation that follows is to "believe in the good news"—or, in other words, to trust Jesus for

---

2 McClendon, *Ethics*, 351.

his.[3] *Turn*—give up your agendas and trust me for mine. *Come*—join in self-giving sacrifice, repudiate arrogance and dominance over others. *Risk*—what you seek to save you will lose; defend it and you will destroy it. *Connect*—truly connect with others in common life. *Resist*—refuse the promises of safety and security through idolatry. *Die*—in counting egocentric agenda items as dead, we let go serially, progressively, in many little deaths that prepare us for the big one. *Jesus's agenda*—there is no King but YHWH, and the Reign of God is here, now. Join in.

Israel's God is becoming king, but not in a political theocracy. God will be king in the breakthrough of justice and compassion according to Isaiah 2—a worldwide transforming people's movement of radical allegiance to a new way and a social revolution of moving from self-defense and exclusive self-care to equal care for others. He is calling us to action and ethics—not to mysticism and interiority but to practice deeds of faithful love (Hebrew, *mitzvot*) and mutuality (Hebrew, *hesed*; Greek, *agape* and *koinonia*). He is asking us to abandon any crazy dreams of a nationalist revolution based on force, violence, and abusive power because it is too weak, it inevitably fails, and it betrays God's vocation to be the light of the world through self-giving neighbor and enemy love.

This vision of YHWH as king is like no other king in all human history. Jesus prays, *YHWH, King, Parent, may Your reign come on earth.* This king calls us to become the one true humanity serving the one true God. Jesus offers an utterly new agenda; his agenda calls us to a radically new way of being:

- a way of creating change by claiming a new basis for happiness (read the beatitudes);
- a way of unconditional love (read the story of the Prodigal Son);
- a way of forgiving in love on the street, not in holy places, and above all, not reacting in retaliation and revenge (read Jesus's last words);
- a way of reverence and respect for the worth and preciousness of everywoman, everyman (read the story of the Good Samaritan);
- a way of caregiving for the poor, the oppressed, the neglected, the unprotected (read what he said about the orphan, widow, troubled in mind, those he called "the least of these");

---

3 See Wright and Borg, *Meaning of Jesus*, 38–39.

- a way of prayer and reliance not self-advancement and self-protection (read the night in Gethsemane account);
- an utterly risky way of being disciples, a way of turning the other cheek, walking a second mile (read the Sermon on the Mount);
- a way of justice and jubilee, not entitlement and greed (read Jesus's first sermon in Nazareth);
- a way of leveling entitlements and sharing breathing room, sharing the road with both men and women (read all the accounts of his respect for women in a culture where they were presumed to have no souls);
- a way of renouncing xenophobia, including all, considering no one as outside grace (read of his visit to Samaria);
- a way of noncooperation with oppression and violence (read the Sermon on the Mount);
- a way of concern for the chronically ill and excluded pariahs (read how he responded to mental and physical illness and un-deified the demons so they could go home again);
- a way of joining a fictive kinship group that includes the rough, the riff-raff (read of his twelve associates, the tax-man Zacchaeus, shady woman Mary, alleged prostitutes, invisible lepers, despised aliens, Roman oppressors, mentally troubled);
- a way of confronting and correcting traditions of temple worship and going out to meet God among the people (read of his roadside conversations, his Samaritan surprise, the cleansing of the temple);
- a way of breaking free from fear and a paranoid defense agenda (read the accounts of his trial);
- a way of letting go of ancestral codes, rules, and laws (read Mark's gospel);
- a way of abandoning all other visions of empire and joining with his reign (reevaluate who gets to create us, whose representations define our lives, whose agenda sets our goals).[4]

Discipleship is embracing his way, his agenda, his dream. Discipleship, as living out the teachings of Jesus, can be separated neither from the cross nor from the beatitudes and the Sermon on

---

4 My summarization is indebted to N. T. Wright. See Wright and Borg, *Meaning of Jesus*, 36–45.

the Mount, nor from the path of suffering, nor from daily walking in the way we see in the Jesus story. That was his agenda.

The temptation of Christendom has been to separate Jesus as Savior—our salvation through his transforming death and resurrection—from Jesus the teacher above all teachers, the Lord beyond all Caesars, the example above all models of personhood and wholeness. Our embarrassment before the Sermon on the Mount has led to this giant leap from the incarnation of Christ to the passion of the Christ, while ignoring and omitting his life, teaching, and ministry, with the resultant loss of the soul of authentic discipleship. The call to return to the way of the disciple comes most poignantly and powerfully in our day not from within Christendom but from Christianity in the Eastern and Southern Hemispheres. A new commitment to faithful discipleship is voiced in these settings where opposition, persecution, and costly sacrifice are often inevitable for the believer. In accepting Jesus's agenda, we step into the footprints he has left behind, and we follow him in life.

This man named Jesus

The late Clarence Bauman, my former teaching colleague at Anabaptist Mennonite Biblical Seminary, suffered for the last twenty years of his life from slowly advancing Parkinson's disease. Gradually his speech became more indistinct. However, he would sit in on the oral examinations given to graduating master's students, and he often claimed the final question. Slowly, haltingly, he would ask a fourfold puzzle: "Do you have a clear understanding of what belief in Jesus means? Or do you believe in Jesus? Or do you believe Jesus? Or do you believe what Jesus believed?"

The perceptive student realized that she or he had just been asked to talk of the wide differences among belief as (1) orthodox definition, (2) experiential pietism, (3) encounter and obedience, and (4) radical discipleship. No amount of excellence in the answers to the first three would satisfy Bauman until the student had come to grips with the fourth. To believe what Jesus believed is to risk all, plunge into the heart of God's call to unconditional love, and choose a life of utter caring, regardless of the cost or the consequences in an uncaring world.

Few Christians move beyond questions one and two in their understandings of Jesus. So the question must be asked again: *Who is this Jesus?* He is not whoever we want him to be, the "selfie" mirror of our "true selves," the idealized expression of our highest goals of personhood, the blank slate awaiting our list of perfect traits or states. He is not the IMAX screen for the projection and sacralization of our larger than life hopes and dreams of goodness—as we visualize it in our own ideal image. When we recreate Jesus to be our imaginary ideal self, this is not only heretical but delusional, not just heresy but apostasy. Jesus is the unparalleled, unique, unrepeatable, radically human Other—so we are called to meet the other who constantly confronts and challenges us while at the same time inviting us to repeat the unrepeatable. We are to imitate the inimitable, imitate the ultimate non-imitator.

Who do we say this Jesus is? How far do we go in pursuit of him? Who is this man? A good man? A great teacher? A religious leader? A mystic companion? A sacrifice and savior? A perfect being? A moral exemplar? An ultimate master?

What is his role in our lives? Ideal type? Wise prophet? Spiritual guide? Presence? Atoning offering? Model? Example? Lord?

What is our role in this relationship? Admirer? Learner? Seeker? Friend? Believer? Imitator? Follower? Dissident disciple?

Where do we find this Jesus? In the person next to you.

Who do I see? My neighbor.

"You want to see God, look at your brother" said second century Christian leader Chrysostom, quoting the Epistle of 1 John. No idols, no pseudo-sacred stand-ins, no holy mannequins—real people image God to us. Jesus recovers the prohibitions of the Jewish tradition that eliminate all images of God except one—humanity. He is the truly human one. The neighbor stands before us as representative of humanity as such, the sacred embodiment of human life as humanity as a whole. The neighbor represents humankind, both as metaphor and as reality, as a particular human. Seeing the other as metaphor is recognizing the larger whole, the preciousness of our status as creatures. Seeing the particular neighbor is seeing the worth of the other.

"Do you mean that I may be ignoring Jesus when I pass by the homeless man who lives under the bridge?" a Chinese seminarian asked my daughter Kate who teaches at a Theological Seminary in Nanjing, China.

"Does that come to you as a new thought?" she asked in reply.

"Oh yes, when you explained what Jesus meant by the words 'the least of these,' my heart sank. What I do to 'the least of these' in my world I am doing to him? When I read the Chinese translation of the Gospels, I completely missed what this actually means. I will think about it every day."

That is the struggle of a follower of Jesus. His agenda must become my agenda.

This act called following

Following Jesus is not a cognitive act of assent to a proposition, not adoption of a formulaic set of beliefs, but obeying the command to love; it is a moral, social, and political vow of tracking this Galilean prophet in his radical practices of compassion. It is not just to understand Jesus but to follow him; not to cite a slogan or master a mantra but to join a movement, to risk safety and security, to follow a subversive agenda, to bear a cross.

Discipleship is necessarily subversive and dissident because in following Jesus we defy and reject all popular images and stubbornly insist that in both the creation image and the incarnational image we see the divine image intended as the measure of humanity fully revealed in Jesus. This means that when asked to replace Jesus with Constantine (or Caesar, Pentagon, Kremlin, etc.) we say no. When invited to substitute any political project with the political vision of Jesus to act, serve, give, care in compassion, we say no. We say no to any project that does not share in the face of need. "Share" is the word for redistributing needed food and clothes, and that calls us to share power, share opportunity, share the possibilities of creating a meaningful life, and share in common community. We thus say no to any social, political, ethical, or religious perspective that does not seek to love the enemy or demur from empire.

Following Jesus means pursuing his stunningly creative politics, his subversively transformative imagination, and his agenda of re-humanization after the model of the Sermon on the Mount. Wherever and whenever anyone follows the Jesus way of radical and utter humanization, they follow the earthshaking but largely overlooked humanism of the language of Genesis. They reject any image of the divine except the other. Every man images the divine to us; every woman is in the image of God.

If one steps into this Jesus way of construing existence we call discipleship, one makes a radical commitment to practice a life agenda that is rooted in the life of Jesus. In Christian usage, a disciple is a follower-learner-adherent of Jesus as master, teacher, Lord (Matt. 7:28–29; 8:25; Luke 8:24). In Greek usage, the disciple was an apprentice, an adherent to the teaching of a particular school or person; in Hebrew there is no clear antecedent with several possible references (Isa. 8:16; 1 Chron. 25:8), although rabbinic practice taught through the teacher-disciple commitment for passing on wisdom and tradition.

The need for cotravelers

Discipleship should not be tried alone. Even those who have few connections with other disciples connect with a community of fellow disciples through active conversation with the Gospels, the Epistles, the rich library of Christian classics, the friends afar who can be reached by media, and the one or two persons important to their lives who share the pursuit of Jesus. Following Jesus closely makes us hungry to connect with others, as did Jesus himself, to get together and learn from each other's constantly fresh discoveries. We are not human alone, but we need more than a nudge to keep connections tight.

In his journals, Philip Hallie—the chronicler of the French mountain village of Le Chambon where a community of disciples led by André and Magda Trocmé saved thousands of Jews from Nazi occupation—wrote his metaphor of human existence in words from his WWII experience: "On July 18, 1943 I spoke of moral support by means of two foxholes connected by a trench. Life is so very much like this. Each man (in his foxhole) follows the configurations of his own personality, but in one wall there is a passage leading to his fellows."[5] Every man's life is expressed in this metaphor—we live in our own little holes but to be authentically human must constantly dig and daily clear those passages that lead us to our fellows. As we have maintained, discipleship is a friend-ship, a fellow-ship, a mutual-ship of joint service-ship. We do not do it alone.

When discipleship provides the paradigm for Christian living, then one sees the church as a body of believers (disciples) who commit themselves to following Jesus Christ together. It roots the identity of the church in the New Testament disciple-story, extends it as a contemporary, culturally appropriate expression of the biblical story of communal faith, and links the practice of being the church today to the church portrayed in the biblical account of Acts and the Epistles. The emphasis on imitation-participation creates a close continuity between the biblical accounts of the disciple's attachment to Jesus and the believing community's current pursuit of a similar attachment. "No one can know Christ truly

---

5 Hallie, *Tales of Good and Evil, Help and Harm*, xii.

except those who follow him daily in life," wrote Hans Denck, a sixteenth century Anabaptist theologian and martyr.[6]

Discipleship as radical obedience

Discipleship is entirely rooted in and dependent on Christ. One is a disciple to Jesus Christ, not to a theory, theology, or life-style. Discipleship means accepting authority offered in Jesus's characteristic humility, with compassion that transforms the act of caring to a moment of God's grace. In the turbulent years of the 1930s, German Lutheran theologian Dietrich Bonhoeffer articulated a radical theology of discipleship in his classic book *Nachfolge* (*Discipleship*) that offered an impassioned call to follow Jesus Christ in a personal and corporate obedience that was guided by Jesus's own teaching, example, and radical obedience to his Father. "Christianity without discipleship is always Christianity without Christ," wrote Bonhoeffer. Linking discipleship to radical obedience to Christ, he pronounced the dictum, "Only the believers obey and only the obedient believe."[7] He insisted that Jesus didn't simply teach personal, moral, vocational, relational, and devotional obedience (which is more easily assimilated into traditional religious categories of practice and thought), but he required political and ultimately life-and-death obedience.

Bonhoeffer contrasted cheap and costly grace: "Cheap grace is grace without discipleship, grace without the cross, grace without Jesus Christ living and incarnate. Costly grace is the gospel which must be sought again and again, the gift which must be asked for, the door at which one must knock. Such grace is costly because it calls us to follow Jesus Christ. It is costly because it costs us our lives. It is grace because it gives us the only true life."[8] Evidence suggests that Bonhoeffer's pursuit of a courageous ethic led him to give up his earlier position of the nonviolence of the Sermon on the Mount and support an attempt to remove Hitler from office. He was one of the last persons to be executed before the suicide of *Der Fuerher*. Whether or not one agrees with his choice to take another's life, one cannot escape acknowledging the radical obedience of his faith and life in his years of risky and subversive action.

Bonhoeffer's costly discipleship has had a strong influence on many other theologians who have written incisively on

---

6 Hans Denck, "Whether God is the Cause of Evil (1526)," 88–111.
7 Bonhoeffer, *Cost of Discipleship*, 55.
8 Bonhoeffer, *Cost of Discipleship*, 45.

discipleship—including Jürgen Moltmann, Stanley Hauerwas, James McClendon, Miroslav Volf, Glen Stassen—and movement leaders such as Ron Sider, Jim Wallis, Lee Camp, and Brian McLaren. The wide recognition of the centrality of discipleship as the heart of faithful obedience to Christ appears in theologies emerging from Asia, Africa, and Latin America. Wherever discipleship is taught, the call is to follow Jesus, not just to admire or respect him. He is commander of our lives, not just someone to be depended on for a special spiritual transaction called salvation.

Discipleship as death and resurrection

Discipleship to Jesus means following a leader from long ago whom we claim is our contemporary through the mystery believers call the resurrection. If one is a disciple to this Jesus whose life history ends in an empty grave story, if this disjunction with the old life and conjunction with a new way of being is true, then it matters above all else. As I've said many times over the years, *If the Resurrection is true, nothing else matters; if the Resurrection is not true, nothing matters.*

If the Jesus story is true, if it calls to you to walk with him and pick up his practices in discipleship, then it matters more than anything else. If it is not true, then everything else matters only for the time being. Saint Paul put the syllogism a bit differently, when writing to disciples at Colossae: If you as a disciple have been raised with Christ—and that is exactly what your dying and rising in the pledge of baptism means—then live out the love of Christ, the radical, self-giving, earth transcending, self-forgetful care for neighbor-stranger-enemy-brother-sister that creates a stubborn resilient reconciling community. If you have been sprung from the prison of death to run freely in the open world of God's confidence, then go out and do it joyfully (Col. 3:1–3, author's paraphrase).

The contrast is clear: you have died; you have been raised. You have died to the old values, to the old defensiveness, to the old competitiveness that leads to conflict, to the desire to win; you have been raised to collaborating. You have died to the old life of seeking your own way, of needing to be right (or at least seen to be right); you have raised to practice humility. You have died to suspicion and dissention that destroys community; you been raised to a new unity, a new solidarity, a new Spirit-shaped-life called *koinonea*. Paul's logic on the gritty reality of discipleship is tight: Jesus is alive, the resurrection is true; if being his disciple grips you, nothing else matters.

Costly discipleship

"I too would have turned back when my pursuer broke through the ice. I would have put my foot on his head and held him under," said an Asian pastor addressing a conference of Asian pastors in Canada, meeting in Rosthern, Saskatchewan, and hosted by Mennonite pastors. Before coming to Christian faith and becoming a Christian minister, the guest speaker had led a violent life in a dog-eat-dog profession. Now he was telling the story that changed him from being a nominal Christian to a radical disciple. "When I heard this bit of Dutch history, it challenged my basic survival assumptions," he said, "It revolutionized my life and how I read the Gospels."

Here is how he tells the decisive story:

A man is imprisoned for his faith, and for hosting secret meetings of a house church in his home. Somehow, he is able to escape from a window with a knotted bed sheet and make a run for it, but he is discovered and pursued by a sheriff and his deputy. Starved to skin and bones, he runs lightly across the thin ice of the moat, but the well fed deputy breaks through and is sinking beneath the ice while his commander, the sheriff, shouts orders from the shore. The escaping prisoner turns back and plants his foot on the man's head, holds him underwater, and then kicks his body under the ice and makes good his escape.

"At least that is what I would have done," confesses the pastor. But that is not what the man in the story did. The real story comes as a total surprise. Instead of ignoring or drowning the helpless pursuer, the fugitive turns back, reaches out, and pulls the deputy to safety on firm ice.

The sheriff shouts, "Arrest that man," and the deputy seizes his savior and takes him back to be burned at the stake in a long and painful death. "The drowning man he saved became his executioner. He did what was right without considering the unknown but possible consequences. That is how a follower of Jesus treats his enemies," the pastor concludes.

The enemy is not an abstraction or hypothetical for this pastor. As a former member of the communist party, his conversion to Christianity cost him his safety. He made many enemies when he left the party. His new understanding of Jesus's teaching ended reliance on violence but opened a new world of a kingdom of love for the enemy. The audience of Anabaptist pastors, familiar with the account from *The Martyr's Mirror* of Dirk Willems and his rescue of the enemy and his death by fire, heard it told as if for the first time. It was the essence of costly discipleship: give up your agendas and trust Jesus for his.

Bibliography

Augsburger, David. *Dissident Discipleship*. Grand Rapids: Brazos, 2007.

Bonhoeffer, Dietrich. *The Cost of Discipleship*. New York: Macmillan, 1963.

Denck, Hans. "Whether God is the Cause of Evil (1526)." In *Spiritual and Anabaptist Writers: Documents Illustrative of the Radical Reformation*, edited by George Williams and Angel Mergal, 88–111. Philadelphia: Westminster, 1957.

Hallie, Philip. *Tales of Good and Evil, Help and Harm*. New York: Harper, 1997.

Hauerwas, Stanley. *The Peaceable Kingdom: A Primer in Christian Ethics*. Notre Dame, IN: Notre Dame University Press, 1983.

McClendon, James Wm., Jr. *Biography as Theology: How Life Stories Can Remake Today's Theology*. Philadelphia: Trinity, 1991.

_____. *Ethics: Systematic Theology*, vol. 1. Nashville: Abingdon, 1986.

Moltmann, Jürgen. *Following Jesus in the World Today: Responsibility for the World and Christian Discipleship*. Elkhart, IN: Institute of Mennonite Studies, 1983.

Stassen, Glen, and David Gushee. *Kingdom Ethics: Following Jesus in Contemporary Context*. Downers Grove: InterVarsity, 2002.

Wright, N.T., and Marcus Borg. *The Meaning of Jesus: Two Visions*. New York: HarperOne, 1999.

Volf, Miroslav. *Exclusion and Embrace: A Theological Exploration of Identity, Otherness, and Reconciliation*. Nashville: Abingdon, 1996.

Chapter 11

Men in Community

Gareth Brandt

I begin writing on the topic of community while sitting alone in an office with my only companions being the books on my shelves and the music coming from inanimate speakers. I am an introvert who is energized by solitude and silence and already drained by the mere idea of sitting in a meeting with fifty other people for the rest of the afternoon. I am presently suffering from post-traumatic stress when the default impulse is to withdraw from public assemblies into the safety of my own cocoon where nothing unpredictable or overly stimulating will assault my little world. Yet I yearn for the healing balm of the community of faith, and I envision a spirit of collaboration and cooperation between women and men—and among all people.

I grew up with the image of the solitary cowboy riding off into the rugged west as the archetype of what it means to be a real man: independent, in control, and heroic. This is the representation of masculinity that appears to have inspired one popular Christian men's movement author to suggest that "every little boy has dreams, big dreams: dreams of being the hero, of beating the bad guys, of doing daring feats and rescuing the damsel in distress."[1] But as Don Neufeld observes,

> Unfortunately it also represents deep themes of isolation and loneliness that many men experience. With learned aversions to vulnerability and often inadequate lessons and role models for healthy relationships, men find themselves surrounded by people but too often longing to be known fully and to be loved by others in spite of their inadequacies. Men often end up hurting the people closest to them while trying desperately to gain their love. Christian community, as it is envisioned as the humble gathering of God's children around a common experience of grace, offers a rich alternative to this seclusion. As a place of unconditional welcome for

---

1 Eldredge, *Wild at Heart*, 9.

a growing boy, for a struggling man, or for the stranger who comes through the door, Christian community can be the place of safety for men to be known fully and to experience unconditional love . . . the freedom from the compulsive strivings to measure up . . . the freedom to be real and vulnerable . . . the freedom to voice the desires for healthy human relationships with women and men and to have this longing nurtured by caring brothers and sisters.[2]

In this chapter I provide a sketch of what such a community might look like. I begin by offering a theology of community and conclude by providing some particular stories of men in community.

A theology of community

Christian orthodoxy holds that God exists as a trinitarian community; it is therefore divine nature to be particular person in close relationship. The first creation story says that humans were made in the image of this communal God (Gen. 1:27); therefore it is also human nature to be in relationship. The second creation account continues in the same vein. After God formed a man from the dust of the ground and put the man into the garden (Gen. 2:7–8), God said, "It is not good that the man should be alone" (Gen. 2:18). "Man" here is not necessarily meant to be gender specific, but it is not unreasonable to apply it to men. Men are not meant to be alone and independent of others even if our cultural archetypes and stereotypes would have us believe this. All people are created to thrive in community, men included. And men in particular need encouragement and inspiration toward living in community, especially considering the Western cultural bias toward rugged individualism.

Throughout the Scriptures the primary attribute of God is that God is loving—indeed, that God is Love (1 John 4:7–12). Love is about relationship. Love is not a private emotion but a communal action. God demonstrated the vulnerability of love in becoming human in Jesus of Nazareth. This means that it was not so much God's vengeful hatred of our sin that sent Jesus to the cross as it was Jesus's passion for God's kindom[3] of love that caused the

---

2 Neufeld, "Men and Masculinity."
3 My use of "kindom" instead of "kingdom" is deliberate in order to be more gender neutral but even more so to indicate the personal and familial nature of God's reign.

rulers of the violent kingdoms of the day to execute him. Male spirituality is then about giving up control and embracing others with the powerfully transforming, self-giving, reconciling love of Christ. As David Augsburger writes, "Christian spirituality is not, as popularly believed, a matter of individual salvation leading to a life of individual self-realization and pointing toward individual growth and perfection. It is a public encounter with a God who meets us in community. . . . The natural habitat of any true disciple of Jesus is community."[4] Part of the problem with the idea that individual salvation leads to a life of individual self-realization and toward individual growth and perfection is that this was the Christian life articulated in the terms of a modern Western view of manhood and, subsequently, personhood. To change this view of spirituality to be more communal will benefit not only people in general but also men in particular.

Mennonites have a particular claim to a communal theology and spirituality because of our roots in the Anabaptist movement of the sixteenth century. Anabaptist spirituality can be summed up in the word *Gelassenheit*,[5] which can be translated as "yieldedness" or "voluntary commitment." In this case, *Gelassenheit* means not only yieldedness to Christ but also yieldedness to the body of Christ, the church. As C. Arnold Snyder observes, in *Gelassenheit* we see "the distance the Anabaptists maintained from the potential of individualism of the spiritualists or a private spirituality of some later Pietists: the Christian life is not simply a matter of an inner baptism (being right with God personally). . . . Rather, the faithful Christian life must be manifested in, and tested publicly, by the community of believers."[6] Each person gives himself or herself freely to love and be loved, to admonish and be admonished. In modern terms, this is the idea of accountability, the positive support that brings people to an honest consideration of how their own behavior might be unhealthy for themselves and for others around them. When this happens a wonderful picture of individual health and community can emerge.

Communal life was not an idyllic utopian existence in early Anabaptist communities—nor is it today. The communal Anabaptists not only experienced severe persecution from the outside (part

---

For an extensive treatment of this view of the atonement see Weaver, *Nonviolent Atonement*.

4 Augsburger, *Dissident Discipleship*, 64–65.

5 See Snyder, *Following in the Footsteps of Christ*.

6 Snyder, *Following in the Footsteps of Christ*, 79.

of the initial catalyst for various Anabaptist groups holding things in common), but there were also internal disputes and tensions as the structure of communal life was developed. There were struggles with church discipline, applying the ban, unequal distribution, and issues over leadership. A theology of community is messy because it involves real people in real relationship, but that is also its glory and beauty.

Men face some unique challenges when it comes to experiencing community. Sometimes there is difficulty with being vulnerable. The strong silent type was modeled by many fathers of the builder generation, and subsequent generations of men have to work hard to break out of this stereotype. Men are afraid of being judged and not being accepted. Men's self-esteem is often tied to athletic prowess, to body image, to perceived parenting success, to sexual orientation, and—perhaps most acutely in North American culture—to work. When any of these merit markers are taken away or not going well, men often withdraw from rather than gravitate to community. Work can also keep men from community because it can be all-consuming at times, leaving men exhausted and wanting to cocoon rather than engage with a community. Selfishness can often keep men from experiencing the fullness of what community should be about. Too often men's interaction is on a surface level. Men talk about sports in a bar after a few beers to relax or go hunting or fishing or golfing where talking at all is bad etiquette. But what is needed is connection on a deeper emotional level. That is not only what women want and need from men but also what men need from each other.

God's love, presence, and guidance is mediated through others in community. We men must get with God's agenda and embrace a more communal spirituality where reconciliation and friendship are the preferred metaphors for salvation and spirituality. Doing so will have profound implications for us, for our families, and for the world. We will have more mutually respectful marriage and family relationships, and someday there may even be peace between warring nations as a result. It starts with how we see God's relationship to us and becomes our model for a life that includes vulnerability, forgiveness, reconciliation, friendship, and community.

Stories of men in community

There are many and varied shapes of men in community. There are accountability partners or small groups where men keep each other accountable for sexual behavior, balance between work and home life, spiritual disciplines, and relationships. Therapeutic groups are powerful ways that men can work through issues of power, abuse, self-esteem, and vulnerability. Then there are special men's events that provide community such as work bees,[7] weekend retreats, prayer breakfasts, seminars, and workshops.[8] Men are stronger and more authentically human in community.

My own experience of men in community began with a sabbatical project exploring men's spirituality. The project began with solitary reading, but I quickly realized that I could not do this alone and that many men shared my quest. I emailed a few dozen friends from my church and colleagues at work, and in less than twenty-four hours I had a table full of men (and a waiting list!) who were interested reading my writings and then meeting together at Mission Springs Brewery and Pub on a regular basis to talk about men's spirituality.[9] In 2008 I sent out one chapter a month for twelve months, and the men read each chapter in preparation for our discussion meetings.

In conversation I began mentioning to people what I was working on during my sabbatical and found an unexpected and enthusiastic interest in this men's spirituality project. Because of the interest I thought I might increase the circle of conversation by starting a virtual group, so I contacted acquaintances across the continent. Again, within a very short time I had a response of about thirty people (mostly men) who were interested in reading and responding to what I was writing, and a number suggested others they knew who would be interested. I then rewrote every chapter using anecdotes, stories, and critiques gleaned from the group that met at Mission Springs once a month and from all the email responses collected electronically. I learned a lot during this process and had good conversations with many people. One of the people in my electronic group put me in touch with Mennonite Men, who became interested enough in the project to provide

---

7 A gathering for mutually accomplishing a task or for communal fundraising.

8 It is important for men to also be in community with women, but for the purposes of this chapter the focus is on the importance of men in community with other men in the context of a culture that sees strong men as solitary.

9 It seems we were part of a trend. In her article "Go on, have a pint with the Lord," Wendy Leung describes the increase of men's religious groups meeting in pubs. She quotes one pastor who describes the appeal of meeting in a pub: "Without the religious setting, you get more authentic discussion, more honest questions, and a little more honest sharing."

funding.[10] The result was my book *Under Construction: Reframing Men's Spirituality* (Herald, 2009).

It was an amazing experience for our group of seven who met every month that year. We did not talk much about sports, politics, or our workplaces. Instead we mostly talked about our relationships with our fathers, spouses, children, and God, about how all those relationships are related, and about what goes on beneath the surface: our feelings, doubts, questions, and fears. There was lots of laughter, but there was also heartache, frustration, and compassion. Emotional depth and spiritual vulnerability in a small group of men were not things we had in any structured form before we took the risk to get together. Our meetings met a need, but the project came to an end after a year. About six months later, one of the members called us back together with the suggestion that we should continue to meet regularly for no other reason than that we needed and enjoyed each other's company. Other men from our church were invited, and the group expanded.

Now it is ten years later, and we are still meeting once or sometimes twice a month. The agenda is less formal and structured, and with almost a dozen men involved somewhat regularly, there is always a table full of men. With no agenda we now talk about everything from sports to church, from family relationships to global politics, from IBUs to MCC.[11] Most importantly, it has become an important expression of church community for all those involved.

Although the writing of this chapter began in solitude, it ended in community. We gathered together at Mission Springs as usual on the first Thursday of the month, and the table was even fuller than usual (even though I had coopted the usual informality with a specific agenda). I asked the men in the group to think about the following questions and write or speak an answer to one or more of them:

- What does community mean to you? Why is community important for you? For men?
- What does an ideal community look like for you? How do you like to experience community?
- How have you experienced community (or lack of community) in church?

---

10 See www.mennonitemen.org.

11 IBU stands for International Bitterness Unit, one of the measurements for the taste of beer. MCC stands for Mennonite Central Committee, the organization that coordinates relief, development, and advocacy work on behalf of Mennonite churches.

- How have you experienced community uniquely in a group of men?
- What unique challenges do men/you face when it comes to experiencing community? Why is community sometimes hard for men/you?

Here are a few testimonials of men in our group, which highlight some themes that arose in our discussion that night:

> I did not realize how hungry I was to be deeply connected with other men until I had seen the invitation to join the men's group at the pub. I needed to be known and to know other men. To find commonality and to understand my uniqueness. I needed to trust and be trusted. That was the beginning of really understanding community as a man. Over time I have seen the fruits of that connectedness: a genuine openness and a level of support to those who share in this community. My intentional connections to other men over a raised glass of beer have helped me to deepen that sense of community and challenged me in untold ways to be a better man.

> In our world of social media, people are more connected to each other than ever before, and yet at the same time we have a deep need for personal face-to-face connection. The need to connect with other people is a deep and primal need. I was unaware of my need for this connection until I was invited to be part of this group. I was nervous at first because I was being invited into an existing group who had met for a year, but it did not take long for me to feel like I had things in common. The thing that drew us together was our need for real human connection. When we meet a stranger or are introduced to a new person, the automatic response is to attempt to find some commonalities. Among Mennonites it is sometimes called "the Mennonite game" when we try to find out if we are related somehow or if the new person knows somebody that we know, but this need to find commonality is universal.

> For me community is like a well-worn old jacket I don't even realize I have on because it is so natural and comfortable, yet when I don't have it I notice it acutely. It is important to be intentional about community, but it

truly becomes community when it "just happens" and later you notice how special it was.

One of my best memories of community in this group is when one of our participants lost his mother to cancer. It was a rather somber gathering that Thursday as we knew what our friend had just gone through. He was able to talk about the funeral and the responses of different family members and just to process what it meant to lose a loving mother at a relatively young age. But the evening was not focused only on his loss; we all began to share about the impact our mothers had had on our lives and how they had shaped the men we had become. It is common to talk about how our fathers had been good and/or bad examples of manhood, but it was a unique exercise to talk about our mothers in this way. It made for a deep and memorable conversation.

The experience of getting together to discuss issues related to men's spirituality was profound for me, and when it was over, I really missed it. It was being together with men, talking about stuff we don't usually talk about, and taking some risks. What we have now is different, but I enjoy hearing about the everyday life of the guys as well as digging into current issues. This is punctuated by times of more introspection and vulnerability, and I appreciate it when someone moves the conversation into those areas as well. We often jokingly refer to it as church and use a lot of religious references to describe our gatherings—and there is some truth in this.

Community is sometimes a difficult dance because we are men who have been taught to be independent and self-reliant. Because all men are welcome in our group, numerous men have showed up once or twice or attend sporadically. I wonder why some have uninvited themselves. Do they feel threatened by the intimacy?

At one point a wife of one of the guys said that it would be fun for some women to join us, and I reactively said, "No! This is just for men. We need a place to be just us. Women will change the dynamic, and some guys won't talk. The topics will change, the responses might change, and we will lose something special." I think they were taken aback, but I felt very protective. We need to be together as just men. This was sacred space. Our wives have told us that the group has been great for their partners and their marriages.

On a simple level, community to me means being with a group of people with some likeminded purpose. There may be a lot of differences in the group, and it can be quite flexible, but true community needs a connecting point, a common shared purpose. Community happens when there is a center. As an introvert, I like my space, and having a specific purpose to a group makes it easier for me to start conversations, form relationships, and get to know people. A story that illustrates the importance of purpose in a group is when my son became part of an outdoor leadership (OL) program at a Christian college. Even though he had been with the same friends through six years of high school, when he came back from an OL trip after being in the program for only several weeks, he said, "I've gotten to know more about these people and told them more about myself than I have with friends I've had for six years! It's a safe place for people to tell their story. People want to know, and they care." This community experience in the OL program made a huge impact on him and his understanding of faith because they shared a common purpose.

Community does not mean everyone has to agree on everything; that is uniformity. Unity requires some diversity. There has been much frustration in our denomination over the question of inclusion of LGBTQ+ people in our churches. Sometimes people have suggested we should just have separate churches, but I disagree. Why? I need to be with people who think differently than I do and who can challenge my beliefs and my natural responses. I don't need to be with just likeminded people. What is needed in all the difference, though, is humility, mutual respect, a willingness to listen, an openness to not having all the answers, and a willingness to embrace diversity while focusing on what holds us together. Lack of community is when these things are missing.

As a man engaged with the church, I have grown to understand my need for connection and community, while at the same time having tendencies to fly solo. My ideal community is when members are transparent and accountable with other members and find support, encouragement, and hope. It gives when there is need. It comforts when there is sorrow. It is welcoming and inclusive. And while I value inclusivity, I know at times I also struggle with being inclusive of others. I have much to learn if I am to live in a model of the ideal community. By my nature I am a closed book—something I learned from my father—and sharing deeply and being accountable as part of a community have been a stretch. While I am comfortable and thrive in social settings, the paradox is that I am sometimes reluctant to step out and make those connections.

I experience community in a weekly potluck care group. I have made a commitment to be present with these people with whom I break bread and with whom I have developed strong and supportive relationships. I am amazed at our differences and yet am grateful for these people and how they enrich my life and provide unfailing support when we have need or experience loss. Joy doubled or grief halved are the result of living in community. On a larger level, my church is a perfect example of real community: a diverse group of people who share faith and yet practice it in very different ways. As one who can tend toward loneliness and isolation when life closes in, I need community to encourage me, to take me outside of myself, to share in joys and sorrows, and to remind me I belong to a living body that is reliant on the other parts.

I experience community best around a table—whether that is at home or at the pub. Community involves shared experience, celebration, practical action, and honest dialogue.

In some ways our group is quite homogeneous; the regular attenders are all heterosexual, middle-aged, white fathers who are connected to the same Mennonite church. We all value inclusivity and openness. At the same time, we have very different personalities, we come from different ethnic and family backgrounds, and our work life varies greatly, including business, trades, education, and non-profits. We wear white and blue collars. When we come together, we share stories about how we are doing and then find connections with what others are going through. We look for commonalities. We begin to trust each other with our lives and become like a surrogate family, especially for those who do not have any family close by. We are men who have realized our need for community and are willing to take the risk to make it happen.[12]

These testimonials are from a specific group of men from a specific geographical area with a specific purpose for meeting, but I hope they provide inspiration for other groups of men in other regions with other purposes. The bottom line is for men to be in community, especially a peaceful spiritual community that is open, vulnerable, mutual, and supportive.

Bibliography

Augsburger, David. *Dissident Discipleship: A Spirituality of Self-Surrender, Love of God, and Love of Neighbor.* Grand Rapids: Brazos, 2006.

Brandt, Gareth. *Under Construction: Reframing Men's Spirituality.* Scottdale, PA: Herald, 2009.

Eldredge, John. *Wild at Heart: Discovering the Secret of a Man's Soul.* Nashville: Nelson, 2001.

Leung, Wendy. "Go on, have a pint with the Lord." *Globe and Mail.* October 12, 2009.

Neufeld, Don. "Men and Masculinity—a Vital Focus for Peacemaking." Paper presented at Global Mennonite Peacebuilding: A Conference and Festival, Conrad Grebel University College, Waterloo, Canada, June 2016.

Snyder, C. Arnold. *Following in the Footsteps of Christ: The Anabaptist Tradition.* Maryknoll, NY: Orbis, 2004.

Weaver, J. Denny. *The Nonviolent Atonement.* Grand Rapids: Eerdmans, 2001.

---

12 Repondants include Gareth Brandt, Brian Bergen, Phil Davis, John Dawson, Al Friesen, Anthony Klassen, Jon Nofziger, Terry Penner, Steve Schroeder, and Gerhard Wiens. Responses have been lightly edited for clarity.

Chapter 12

The Gospel Gift of Peace

Marty Troyer

Scott Brown was a model peace activist. Environmental protector, restorative justice facilitator, criminal justice reformer, anti-war activist, he was an author, public debater, and leader of movements. He was informed, passionate, funny, and, perhaps most importantly, available. His mission statement was *Be right, win every battle, and help save the earth*. If there was something to do with peace and fighting violence, Brown was there. He was the essence of protagonist, antagonist, and pacifist. When he told his story to my church and friends, I couldn't help thinking, *This is the kind of man I want to be when I grow up*.

There was only one problem: Scott's inner life was a complete mess. He was a broken man inside. His marriage fell apart, his coworkers had to walk on eggshells around him, and he was motivated by a wounded soul that needed to earn worth through works. His tactics included shaming, blaming, and creating enemy images of the very people he was trying to convert. He once screamed to a scientist in a radio interview, "Stop lying to people!" so many times they eventually cut him off.

Brown's story is not unusual to me as a pastor-activist in Houston. Many times have I witnessed men passionate for the cause of peace but noticeably without peace in their hearts. Ironically, peace activists can be some of the hardest people to work with. Brown's story also connects with me personally, as I long to live with the peaceful skills of parenting, conflict transformation, and peace witness that I preach week in and week out. All of us men some of the time and some of us men all of the time live in a disturbing world without peace, both in our public selves that perpetrate havoc on those around us and with the private hidden corners of our deeply troubled inner worlds. But Scott Brown couldn't see any of this. He later reflected, "I was about as in touch with my feelings as I was the Rings of Saturn."[1] When his life finally scraped bottom, he was filled with sadness and uncertainty and was bored with being angry.

---

1 S. Brown, *Active Peace*, 3.

It seems like Brown got it half right. He mastered *doing* peace work but flunked *being* a peaceful man. Though his cause was right, his soul was a muddled mess impossible to want to emulate. There has to be an alternative to burn out, on the one hand, and content passivity, on the other. We don't have to choose between heroism and health. In this chapter we explore what men can do if they want to make peace in their relationships yet find inner peace elusive.

A true model of peace

More than anyone else in history, Jesus models the kind of healthy lives men are meant to live. He embodies being peaceful at heart, or what sociologist Brené Brown calls "wholeheartedness."[2] Jesus's genius at keeping the inner and outer life connected means he had both what Scott Brown had and what he didn't have. We all know Jesus was a radically ethical man. But he also tended his soul and still needed to hear God say to him, "You are my Son, the Beloved; with you I am well pleased" (Luke 3:22).

Jesus promised the blessing of finding our core identity as children of God when we make peace. He unashamedly spoke of his male protégés as his "beloved" while expecting them to live robust lives of justice for the hungry, poor, sick, migrant, and prisoner among them. As followers of Jesus, our capacity to radically love is directly tied to our capacity to vulnerably accept his love and our need for it (1 John 4:19). Rather than Scott Brown, Jesus was the kind of peaceful at heart peacemaker we should all long to be when we grow up.

As Anabaptist Christians, Mennonites are at our best when inner and outer peace are embodied as two parts of the same whole. Early Anabaptist writer Hans Denck does a fantastic job of poetically capturing the tension of all Anabaptists between the inner life of trusting Jesus (spirituality) and the public living of a Jesus-centered life (mission): "No one can truly know Christ unless you follow him in life; and no one can truly follow him unless first you have known him."[3]

As cultures and contexts have changed, Mennonites haven't always held them together well. On the one hand, the modern mental model of "missions" has left many in the church removed from the action and forced to define discipleship in terms of being good church members. On the other hand, when the world seems

---

2 See B. Brown, *Gifts of Imperfection.*
3 Klaassen, *Anabaptism in Outline*, 87.

especially messy, we often focus too strongly on action and suffer from spiritual poverty.

Today many of us are passionate for both a new spirituality and a new world. We're not interested in workaholic absentee parenting for the sake of the cause or in staying at home when it feels like the world is burning. Menno Simons, our namesake, has a sharp, compelling statement about Christian action that's often quoted in Mennonite circles:

> True evangelical faith is of such a nature that it cannot lie dormant, but manifests itself in all righteousness and works of love; . . . it clothes the naked; it feeds the hungry; it comforts the sorrowful; it shelters the destitute; it aids and consoles the sad; it returns good for evil; it serves those that harm it; it prays for those that persecute it; [it] teaches, admonishes, and reproves with the Word of the Lord; it seeks that which is lost; it binds up that which is wounded; it heals that which is diseased and it saves that which is sound.[4]

Add stopping nuclear war to that list and I'm all in. But the temptation to act removed from the power of the Spirit is hard to resist. We're supposed to be self-made courageous men who shed our blood to save our people. Simons saw it differently. For him, action is rooted in personal transformation. What we don't see quoted as often is what Simons says immediately before telling us our faith can't be passive:

> If you sincerely accepted and believed the divine goodness, mercy, and the boundless love of our beloved Lord Jesus Christ toward you . . . if you believed all this, you would doubtlessly love Him in return, Him who has shown you such great love and grace without any merit on your part. And if you would return the love with which He has loved you and yet loves you, you would, believe me, not tire of seeking and following Him.[5]

We too often think of Jesus's call to discipleship as a call to morality. It isn't. It's an invitation to live the abundant life he promised of becoming fully human and fully alive. Yes, the dignity of being God's partner in making peace in our violent world is

---

4 Simons, "Why I Do Not Cease Teaching and Writing," 307.
5 Simons, "Why I Do Not Cease Teaching and Writing," 306–307.

0.0

essential to becoming fully alive. But so is doing our inner work; we just don't stop there. As I write in *The Gospel Next Door*, "In his living and loving we see who we are meant to be: intimately connected to God, free to fully be ourselves, connected passionately to community, and committed to creating shalom in our world."[6] In order to do the things that Jesus did, we must become the kind of man that Jesus was.

Jesus once said, "You will know them by their fruits. Are grapes gathered from thorns, or figs from thistles? In the same way, every good tree bears good fruit, but the bad tree bears bad fruit. A good tree cannot bear bad fruit, nor can a bad tree bear good fruit" (Matt. 7:16–18). We've got to become the kind of men who naturally live the life of Jesus and his teachings found in the Sermon on the Mount and elsewhere throughout the Gospels—men of integrity whose peaceful hearts pour out into peaceful living.

Jesus's story is as much about violence as it is about anything. In the face of a #MeToo moment of violence against women, Jesus non-anxiously dispersed a lynch mob (John 8:1–11). When everyone was watching, he called out his buddies to stop pretending violence works (Luke 9:54–55; 22:49–51). He was tenderhearted to those who didn't get it, took time to relax by himself, and asked for help when needed. And then he was killed and resurrected, where unspeakable violence was met with the unspeakable gift of friendship and offer of peace (John 20–21).

What we're up against

We live in what military and business leaders call a VUCA world: volatile, uncertain, complex, and ambiguous. VUCA fits my experience as a dad and a pastor like a glove. It's not that our list of public sins is longer than before; it's that we're more aware. We're pushed to deal with racism, sexism, homophobia, militarism, police brutality, Islamophobia, poverty, and climate change in ways that are near impossible to understand through the idolatrous lens of American exceptionalism.

Our new normal is kids being shot in schools, church members being shot during worship, so-called enemies being killed by our drone missles, and nuclear threats by ego-obsessed men in power. We have the names etched in our minds of victims of police brutality: Michael Brown, Alton Sterling, Tamir Rice, Stephon Clark, Yvette Smith, Miriam Carey, Eric Garner, Philando Castile.

---

6 Troyer, *Gospel Next Door*, 67.

These problems and the speed with which we're expected to address them are part of what scientist Will Steffen calls the Great Acceleration.[7] Life and the news cycle move fast. The problems we face are global yet painfully personal, complex yet close to home. Trying to think our way through them feels like trying to imagine a billion grains of sand.

Our inability to respond to every major crisis can feel like a lack of caring. We often feel paralyzed when confronted with the massive number of causes, needs, caring opportunities, and calls to get involved *now*. From the scroll of Facebook to our news apps, we see the brokenness of our Great Acceleration everywhere, and we are overwhelmed.

No dad should have to involuntarily remember the names of men and boys who killed kids like mine in places called Santa Fe, Parkland, Newtown, West Nickel Mines, and Columbine. No teacher should have to consider whether he'll need to choose between keeping his students or himself safe in an active shooter scenario. No husband should need to worry about his wife walking on a public trail in Toronto or running the marathon in Boston. And no boy should have access to his parent's gun when psychologically tormented and struggling to make his way in the world.

And yet we do.

Scripture has its own ways of talking about broken societies and worldviews. When groups stray from God's agenda and pursue their own, they're being *unrighteous*, or not right with God and others. When holistic shalom is held back for some people, groups slide into *injustice*. *Corruption*, *wickedness*, *evil*, and *sin* are words used to flesh out the state of societies. So we read stories about unjust empires like Egypt and Israel that deserve to be in ruin. We're introduced to kings God never wanted to appoint who stray repeatedly into hoarding and violence. We know by heart the story of God's flood to reset the human project because "the earth was corrupt in God's sight, and the earth was filled with violence" (Gen. 6:11). Jesus says the wealthy "devour widows' houses" (Mark 12:40), and he weeps because society does not know "the things that make for peace" (Luke 19:42). This all sounds too familiar. Things are not as they're intended to be.

---

7 See Steffen et al., "Trajectory of the Anthropocene."

Peaceless at heart

It gets worse. These cultural problems have a profound impact on us psychologically. A 2018 study by insurance giant Blue Cross Blue Shield reports that the number of people experiencing depression skyrocketed 33 percent between 2013 and 2016.[8] Every individual suffers for unique reasons, and their care needs to match their particular set of circumstances. But there are also shared root causes that may help us understand this mental health pandemic. Conflict studies professor Vern Neufeld Redekop provides a helpful analysis of human identity needs, as Don Neufeld discusses in his chapter above.[9] Based on Redekop's analysis, I wonder whether our deteriorated notions of action, security, and connectedness leave us hollowed out and traumatized.

Many Christians find it hard to connect their vocation to their call to Christian action. Action for ordinary Christians has often been reduced to performing the duties of a good church member. This largely entails providing financial support, supporting the church in its activities, and putting in time as church volunteer. It hasn't always mattered what one's job is so long as it produces income to donate and save.

And that's not good enough. According to David Graeber's research,[10] 37–40 percent of workers believe their jobs don't make a meaningful contribution to the world. That's millions of people who think if their job disappeared it wouldn't matter—millions of people locked into boredom, lethargy, lack of dignity, and feelings of despair and worthlessness. Though "created in Christ Jesus for good works" (Eph. 2:10), we do meaningless work disconnected from the common good or righting the felt wrongs of the world. We're meant to be healers of the world who seek above all else the public kingdom of God's shalom for all. And yet for forty to sixty hours a week we labor to buy a bigger house.

Heart of Darkness author, Joseph Conrad, cuts to the core: "A man is a worker. If he is not that he is nothing."[11] Real life, our culture tells us, is about money, security, position, power, and happiness. Christianity defines real life differently. We're called to follow Jesus in specific actions like protecting widows, defending migrants, providing health care, and letting "the oppressed go free"

---

8 "Major Depression: The Impact on Overall Health."

9 See Neufeld's discussion of Redekop, *Violence to Blessing*, in chap. 1 above.

10 Graeber, *Bull Shit Jobs*.

11 Conrad, *Notes on Life and Letters*, 150.

(Luke 4:18). Excluding peacemaking from our concept of vocation and action neuters us in the face of the violence mentioned above. Our work should build the common good; our vocation should connect to our call to Christian action.

Redekop includes security as another human identity need. Many of us no longer feel that our world can be trusted to provide security. The religious-like promises of capitalism tempt us to believe that the GDP and a 401(k) are the seeds of security.

But there's an extraordinarily close connection between income inequality and individual health and security. The research of Richard Wilkinson outlines how the world's most economically unequal countries experience the most crippling social and personal dysfunction.[12] Life expectancy, infant mortality, gun violence, teenage births, child well-being, social mobility, and mental health are all devastatingly worse. Canada is in the middle of the pack of these, while the United States is off the charts. When it comes to mental health, for example, countries with unjust economies have three times more people who suffer from depression. We're wired to be drastically impacted by our cultural problems. In this case the very strategy used to pursue security undermines our security. As Wilkinson says, "If you want to live the American Dream, you should go to Denmark."

Finally, Redekop identifies connectedness and relationship as human identity needs. Gone are the days when we knew our food's producer by name and "Made in America" was a trusted label. In its place is our growing awareness of sweatshop labor, slaves used to produce our chocolate and coffee, and North American energy consumption that degrades the environment of the poor more than the rest of us. We know those things; we may feel them. Yet these unintended consequences of our lifestyles feel impossible to undo. We feel a global connectedness in its negative reality, without a positive spirituality of global oneness to shape our actions. Part of our peaceless inner malaise is due to our complicity in a system we helped build that negatively impacts the poor, marginalized, and oppressed.

Coping 101

When confronted with the social dysfunction of our VUCA world, many of us choose denial to cope with the trauma. We've embraced what Canadian novelist Douglas Coupland calls a "culture of perki-

---

12 See Wilkinson, "How Economic Inequality Harms Societies."

ness" to deny our fears.[13] Some self-soothe with the belief that, with God on our side, our planet is too big to fall. And we men have been socialized to cover up and hide our insecurities—though, to be fair, news about a fourth straight Warriors-Cavaliers NBA finals gets more coverage than disaster relief, men mentoring boys, or churches who work for nonviolence.

One character trait of spiritually healthy people is their ability to accept reality as it is. We've got to stare social dysfunction in the face and not blink. Psychologist Mary Pipher writes, "Our emotional and physical survival depends on our ability to tolerate reality at least some of the time. We cannot act adaptively if we don't face the hard truths of the day."[14] And that takes a lot of emotional bandwidth. The real question isn't whether we see reality. It's impossible to miss. Rather, the question is whether we see that our own spiritual immaturity is directly tied to our political and cultural problems.

I used to think I was brave just to see reality clearly. But now I know that's not bravery but perception. Bravery is naming our complicity in the state of the world and the land where we live. Our quietude is linked to the increased war budget. Our turn of the eye is linked to the abuse of women. For those of us not in the minority, our unanalyzed white male privilege leads law enforcement to believe they can act with impunity against our black neighbors.

And here's something easy to miss about the psychological impact of our cultural problems: as bad as this can be for church people, everyone else is just as conflicted and hurting. We have bored coworkers, spiritually dead friends, and emotionally frazzled family. All of us are trying to cope and make our way in this VUCA world.

The gospel gift of peace

The good news is that we are not left to fend for ourselves. Christianity is about God's love for the whole world and our part in bringing God's kingdom to places like my hometown of Houston "as it is in heaven." Whether we're talking about our cultural problems or their pyschological impact on us, peace is God's answer. Shalom equips us to take responsibility for the trauma of our personal lives, which is directly linked to the brokenness of our land. In this sense peace is the Bible's biggest word, encompassing all the good gifts of

---

13 See "Douglas Coupland's Guide to the Next Decade."
14 Pipher, *Green Boat*, 47.

God. Salvation, wholeness, safety, justice, restoration, meaningful action, peace-of-mind, the common good, and caring relationships are all part of God's peace, a gift that is freely offered to us.

The Hebrew Scriptures use the word *shalom* for peace, along with a host of other synonyms. Shalom is peaceful relationship with ourselves, God, others, enemies, and all creation. When things are working well, shalom is present. When social dysfunction and violence are present, shalom is missing. Shalom's connection to social justice can be seen in some of the more colorful images the Hebrew Scriptures use to illustrate it. Isaiah envisions a land filled with an overabundance of camels that produce economic stability (Isa. 60:6); Zechariah envisions streets full of boys and girls playing safely (Zech. 8:5); and Micah envisions security where everyone fearlessly sits in his or her own vineyard (Micah 4:4).

I have friends who have attended every Houston public schools board meeting for years because they know schools are at the intersection of racism, poverty, and inequality and because their Christian faith commits them to the common good of all students, particularly those without a voice. It's tedious work that's outside of the limelight, as is most good peacemaking work. And yet in their pursuit of just education for all, these friends are seeking the shalom of their city.

Mennonites often say that shalom is more than just the absence of violence. Shalom is about creating what civil rights leaders called the beloved community and what the prophet Ezekiel calls return to Eden (Ezek. 36:22–38). It's the presence of all good things, not just the absence of evil. Shalom suggests that personal healing and healing our world are one and the same. The ministries of Mennonite Men, Mennonite Central Committee, and Mennonite Disaster Service are all missions of shalom to restore our world to God's intended design. Without these positive restoration projects, our traditional "quiet in the land" pacifism mentality falls flat.

But shalom also very much does include the removal of violence. Weapons shall be beaten into farm tools, soldiers' clothes shall be burned as useless, and the wolf shall live with the lamb. God protected Cain from the death penalty and tried to remove violence from the world with a flood. And Jesus repeatedly removes violence from a situation through word or deed. Knocking out a tooth from the person who knocks yours out is common sense, but Jesus calls his followers to stop violence with love for our enemies. The essence of violence is sin, and Jesus is "the Lamb of God who takes away the sin of the world" (John 1:29).

Overflowing with peace

We men must stay committed to nonviolence. It is a gospel life-style. As I write in *The Gospel Next Door*, "It's not extra credit, or an elective, or a special track of special action for special people, the privileged few. This is the kind of life we'd naturally live if we truly believed Jesus' gospel. It is action rooted in theology, behavior rooted in belief, and discipleship rooted in the story of Jesus."[15]

What Menno Simons wrote in 1552 still needs to be our agenda today for the sake of our kids and our government's enemies alike: "The Prince of Peace is Jesus Christ. We who were formerly no people at all, and who knew of no peace, are now called to be a church of peace. True Christians do not know vengeance. They are the children of peace. Their hearts overflow with peace. Their mouths speak peace, and they walk in the way of peace."[16] A Christian message of shalom from an Anabaptist perspective offers a consistent vision for peace as an inner experience of salvation that overflows into specific peaceful action. One cannot disconnect the two anymore than one can separate spaghetti from its sauce.

I'll never forget a story the Anglican priest Kenneth Leech told just as I was beginning to see myself as an activist. In the story he had just completed a lecture on Christian social justice when a woman approached him and said, "Isn't it just so interesting that there is another Kenneth Leech out there who writes and speaks beautifully about prayer? I came because I'd seen your name and assumed you were him." Leech replied, "Ma'am, there is no other Kenneth Leech. I'm one and the same. I write about both prayer and justice—usually at the same time." That is the kind of men we need to become: men whose hearts overflow with peace.

In order to be peacemakers, we need to choose to act like them. And choice is a powerful force. Canadian novelist Louise Penny puts these strong words in the mouth of her famous detective Gamache: "We can choose our thoughts. We can choose our perceptions. We can choose our attitudes. We may not think so, we may not believe it. But we can. . . . Life is a choice. All day, every day. Who we talk to, where we sit, what we say, how we say it. And our lives become defined by our choices. It's as simple and as complex as that. And as powerful."[17] Choosing to identify our guiding principles today can empower us to choose peace when

---

15 Troyer, *Gospel Next Door*, 93.
16 Simons, "Reply to False Accusations."
17 Penny, *Still Life*, 76.

the situation demands it. Strong restorative intentions regarding nonviolence for us men are essential or we'll remain paralyzed by the Great Acceleration of our VUCA world.

One of those intentions should be connecting our vocation with the common good. When we think about bringing faith into the workplace, we should refuse to limit it to hosting Bible studies and putting Christian messages on our marque; instead we should find work that is by nature building the common good. No more value less capitalism and working for the weekend. Our Christian vocation is no more or less than to "seek the welfare [shalom] of the city" where we live (Jer. 29:7). That's not something we're meant to accomplish with a monthly service project. That's meant to be the agenda of our 9 to 5, Monday to Friday vocations as well.

Another strong restorative intention is to learn the skills needed to stop violence. Let's put peacemaking back on the agenda. To do that churches will need to adjust their adult curriculum from only learning *about* peace to learning *how to make* peace. That includes stopping violence in our own hearts by learning to name and manage our anxiety. It requires learning how to "fight" well and deal with conflict in our marriages and friendships. And for some of us, it involves learning how to organize a peace march, lead nonviolent direct action training, or even be arrested.

Men often hold power and privilege that position us to uniquely defend women, children, and the vulnerable "other." And we should. Social media and church open mic sharing provide opportunities to speak against duplicitous and inconsistent messages regarding violence. And we should. Schools are usually open to displaying alternatives to military recruitment brochures and legally permit our boys to abstain from saying the pledge. And we should. Ephesians says that Jesus came to make and to proclaim peace (2:14–17). And we should do it too.

That's the importance of choosing guiding principles today so that tomorrow our behavior follows. Let's give our word to seek the shalom of our city. Let's commit to co-create with God a better world. As God's partners in justice, we're part of something larger than ourselves. We're part of a cosmic story about the restoration of all creation that's far bigger than we often know. Naming and nurturing strong restorative intentions for ourselves can give us the dignity we need to see ourselves as part of the solution to the world's great problems. And like solving most problems in life, it all begins with us.

Becoming peaceful at heart

Perhaps the most difficult action we can take is becoming peaceful at heart. We cannot expect to live like Jesus if we do not become Jesus-like. So another strong restorative intention is personal formation. We men experience great insecurities, and many of us are motivated by psychic wounds. We resonate all too well with rocker Ozzie Osborne when he sings, "Mental wounds not healing / Life's a bitter shame / I'm going off the rails on a crazy train."[18]

I'm in a group of fifteen pastors where every single one us admitted to using quality performance as a way to earn love. Don Neufeld writes that, for men, lack of recognition "can crush our sense of self."[19] This reminds me of a story of comedian Tom Arnold who, when asked why he wrote a certain book, is said to have replied with shocking honesty, "I did it because I want you to like me." To be peacemakers we're gonna have to deal with our own insecurities.

Grace is what allows us to face our personal shame and unevangelized zones with vulnerability and courage. And there will be no peaceful heart without vulnerability. It's the engine that drives spiritual growth. As Bob Dylan says, "Behind every beautiful thing there's been some kind of pain."[20]

Scott Brubaker-Zehr names the difficulty and necessity of finding safe places for men to be vulnerable and "to find a healthy integration between the outer and the inner."[21] While he zeroes in on the importance of cultivating an inner spiritual life, I confess that as a young adult this kind of talk left me cold. I was all about action, about *doing something*. Now I know better. Without this difficult self-reflection, we're destined to remain stuck on autopilot, incapable of loving and receiving love well.

Which brings me back to the model peace activist Scott Brown I opened the chapter with. Without healthy masculinity his peace activism nearly killed him. Like so many of us, he had to hit rock bottom before his journey to being peaceful at heart could begin. The core of his wake up was the need for personal transformation as foundation for living. His book *Active Peace: A Mindful Path to a Nonviolent World* chronicles his journey "from operating on unconscious autopilot with a lot of anger and resentment, to a place

---

18 Osbourne et al., "Crazy Train."
19 See chap. 1 above.
20 Dylan, "Not Yet Dark."
21 See chap. 14 below.

of inner peace and empowerment."[22] And here's the thing he gets that many church discipleship programs miss: It's not about more information. It's not about another book study, sermon, or podcast. It's not as if we don't know what following Jesus means.

The struggle is having the inner resources to live the kind of lives we are called to live. Becoming peaceful at heart is about formation, a long journey of effort, vulnerability, and personal healing—none of which we are meant to do alone. Being in a community of common-cause Christians is necessary for spiritual and missional vitality.

The psychology of peacemaking

Our inner peace drives our lifestyle of peace—and vice versa. Living peaceably can have a profound positive impact on us psychologically. Action is a powerful antidote to despair. Scott Brown chronicles a long list of psychological benefits of living peaceably. Intentional action is linked to "psychological health and maturity," "wellbeing, vitality, and flourishing," and "a greater sense of aliveness." As Brown observes, "We come alive to ourselves and everything that supports life."[23] People who take responsibility for the health of the world feel empowered, confident, and compassionate.

I know countless people in Houston whose faith is flourishing because they've joined God on mission. My friend Bob Baldwin talks about the triple bottom line of active faith: it solves problems, strengthens the reputation of God, and changes us personally. Decades ago Abraham Maslow researched the connection between action and health at length and concluded, "Self-actualizing people are, without one single exception, involved in a cause outside their own skin, in something outside themselves. They are devoted, working at something . . . which fate has called them to somehow and which they work at and which they love, so that the work-joy dichotomy in them disappears."[24] Early Anabaptist writer Pilgram Marpeck observed this truth as well: "Service is commanded by Christ, and it is the means by which, according to the commands of Christ, [Christians] are prepared."[25]

Jesus was right when he proclaims that peacemakers are blessed. In that same sermon he promises us that when we live by his

---

22 S. Brown, *Active Peace*, 6.
23 S. Brown, *Active Peace*, 171.
24 Maslow, *Farther Reaches of Human Nature*, 43.
25 Klaassen, *Anabaptism in Outline*, 79.

teachings we'll be as secure as a man who built his house on solid rock (Matt. 7:24–27). Jesus is recreating a beautiful new world out of the old filled with justice, joy, and peace, and he invites all of us—men included—to be transformed into people who can help make that reality. This is what we were created for: peace within and peace for all. As Dallas Willard says, "Nothing less than life in the footsteps of Christ is adequate to the human soul or the needs of our world."[26] This is God's gospel gift of peace. "Blessed are the peacemakers, for they will be called children of God" (Matt. 5:9).

Bibliography

Brown, Brené. *The Gifts of Imperfection: Let Go of Who You Think You're Supposed to Be and Embrace Who You Are.* Center City, MN: Hazelden, 2010.

Brown, Scott. *Active Peace: A Mindful Path to a Nonviolent World.* Santa Margarita, CA: Collins Foundation Press, 2016.

Conrad, Joseph. *Notes on Life and Letters.* Edited by J. H. Stape. New York: Cambridge University Press, 2004.

"Douglas Coupland's Guide to the Next Decade." Interview with Guy Raz. All Things Considered. NPR. October 17, 2010. https://www.npr.org/templates/story/story.php?storyId=130631043.

Dylan, Bob. "Not Yet Dark." *Time Out of Mind.* Columbia Records, 1997.

Graeber, David. *Bull Shit Jobs: A Theory.* New York: Simon and Schuster, 2018.

Klaassen, Walter. *Anabaptism in Outline: Selected Primary Sources.* Scottdale, PA: Herald, 1981.

"Major Depression: The Impact on Overall Health." BlueCross Blue Shield: The Health of America. May 10, 2018. https://www.bcbs.com/the-health-of-america/reports/major-depression-the-impact-overall-health.

Maslow, Abraham. *The Farther Reaches of Human Nature.* New York: Viking, 1971.

Osborne, Ozzy, Randy Rhoads, and Bob Daisley. "Crazy Train." *Blizzard of Ozz.* Jet Records, 1980.

Penny, Louise. *Still Life.* New York: St. Martin's Press, 2007.

Pipher, Mary. *The Green Boat: Reviving Ourselves in Our Capsized Culture.* New York: Riverhead, 2013.

---

26 Willard, *Great Omission*, 93.

Redekop, Vern Neufeld. *From Violence to Blessing: How an Understanding of Deep-Rooted Conflict Can Open Paths to Reconciliation.* Ottawa, ON: Novalis, 2002.

Simons, Menno. "Reply to False Accusations" (1552). In *The Complete Writings of Menno Simons, c. 1496–1561,* translated by Leonard Verduin; edited by John Christian Wenger, 541–77. Scottdale, PA: Herald, 1956.

_____. "Why I Do Not Cease Teaching and Writing" (1539). In *The Complete Writings of Menno Simons, c. 1496–1561,* translated by Leonard Verduin; edited by John Christian Wenger, 289–320. Scottdale, PA: Herald, 1956.

Steffen, Will, Wendy Broadgate, Lisa Deutsch, Owen Gaffney, Cornelia Ludwig, "The Trajectory of the Anthropocene: The Great Acceleration." *Anthropocene Review* 2, no. 1 (2015): 81–98.

Troyer, Marty. *The Gospel Next Door: Following Jesus Right Where You Live.* Harrisonburg, VA: Herald, 2016.

Wilkinson, Richard. "How Economic Inequality Harms Societies." TEDGlobal 2011. July 2011. https://www.ted.com/talks/richard_wilkinson#t-882758.

Willard, Dallas. *The Great Omission: Reclaiming Jesus's Essential Teachings on Discipleship.* New York: HarperOne, 2009.

Part
4

Practices

Trading Manpower
for the Power of Love

David Evans

"How did you learn to be a man if you didn't have a father to show you?" That's the question a college student affiliated with Campus Crusade for Christ asked me while at summer camp my senior year of high school. I had explained to him that my father had left my home when I was six years old and that I hadn't been in contact with him for the last twelve years. His assumption that boys need fathers to lead them to manhood was one he shared with much of evangelical Christian America. Black Americans also shared this assumption and engaged efforts to fill the assumed void through mentoring programs and rhetorical strategies to encourage fathers to stay active in their children's lives. The assumed problem and remedy were so pervasive that President Barack Obama created the fatherhood initiative to that end.

The problem with being a man, however, wasn't a problem of fatherlessness. I didn't need a father to learn how to be a man. The pervasiveness of structures, symbols, institutions, and media that championed the essential dominance of manhood in society—what I call "manpower"—taught me how to be a man every day of my life. The problem was that the lessons I learned of manhood were lessons of domination, intimidation, homophobia, misogyny, and ultimately fear of losing power. In short, the problem is not that some of us do not know how to be men; patriarchy makes it impossible to know otherwise. The problem is that men do not learn how to love. The solution to learning to be a man, then, was not to spend more time with men who had essentially learned the same lessons. Rather, by rejecting manpower as expressed by the majority of American institutions, Christian and secular, the solution to the problem of the crisis in manhood is for men to learn to embrace the power of love.

Manhood is a myth of power, sustained and supported by stories and expectations of socially prohibited and encouraged behaviors. The stories and expectations of manhood are sustained and supported by fathers but also by mothers, individuals, institutions, groups, and systems. The myth of manhood is not fiction, though many of the narratives that give it power reside in the worlds of comic book superheroes, science fiction, and fantasy—I'm thinking here of the likes of Superman, Luke Skywalker, and King Arthur. Manhood is socially constructed by narratives that produce social systems and meaning in society. The system of patriarchy is the main purveyor of this message, and the power—represented in institutions, from schools to media—produce and empower its messengers. According to patriarchal narratives, men are supposed to overcome seemingly insurmountable obstacles to heroically save the vulnerable and to do so as individuals who lord over masses of followers. No matter how fantastical or unattainable the narratives may be, they influence the rules of what constitutes manhood even as they vary from one place and time to another.

To demonstrate that manpower is an oppressive problem that can only be solved by the power of love, I share below my personal experience of struggling with the expectations of US American manhood as a secular adolescent and then as an evangelical Christian as a teen and young adult. I use my personal narrative to demonstrate the inescapable influence the patriarchal systems and institutions have on individual male lives. As Carol Hanisch famously said, "The personal is the political."[1] Such feminist insights guide my investigation of manpower throughout this essay, especially ideas expressed by bell hooks, who warns, "Anyone who claims to be concerned with the fate of black males in the United States who does not speak about the need for them to radicalize their consciousness to challenge patriarchy if they are to survive and flourish colludes with the existing system in keeping black men in their place, psychologically locked down, locked out."[2]

While it may appear counter intuitive to employ the insights of women's analyses to teach us about manpower, my fundamental assumptions regarding power begin with the insight that those who know most about power are those who are most oppressed by it. Audrè Lorde argues that the oppressed must know because "we have recognized and negotiated these differences, even when this recognition only continue the old dominant/subordinate mode of human relationship, where the oppressed must recognize the masters' difference in order to survive."[3] The effects of manpower are inescapable. Those most harmed by manpower tend to have spent

1 Hanisch, "Personal Is Political," 76–77.
2 hooks, *We Real Cool*, xi.
3 Lorde, "Age, Race, Class, and Sex," 114–23.

the most intellectual energy and effort researching it because they cannot thrive without deeply understanding its effects and how it works. Thus, I privilege their voices to understand the far-reaching influence of manpower and the remedy for the harms it inflicts in our collective body.

Manpower, authorized by nearly every system and institution in our society to dominate others, is a seductive and often blinding force for those who are privileged by their social locations to possess it. Oftentimes oppressive actors are not aware of the constitution of their power and how it affects them or the people around them. While they may have some tacit sense of leadership and authority, that those under their leadership and authority must listen to or follow them, they take their force, possessions, and ability to act on the world for granted. The identities that form and the privileges afforded to them as a result of their oppressive power remain largely unexamined precisely because the benefits of oppressive power cause little to no visible discomfort. In short, power in our white-supremacist-capitalist-imperialist-patriarchal society works for the economy in which it was designed, and it works economically for those endowed with manpower. Thus the need for them to question it does not emerge apart from some outside intervention.[4] The possibility of outside intervention is also an acknowledgment that manpower is not the only type of power. Even oppressed people have agency. If people endowed with manpower decide to relinquish or share power, it is often because people oppressed by manpower confront them with grievances and demands to end their oppressive practices. For love to be possible, oppression must end. However, it will not end until men fully learn the harms of manpower and, conversely, the power of love.

Growing in manpower

I learned to be a man on the streets of Lansing, Michigan, in the 1990s. Here I also learned that to be a black man held different responsibilities than being a white man, and it carried different connotations than the masculine ideal James Baldwin had to contend with in his Harlem neighborhood of the 1930s. The lessons I learned of manhood were more similar to the manhood of other urban communities of the United States in 1990s; Lansing manhood was less dependent on combative conquests than it was on sexual conquests. Still, what Baldwin called "the myth of manhood" was

---

4 Foucault, "Subject and Power"; Freire, *Pedagogy of the Oppressed*, 175.

not so foreign to black boys in Lansing that his insights can be dismissed as irrelevant. As Baldwin points out, "The American ideal, then, of sexuality appears to be rooted in the American ideal of masculinity."[5] To the contrary, the myth of manhood is a deeply rooted US American ideal. While "manhood" is social, it is also historical. Its social construction explains why men—black, Asian, Latinx, American Indian, white, cis, trans, straight, queer, urban, rural—experience it differently depending on social and geographical location; and its multiplicity is rooted in histories on which current iterations of manhood depend.

Gale Bederman captures this history in her description of the events leading up to the heavy weight title fight between Jack Johnson and Jim Jefferies in 1910. Jack Johnson, a black heavy weight boxing champion, defied common white myths of black men. White society taught that black men, though often exploited for physical labor, were physically inferior to white men and were more emotional, which explained the centrality of religion, a feminine domain, in black culture in the nineteenth and early twentieth centuries. Johnson's boxing successes posed a symbolic threat to the myth of white male power. Thus, a chorus of white people, young and old, cried out for the retired white heavy weight champion, Jefferies, to challenge Johnson and save the future of the United States. Prognosticators predicted that Jefferies, with his physical strength and cunning, would beat Johnson, who relied on his passions and savagery. When Johnson beat Jefferies by knockout, media described him as a menace to society. His flamboyant dress and his propensity to parade white women on his arm did nothing to rebut the white gaze. Instead, he was targeted for a capital crime he did not commit and died in prison. The fragility of manpower is evident in Johnson's story as is the complexity of black men's proximity to it. Society tasks black men, like white men, to grow in manpower, but black men face limits if their possession of power threatens or rivals their white counterparts.[6]

To survive as a black man, avoid prison, mob violence, and poverty, young Black boys must to learn the obstacles society presents or possibly face a similar fate as Johnson. Fathers are traditionally tasked with the responsibility of teaching these lessons. That explains why the Christian student asked me about my father; he called on that tradition. As a young person, I had no grasp of

---

5 Baldwin, "Freaks and American Ideal of Manhood," 869.
6 Bederman, *Manliness & Civilization*, 1–5.

the power society conferred on fathers to teach their sons about manhood nor the historical factors that would determine what constituted those lessons. While black men who do not live in the homes of their children are the most likely of all races of men to be actively involved with them, my father was not among those who did.[7] He stopped actively engaging me when I was six years old. Thus, my father did not teach me to become a man. In fact, no one explicitly told me how to be a man. Instead, the first lessons I received derived from pejorative childhood gendered interactions concerning what a man should not be.

Teaching someone what they are not to supposed to be is a common identity strategy that Toni Morrison refers to as the "not-me."[8] The not-me strategy defines identity by those identities that the core group excludes, often dehumanizing those excluded identities in the process. In elementary school we played a game called "smear the queer" in which one person, whom everyone called "the queer," carried a football and everyone else attempted to tackle him, at which point "the queer" would release the ball. The goal of this game was convoluted. On one hand, no one wanted to be "the queer" for fear of being annihilated by the other boys. On the other hand, if you were fast enough and agile enough to avoid being tackled, then you could gain fame. While the overt lesson was to not be "the queer" or you will be physically overpowered by other men, the more subtle lesson was one that fetishized "the queer."

The game also taught an important lesson on power. Even as a young boy, I was taught that power was something to covet and convey physically. The opposite of exerting power was being over-powered. The problem with being "the queer" was that you became an object who only responded to another person's aggression and never initiated contact yourself. You acted out what traditionalists refer to as the traditional feminine role. But femininity was not a possession boys were taught to embrace if they wanted to become men. Perhaps the most enduring implicit lesson of the game was that, if a boy could not reject the feminine within, then the other men in his world would beat it out of him. The title of the game set the parameters for how a boy was to self-identify and what the consequences were of appearing to identify wrongly. Inability to

---

7 J. Jones and Mosher, "Fathers' Involvement with Their Children."
8 Morrison, *Playing in the Dark*, 38.

dominate others through physical power attracted ridicule in the forms of being called a "queer," "sissy," "pansy," and often "girl."

A boy who couldn't throw hard, run fast, or endure such games were told they throw, run, or scream "like a girl." To be a boy, or man, meant not being "like a girl." The terms "sissy" and "pansy" were meant to illustrate those feminine qualities— emotional vulnerability, physical weakness, and beauty—that a man was supposed to conquer in others and in himself. It was clear to me well before adolescence that qualities marked as feminine would make me vulnerable to the ridicule and violence of other boys. This meant that if I, as a rather sensitive child, wanted to avoid experiencing pain inflicted on me from the other boys, then I had to completely reject my love for things stereotypically reserved for girls: pink, stickers, ballads, conversation, sadness, affection, and love.

Loving myself as a boy, then, proved to be an extremely difficult concept, first, because it was clear that many of my interests were in direct conflict with the goal of manhood and, second, because loving-self was not something that masculine culture taught boys. Our cartoons—from G. I. Joe to He-Man—always portrayed muscular men performing herculean feats without fear or awareness of pain. They had no concern for their own safety or well-being. I recall a white male Christian leader communicating that self-love was a problematic love that needed to be avoided because it was synonymous with pride. This was a confusing lesson for me.

My mother taught me, as a young black boy, that self-love was extremely important. Black communities across the United States attempted to overcome internalized racial oppression through self-love. Whitney Houston's song "Greatest Love of All" reflected the popularity of this philosophy: "Learning to love yourself / It is the greatest love of all."[9] Thus, for most of my childhood, I felt conflicted between being black and being a man. Many other black boys were sensitive like me. However, when we faced the world around us, it sometimes felt like we were under assault. Our love for self exacerbated the pain we felt when it was obvious that society didn't seem to share that love for us. So our fathers, grandfathers, uncles, mothers, grandmothers, aunts, coaches, pastors, teachers, and peers tried to exorcise our sensitivity to the feminine out of us.

At the same time that our world taught us to reject the feminine within, little outside of my childhood home taught me to love black

---

9 Houston, "Greatest Love of All."

men—something I was destined to become. How could I learn to love myself when the world around me routinely expressed its disdain? According to bell hooks, this experience is all too common: "Sadly, the real truth, which is a taboo to speak, is that this is a culture that does not love black males, that they are not loved by white men, white women, black women, or girls and boys. And that especially most black men do not love themselves."[10] Darkness in my cartoons, television sitcoms, and movies regularly represented evil in the 1980s. With all the negative portrayals of black men in the media, no one debated Tupac's critique of US society, "We ain't ready to see a Black president."[11] Even seemingly unrelated news stories like those about killer bees managed to teach lessons that anything that originated in Africa, like me, was inherently aggressive and savage. I learned to fear other black men and even to fear myself. I also learned that the world around us feared us and used violence to exert control over us. In this environment, our juvenile sensitivity felt detrimental to my survival. So I learned to suppress any feelings that would make me appear weak.

For a black boy, the rules of manpower permitted me to only express anger and stoicism in public. (I assume this is why young black men often refuse to smile in photographs to this day.) The implications of these rules for me, as hooks writes, were that "in patriarchal culture, all males learn a role that restricts and confines. When race and class enter the picture, along with patriarchy, then black males endure the worst impositions of gendered masculine patriarchal identity."[12] I was betwixt and between the expectations of manhood forced on me in US society and the force of white manhood on my young black body, which posed an implicit threat to white manpower. Thus, I learned to embrace manpower—but not too much. I had to restrict my emotional sensitivity, demonstrate the potential of dominance over others, but also confine it to my relationships with black boys and girls and defer to white ones.

Christian manpower

It was not until I converted to evangelical Christianity, through a revivalist campground ministry when I was fourteen years old, that I recall being explicitly taught to "be a man." Today it is commonplace for men and women to tell men to "man up" instead of

---

10 hooks, *We Real Cool*, ix.
11 2Pac, "Changes."
12 hooks, *We Real Cool*, x.

expressing fear or other vulnerable emotions, but in the 1990s and early 2000s, the phrase I heard through Christian groups and books was, "Be a man." These Christian books and groups did nothing to interrupt the lessons of male domination and stoicism I learned in my mostly secular prepubescent years. Instead, I learned that dominance and stoicism were divinely ordained. For a young black evangelical, becoming a man in a divinely ordered fashion appeared both desirable and illusive because in my evangelical community no black men were ordained to lead men's groups or write men's books. Thus, for the remainder of my teenage years and my young adulthood, I wondered what it meant to "be a man."

There's a great amount of history behind my encounter of evangelical manpower. The history of American manpower is an issue not only of gender and race but also of religion. The intersection of gender, race, and religion compounds the issues of power. For most of US history, white people taught that manhood was the God-ordained domain of white men. White men refused to consider black men as worthy of manhood so that they could subjugate them and justify the subjugation of all descendants of Africa. White power exerted over and against black folks had the dual effect of teaching black folks to internalize the debasing attitudes that white society promulgated to justify its exploitation of black bodies and of persuading black men to desire similar types of power. So when black folk broke free from the chains of white institutions to create their own institutions (often churches), many black institutions replicated patriarchy and excluded women from official leadership in similar ways that white men did to white women and black people in general. Richard Allen's exclusive ordination practices against women like Jarena Lee in early the nineteenth-century African Methodist Episcopal Church demonstrates this point.[13] This pattern persisted in other black institutions well into the twentieth century. Pauli Murray, a civil rights leader and attorney, lamented the restrictions placed on women during the 1963 Civil Rights march on Washington: "Not a single woman was invited to make one of the major speeches or be a part of the delegation of leaders who went to the White House."[14] Still, in spite of black men's imitation of white male power over women, white men refused to view black men as equals. And just as white men

---

13 Lee, "Life and Experiences of Jarena Lee," 25–48.
14 Height, "'We Wanted the Voice of a Woman to be Heard,'" 85–87. See also W. Jones, *March on Washington.*

claimed theological authority to make these distinctions, black men did the same to black women.

Though my church family at home was predominantly black, my evangelical campground world was predominantly white. Nevertheless, the lessons I learned on manpower complemented one another. I could not come to these conclusions based solely on my interpretation of the Hebrew Bible or New Testament. Biblical narratives that included women heroes did not lend themselves to see Abraham, Isaac, and Jacob as the only significant actors; they shared narratives with Sarah, Rebekah, and Rachel. Hagar, Rahab, Esther, Ruth, Mary, and other women acted as preachers, saviors, subversives, and teachers throughout the text. To learn the lessons of manpower through Scripture, I needed evangelical Christian books. In the late 1990s there were plenty of them. Men's ministries like Promise Keepers popularized the need for fatherhood initiatives and men's groups, and these movements provided opportunities for authors to teach men how to father and support boys and each other. John Eldredge's *Wild at Heart* emerged shortly after the height of Promise Keepers as the most popular of the men's ministry genre.

Though Eldredge wrote a book for men, unlike the other men's books *Wild at Heart* argues that men do not need to be taught as much as they need to be freed to express their innate manhood. They need to unlock their manpower. In a text replete with dominant metaphors for men—warriors, expansionists, heroes, cowboys, kings—his major argument is that men had been confined by a docile Christianity that subdued and domesticated them. The heart of a man, according to Eldredge, was wild. Eldredge teaches that the secret to men's souls is that they are inherently adventurous and need three things: an adventure to live, a beauty to rescue, and a battle to fight. Though Eldredge tries to distinguish "a false sense of power" from a true God-given power, there is little to distinguish Eldredge's lessons on innate, wild, adventurous warrior power from the secular manpower that I learned as a young person.[15]

The notion that we should define masculinity by the power to dominate, initiate, be aggressive, and act in the world became central to the teachings of men's healing ministries. Andy Comiskey, the founder of Desert Stream Ministries, a ministry that aims to "equip the body of Christ to minister healing to the sexually and relationally broken through healing groups and leadership

---

15 Eldredge, *Wild at Heart*, 152.

training for the local church,"[16] published *Strength in Weakness* as a major teaching tool for this ministry. It defines male sexual brokenness as originating with the original man "cut off from his heart, compulsive and troubled by work-related concerns." This broken man, Comiskey explains, "may use his power harshly toward the woman." The issue here is not the power and authority a man has. "After all," Comiskey writes, "did not God grant him authority over the woman?" Like Eldredge, Comiskey's concern is that a man is supposed to use this power to protect and preserve the honor of women, not to "bolster his own flagging sense of self." The solution to this problem is men and women understanding and expressing their complementary masculinity and femininity. Manpower, in this paradigm, is not a fundamentally flawed concept but rather is simply broken in US American society. To fix or heal manpower, men must learn to use their dominant power correctly.[17] For Comiskey, the problem with homosexual men is not that they misuse their power but that they refuse to use it at all; they are passive or express anger passive aggressively in the way of distorted femininity.

Manpower in both Eldredge's and Comiskey's views needs to be released for the health of men and women. While Comiskey's focus is on the relational world of men, Eldredge concerns himself with men's relationship to the world itself. Perhaps Eldredge's grandiose vision is what allowed him to sell more than four million copies of *Wild at Heart* and for it to remain the top selling book in the Men's Gender Studies section on Amazon. Though I disagree with Eldredge's solution, he highlights a significant problem: "Men are angry, and we really don't know why. And how come there are so many 'sports widows,' losing their husbands each weekend to the golf course or the TV?"[18] He suggests that the problem is that men are bored and lacking adventure. In truth, neither anger or incessant sports watching are the products of men's boredom or wanderlust. Men are angry because it is the only emotion that our society permits them to express. And if men choose sports over their spouses, it is similarly because the emotional world of their partners is not one they have learned to embrace in themselves.

---

16 See http://desertstream.org/.
17 Comiskey, *Strength in Weakness*, 39, 46.
18 Eldredge, *Wild at Heart*, 45.

The power of love

One should not be surprised to find that Eldredge remains so popular after almost two decades, given the popularity of secular masculinity champions like Warren Farrell and Jordan Peterson. One explanation for Eldredge's continued success is that these authors are promoting the same messages and that church groups contain built-in apparatuses for men's groups: preservation of what Farrell calls "the best of traditional masculinity."[19] Farrell's *The Myth of Male Power* first appeared in 1993 but has received renewed attention and been reprinted in the last two years. Farrell and Peterson's message still resonates and appears to be in resurgence among men today. As I write this, Peterson's *12 Rules for Life: An Antidote for Chaos* is the most read book on Amazon. And it has been in the top four best sellers for twenty-one weeks.[20]

In *12 Rules for Life*, Peterson claims that the world is in desperate need of masculine order that can be the antidote for feminine chaos. For Peterson, "the primary hierarchical structure of human society is masculine." He then offers a grand narrative of history to support his thesis:

> It is because men are and throughout history have been the builders of towns and cities, the engineers, stonemasons, bricklayers, and lumberjacks, the operators of heavy machinery. Order is God the Father, the eternal Judge, ledger-keeper and dispenser of rewards and punishments. Order is the peacetime army of policemen and soldiers. It is the political culture, the corporate environment, and the system.[21]

Conversely, he argues that "the feminine is chaos." And men's direct encounter with chaos is represented when "woman as Nature . . . looks at half of all men and says, 'No!'"[22] However, this type of rendering of femininity and masculinity is not historical as much as it is philosophical. The women who ruled Egypt, Carthage, Byzantium, and England and brought about stability in political, religious, and other social structures would, no doubt, refute Peterson's claim. But his point is not that men rule and women cannot; he suggests, rather, that from a male perspective those virtues derived from the

---

19 Farrell, *Myth of Male Power*.
20 See https://www.amazon.com/charts/2018-06-10/mostread/nonfiction/index.html? ref=CHRT_BK_RD_NF_1_DP.
21 Peterson, *12 Rules of for Life*, 40.
22 Peterson, *12 Rules for Life*, 37.

chaos of the feminine must be controlled and that the failure of our language games to recognize the differences between the genders is bringing instability to our societies.

The idea that the masculine should order the feminine is the main theme of Peterson's gender philosophy, but he downplays the importance of the power involved in making that possible.[23] In an imperialist, white supremacist, patriarchal context, this move makes manpower even more potent because it almost renders it invisible; and positions of power are always most potent when people do not to see them, be it due to ignorance or willful refusal. Peterson wants his readers to recognize that power is but one among many factors that determine status in a society, alongside "competence, ability, skill."[24] In failing to recognize these factors as forms of power, Peterson enables unequal power relationships to thrive without challenge. Conversely, acknowledging power makes it possible for people to begin to analyze, divest, use, or even share power in humane ways. Peterson both minimizes the role of power and warns of its abuses. His analysis lacks the capacity to view power with complexity. For Peterson, power is force.[25] Minimizing the role of power in our relationships to others blinds believers in Peterson's patriarchal philosophy to the problems of manpower because they cannot see their source. This is only possible in the world of abstraction and theory; we need historical and practical knowledge to adequately understand and deal with manpower.

For men to replace manpower with the power of love, I propose three steps: (1) engage the worlds of womanist and black feminist thought, (2) love ourselves, and (3) imitate Jesus. I'm suggesting that the path to this way of being begins with the relational world of women—a world that men are routinely taught to ignore so that they might fearlessly lead, stoically overcome, and forcefully dominate. We must engage women first because we have been hampered in our ability to love ourselves and have traded a human Jesus for a manly one. Women, who are most often harmed by these expressions of masculinity, claim that what men are missing is not unbridled permission to be wild or more rules to live by. Rather, men are missing the ability to love themselves, other men, women, and other humans well. We need women to

---

23 Peterson, *12 Rules for Life*, 311.
24 Peterson, *12 Rules for Life*, 313.
25 Peterson, *12 Rules for Life*, 314.

teach us to do that because, as bell hooks writes, "men theorize about love, but women are often love's practitioners."[26]

Women are mothers, sisters, and friends of men. Some women, hooks suggests, do not speak of their deep desire to experience the love of men because too many have been convinced that to do so would threaten the possibility of gaining forms of manpower.[27] The inability of men to love others adequately and the desire of women to gain manpower have produced volumes of literature by women on what it means to "be a man." As a mother reflecting on how to mother her son, Audrè Lorde asked, "What does 'acting like a man' mean?"[28] For bell hooks, questioning what "acting like a man" means is crucial, but the next step must go beyond rejection or redefinition: "To create loving men, we must love males. Loving maleness is different from praising and rewarding males for living up to sexist-defined notions of male identity. Caring about men because of what they do for us is not the same as loving males for simply being."[29]

Love, here, is a power that begins with oneself. Love manifests in the strength to create boundaries and also to confront others when those boundaries are crossed. For women to have survived in the US imperialist, white supremacist, patriarchal context, they have had to learn to love themselves in the face of a rampant misogyny and rape culture that promotes the preposterous idea that women are at fault for the gender violence they endure. Womanists have loved themselves enough to reject this notion and have loved men enough to confront them with the truth that manpower has imprisoned them in a patriarchy they preserve even while it imprisons them. To free men from this prison and into solidarity with women, men must learn to love themselves from early in their development. Lorde gives voice to this love: "I wish to raise a Black man who will not be destroyed by, nor settle for, those corruptions called power by the white fathers who mean his destruction as surely as they mean mine. I wish to raise a Black man who will recognize that the legitimate objects of his hostility are not women,

---

26 hooks, *All About Love*, xx.

27 hooks, *Will to Change*, 4. She writes, "Rather than bringing us great wisdom about the nature of men and love, reformist feminist focus on male power reinforced the notion that somehow males were powerful and had it all. Feminist writing did not tell us about the deep inner misery of men. It did not tell us the terrible terror that gnaws at the soul when one cannot love."

28 Lorde, "Man Child," 72–80, 74.

29 hooks, *Will to Change*, 11.

but the particulars of a structure that programs him to fear and despise women as well as his own Black self."[30]

Within Lorde's desire for her son is both the liberative future for the individual man and a more equitable and just future for everyone else. Liberation for men imprisoned in manhood begins with rejection of manpower, but it moves towards deconstructing the white supremacist, imperialist, patriarchal systems of domination that authorize it. Solidarity with women is essential to this movement, not only because of the wisdom that women hold as those most harmed by manpower but also because women have learned and encouraged one another in the practice of love much longer than men.

In spite of Scripture's teaching that "God is love" (1 John 4:8), patriarchal Christians emphasize the order, sovereign, and monarchical qualities of divine character. For Christians, the most loving human to ever live was Jesus of Nazareth. As the Word made flesh, he instructed his disciples to love God and to love their neighbor as themselves (Mark 12:29–31). However, US men have challenged this depiction of a loving Christ figure for at least a century. In 1925 Bruce Barton's *The Nobody Knows* criticized the idea of loving Jesus because the idea that "Jesus was the 'Lamb of God' . . . sounded like Mary's little lamb, something for girls—sissified. . . . Jesus was also 'meek and lowly,' a 'man of sorrows and acquainted with grief.'"[31] For Barton, the loving Jesus had been portrayed as a weakling, kill-joy, failure. In contrast, Barton writes, "Only strong men inspire greatly and build greatly."[32] Barton concluded that because Jesus was popular and founded a religious movement, he must have been a muscular, strong, popular organization builder. For Barton, this is what it means to be and act like a man. At a time when the domain of men was located in business, commerce, politics, military, and other spaces beyond domestic life and when success demanded physical strength, rugged individualism, and dominance, the meek and mild Jesus had no use to men. So men like Barton made Jesus in their image.

Women, like Catholic theologian Elizabeth Johnson, have recognized the ways in which men have redefined the divine in their own patriarchal image. In her theological text *She Who Is*, Johnson argues that Jesus is not a prototype for patriarchy, except when those allied to patriarchy distort Jesus to meet that end. The

---

30 Lorde, "Man Child," 74.
31 Barton, *Man Nobody Knows*, 4.
32 Barton, *Man Nobody Knows*, ii.

problem, she argues, is not with the meek and mild Jesus; it is with patriarchal interpretations. Those who argue that becoming a man involves growing in dominance and control need to see Jesus as transcendent and divine. In studying the Jesus of the New Testament, however, their Christ seems foreign to the compassionate, power sharing, and self-giving man from Nazareth. Johnson's reading of Jesus does not attack the fact that Jesus is a man; rather, she suggests that his expression of manhood is very different from what patriarchy demands men to become. "The heart of the problem," Johnson argues, "is not that Jesus was a man but that more men are not like Jesus, insofar as patriarchy defines self-identity and relationships."[33]

This Jesus—the God, self, and neighbor loving man—is a man other men can learn from. Ultimately, the lesson we learn from him is how to become a more loving human. The greatest commandments are centered on love, and his relationship to power is a direct response to his relationships with God, self, and neighbors. The New Testament letter to the Philippians claims that his loving response to power involved emptying himself of it. Paul writes that we should imitate Jesus,

> who, though he was in the form of God,
> did not regard equality with God
> as something to be exploited,
> but emptied himself. (Phil. 2:7)

Jesus sought equality with humanity, not lordship over women or other men. He considered himself a brother, a sibling, an equal, not a master. He chose not to dominate. He called his disciples friends, not servants.

Conclusion

Looking back, it is not surprising that the Campus Crusade for Christ student asked me about my father instead of asking if I had considered learning from Jesus how to be a man. Steeped in patriarchy himself, he could not imagine that other sources could offer men something better than the power to dominate and control others. We both would have benefited from a narrative of a man who rejected manpower and embraced the power of love in his relationships to the world—including every living thing and everyone in it. Today I am choosing to learn from women, embrace

---

33 Johnson, *She Who Is*, 24.

myself, and follow the narrative of Jesus. In this way, the power of love enables me to live in a way that empowers me to see that the binary constructions of patriarchy that pit women as my enemies are products of manpower that threatens to destroy us all. I am learning that the power of love can inspire my imagination to conceive of new ways to relate to others. Instead of dominating, I can defer to the wisdom of others. Instead of controlling, I can collaborate with others. Instead of struggling stoically through life, I can express the full range of my human emotions. Only the power of love could liberate me from the prison manpower constructed, and that is a lesson men must share for generations to come.

Bibliography

2Pac. "Changes." Written by Tupac Shakur, Deon Evans, and Bruce Hornsby. *Greatest Hits*. Interscope Records, 1998.

Baldwin, James. "Freaks and American Ideal of Manhood." In *Baldwin: Collected Essays*, edited by Toni Morrison, 814–29. New York: Library of America, 1998.

Barton, Bruce. *The Man Nobody Knows: A Discovery of the Real Jesus*. Chicago: Dee, 2000.

Bederman, Gale. *Manliness & Civilization: A Cultural History of Gender and Race in the United States, 1880–1917*. Chicago: University of Chicago Press, 1996.

Comiskey, Andy. *Strength in Weakness: Healing Sexual and Relational Brokenness*. Downers Grove, IL: InterVarsity Press, 2009.

Houston, Whitney. "Greatest Love of All." Music by Michael Masser; lyrics by Linda Creed. *Whitney Houston*. Arista Records, 1986.

Eldredge, John. *Wild at Heart: Discovering the Secret of a Man's Soul*. Nashville: Nelson, 2010.

——————. *Wild at Heart Field Manual: A Personal Guide to Discovering the Secret of Your Masculine Soul*. Nashville: Nelson, 2002.

Farrell, Warren. *The Myth of Male Power*. New York: Berkley, 1993.

Foucault, Michel. "The Subject and Power." In *Michel Foucault: Beyond Structuralism and Hermeneutics*. 2nd ed. Edited by Hubert L. Dreyfus and Paul Rabinow, 208–228. Chicago: University of Chicago Press, 1982.

Paolo Freire, *Pedagogy of the Oppressed*. 30th anniversary ed. Translated by Myra Bergman Ramos. New York: Bloomsbury, 2014.

Hanisch, Carol. "The Personal Is Political." In *Notes from the Second Year: Women's Liberation; Major Writings of the Radical Feminists*, 76–78. New York: Radical Feminism, 1970.

Height, Dorothy O. "'We Wanted the Voice of a Woman to be Heard': Black Women and the 1963 March on Washington." In *Sisters in the Struggle: African American Women in the Civil Rights-Black Power Movement*, edited by V. P. Franklin and Bettye Collier-Thomas, 83–92. New York: NYU Press, 2010.

hooks, bell. *All About Love: New Visions*. New York: HarperCollins, 2001.

——————. *We Real Cool: Black Men and Masculinity*. New York: Routledge, 2004.

——————. *The Will to Change: Men, Masculinity, and Love*. New York: Washington Square, 2005.

Johnson, Elizabeth A. *She Who Is: The Mystery of God in Feminist Theological Discourse*. New York: Crossroad, 2002.

Jones, Jo, and William Mosher. "Fathers' Involvement with Their Children: United States, 2006–2010." *National Health Statistics Reports* 71, December 20, 2013.

Jones, William Powell. *The March on Washington: Jobs, Freedom, and the Forgotten History of Civil Rights*. New York: Norton, 2013.

Lee, Jarena. "The Life and Experiences of Jarena Lee." In *Sisters of the Spirit: Three Black Women's Autobiographies of the Nineteenth Century*, edited by William L. Andrews, 25–48. Bloomington: Indiana University Press, 2000.

Lorde, Audre. "Age, Race, Class, and Sex: Women Redefining Difference." In *Sister Outsider: Essays and Speeches*, 114–23. Freedom, CA: Crossing, 1984.

——————. "Man Child: A Black Lesbian Feminist's Response." In *Sister Outsider: Essays and Speeches*, 72–80. Freedom, CA: Crossing, 1984.

Morrison, Toni. *Playing in the Dark: Whiteness and the Literary Imagination*. Cambridge: Harvard University Press, 1992.

Peterson, Jordan. *12 Rules for Life: An Antidote to Chaos*. Toronto: Random House Canada, 2018.

Cultivating an Inner Spiritual Life

Chapter
14

Scott Brubaker-Zehr

Early on in my pastoral ministry I was preparing a young couple for marriage. I asked each of them to name something they appreciated about their relationship. The young woman gestured for her fiancé to go first, and I noticed a brief flicker of panic in his eyes. He thought for a moment and then blurted it out, "Summer!"

"Summer?" I responded.

"Yeah, summer," he repeated with nervous conviction. "You can throw a couple of steaks on the barbeque and sit out on the back deck. Summer—that's what I appreciate."

I probed a bit further as to what this might have to do with his relationship and quickly came to the conclusion that he was not trying to be a smart ass. He was simply answering the question to the best of his ability.

As this episode illustrates, it can often be difficult for men to express outwardly what they are feeling inwardly. For those in pastoral ministry, this can leave us with questions like, *What is going on inside the hearts and souls of the men in my congregation? And in the interior lives of my male friends and colleagues? And inside me?* These are all important questions, but they not easy ones to answer.

In this chapter I make the case that, in order to grow in confidence and peace as members of society and as disciples of Jesus, men need to find ways of attending to their inner lives in relation to God. I share results of a study on men's experience of God, which raise further questions and point to ways of engaging men on their inner spiritual journey, a journey that is inseparable from outward behaviour.

The importance of spiritual experience

Awareness of feelings, interpersonal dynamics, and interior states does not come easily for many of us men. But what about an awareness of God, Christ, and the Holy Spirit? As a Mennonite man and pastor, this has become a question of continuing interest to me.

My interest in this question of men's experience of God is rooted as much in my own story as it is in my pastoral vocation. After returning home from working with the Mennonite Church in Colombia, South America, from 1990 to 1994, I was feeling a sense of spiritual emptiness. While living and ministering in a poor neighborhood of Bogotá, I was overwhelmed with serious social problems and economic disparities. It became painfully clear to me that intellectual resources were not enough to sustain me in ministry. I needed a deeper grounding in faith and hope, and so I began to search for a more personal experience of God. This search has been an ongoing journey that continues to the present day.

In her book *A Mennonite Woman: Exploring Spiritual Life and Identity*, Dawn Ruth Nelson recalls a similar experience while working in Northern Ireland. She had studied at the Associated Mennonite Biblical Seminaries (now Anabaptist Mennonite Biblical Seminary) in Elkhart, Indiana, at a time when the ethical, socio-political dimensions of the gospel had been emphasized over the personal and inner aspects. She recounts how the "outer-ness" of a purely political gospel "wore thin" as she encountered loneliness, the breakdown of relationships, and intractable social problems. She began to yearn for an inner life of prayer that could sustain her over the long haul.[1]

For Christian faith to be meaningful and vibrant, there needs to be some primary experience of God. By "experience" I mean an awareness of God's presence or influence that we can personally appropriate and articulate in basic ways. The importance of a personal, experiential dimension is not a strange concept. Think for a moment about the work of business and sales. In order to be effective, the salesperson needs to have an *experience* of their product. Simply knowing the specifications is not enough. They have to be able to say how the product or service has affected their

---

1 Nelson, *Mennonite Woman*, 106. Nelson goes on to describe how the development of a spirituality curriculum at the Associated Mennonite Biblical Seminaries in the late 1980s grew out of similar concerns among certain faculty. Marlene Kropf noted in an interview with Nelson that many of the students in the 1980s were coming to the seminary without a personal knowledge of prayer. They had inherited the ethical call without the corresponding inner life that undergirds that call. Kropf interprets the situation in terms of the breakdown of family and communal structures that happened with increased mobility and urbanization: "It's very possible to live on that heritage without having one's own direct connection to God. . . . As long as you have the communal structures, you don't know that you are spiritually bankrupt. . . . You live off other people's connection to God or the community's inheritance. But I think you spend that inheritance in one generation" (114).

life and work. They need to have *stories* of what the product has meant to them *personally*.

The personal dimension is particularly relevant for those of us in the Anabaptist-Mennonite tradition. Our heritage of faith is an *existential* one since it hinges on voluntary adult baptism. Prior to baptism and membership in the church, we look for a personal awareness of God that can be owned and shared with others. Our Anabaptist forbears spoke of an inward baptism of the Spirit, which comes before the outward baptism with water.

In his book on Anabaptist spirituality, Arnold Snyder writes, "Mystical and Anabaptist spirituality contrast dramatically with Reformation spirituality. The accent falls on the experienced presence of the living Christ within, transforming believers with power, rather than on the historic work of Christ's atonement on the cross."[2] While such a statement may sound overly pious for many Mennonites today, most of us would likely agree that Christian faith is meant to be more than just going to church and believing the correct doctrines. Faith in Christ needs to be experienced personally and fleshed out in our daily lives.

Studying men's experience of God

In a recent Doctor of Ministry project, I set out to investigate how men in Mennonite churches experience God by conducting individual, in-depth interviews with men who were attending churches in the local area, in which I asked an open-ended question about their experience of God, or their spirituality.[3] In preparing for the research, I was often asked why I was focusing on men rather than interviewing women as well. One of the reasons I wanted to work with men was because men seem to talk less about their spiritual experiences than women. As I've participated in spiritual retreats, workshops, and spiritual direction over the years, I've noticed that men are greatly outnumbered by women. This led me to ask, Why? Are men not having spiritual experiences that they want to explore? Are men not as spiritual as women? Or might they have different ways of describing and processing such experiences?

---

2 Snyder, *Following in the Footsteps of Christ*, 65.
3 See Brubaker-Zehr, "Understanding Men's 'Experience of God.'" Throughout this chapter, I refer interchangeably to men's "experience of God" and their "spirituality." Spirituality is essentially our experience of God (however we may understand God) and how that experience influences our beliefs, attitudes, and actions.

The process

For my research, I invited men to confidential, hour-long interviews, in which they responded to the question, *How do you experience God within your congregational setting and beyond?*[4] I chose this open-ended question because I did not want to lead the interviewees into any particular response. I wanted to hear what they would say for themselves. The process was stopped when it became clear that the thematic categories were sufficiently saturated—in other words, when the same themes kept being repeated. I then proceeded to organize, analyze, and theorize about their responses, employing a qualitative research methodology called Grounded Theory.[5]

What I discovered

I discovered that the question, *What is your experience of God?* was not an easy one to answer. The men were somewhat puzzled and stymied. The question involves so much uncertainty and invites further questions: Who is God? How can we know that it is "God" we have experienced? The men talked most readily about their questions regarding God and their difficulties in understanding. To give an example, several men wondered how it was possible to talk about gratitude for God's blessings when so many innocent people were suffering in the war in Syria.

In the post-research reflection meeting, the men all acknowledged that they don't usually talk about their spiritual experiences. This conversation was a new thing for them. Several said it was easier to talk about such things in a one-on-one setting than in a group. One said he'd had a few conversations like this with friends but only after a few drinks. The whole topic felt strange and vulnerable to them.

Even though it was a challenging question to answer, the men were very open to exploring and conversing. One said he found the interview experience to be cathartic. I was surprised that virtually all of the men randomly contacted were willing to be interviewed. My committee and I had assumed that it might be difficult to find willing volunteers, but this was not the case.

---

4 With the help of my advisory committee, a pool of willing individuals was selected at random. The men were chosen from long-established urban Mennonite congregations of European ancestry. Many members of these congregations are professionally educated and tend to describe themselves as theologically progressive or liberal. Ages ranged from the 30s to the 70s, with every decade represented.

5 Grounded Theory methods consist of "systematic, yet flexible guidelines for collecting and analyzing qualitative data to construct theories 'grounded' in the data themselves" (Charmaz, *Constructing Grounded Theory*, 2).

The interviews showed that despite a difficulty in articulating their experience of God, the men shared stories of depth and were very sensitive to spiritual themes. Their responses were grouped into seven major categories.

(1) Awareness of unmerited goodness. The men spoke most often about good things they had witnessed or experienced in their lives that did not seem connected with their own merit or abilities. They commented about goodness experienced in nature, in seemingly coincidental events, and in their work and family lives. They did not use theological language such as "grace." In general, God was experienced in the mystery of blessings. The majority, however, were hesitant to name God as responsible for the goodness. Most of them referred to God as a mystery they could not describe or explain.

(2) Awe. Awe refers to experiences of fascination. Most often, awe was experienced in relation to unmerited blessings: work or skills, witnessing the genuine goodness of others, or the beauty of nature. I found it interesting that none of the experiences of awe were connected to a sense of fear or dread. In the Bible, encounters with God are often accompanied with the assurance, "Do not fear." Rudolf Otto describes religious experience as an encounter with the "mysterium tremendum and fascinosum."[6] He claims that encounters with the divine often provoke a sense of fear or dread. None of the men in this study reported this sort of experience.

(3) Reverence. In response to unmerited beauty or goodness, many of the men expressed feelings and actions of reverence. One man sat down to take in the beauty of a vista while he was skiing. Another took time to kneel down with amazement, observing a small flower at his cottage: "And you look at that flower and just a little bud on it and you literally stand there and watch it. I even knelt down to watch it close, for five minutes, ten minutes at the longest. That flower comes from a little bud and you will see a complete and beautiful open flower. It opens up—unreal—one time."

(4) Trust in a non-malicious universe. The men generally reflected on experiences of goodness by saying that there must be a benevolence to the universe. However, the majority of men were not ready to speak definitively about God's character or role in this benevolence. Many were troubled with the instances of suffering that they observe all around them. As one man reflected, "I have gotten to the point in my life where I actually don't want to come up

6 Otto, *Idea of the Holy*, 16.

with a definitive experience of God. Or maybe that is the definitive experience; not wanting. Or having this experience that there is an underlying non-maliciousness to the universe, and I almost hesitate to say goodness, because that implies, what do you do then with all the horrible suffering?" The men wanted to account for all of the evidence before making a statement of faith. For the majority, trust in a non-malicious universe was as far as they could go.

(5) *Sense of connection*. The majority of men spoke repeatedly about the goodness of being connected to nature, family, meaningful work, and friendships. They also experienced a mysterious and benevolent connection between various events in their lives, such as meeting a spouse, being saved from an accident, or finding meaningful work. Some described a sense of someone looking out for them or something holding everything together. When they talked about experience of God within their congregation, it was this sense of connection or community that was most important.

(6) *Ethical desire*. In addition to feeling connected, the men also expressed a desire to connect, which demonstrated a consistent ethical impulse. While they did not say, "I experience God through the ethical desire that God places within me," this desire came up so frequently that it can be interpreted as an integral part of their experience of God. The men showed a genuine desire to be good and to do good. One man shared, "We recycle Kleenex boxes, I tear out the plastic liners. And the green bin thing is amazing. There was an article in the newspaper a while ago about people not using the green bin because it smells bad. And I'm thinking, you know, I just want to punch those people! Because, like, come on! Pull your head out of your posterior for a minute. Let's think about the long-term implications of this!"

Most often, the ethical impulse seems to grow out of a context of having experienced unmerited goodness. For example, a man experiences the wonder and beauty of the natural environment and then has a desire to care for the earth through recycling. Another man works to form caring relationships with his students because of the caring communal relationships he has enjoyed in his own life. In general, the men were uncertain about Christian doctrine but clear on ethical values. When speaking about Jesus, they referred to him almost exclusively as an ethical role model.

(7) *Awareness of need*. The men did not talk much about their own brokenness or suffering. None of them spoke of sin in the traditional sense of the word or of the need for forgiveness from

God. In general, they talked more about their own vulnerability or the vulnerability of others.

Summary

In this particular Mennonite context,[7] and based on these particular interviews, I would describe the men's spirituality as follows:

- It is a tangible. When asked about their "experience of God," these men reflected on concrete encounters with nature, events, and other people. They tended to respond to what they could observe, touch, and experience with their senses.
- It is external. The men did not describe an active inner life in relation to the question posed.[8]
- It is a spirituality of gratitude for the everyday goodness that surrounds them.
- It is a spirituality of connection. The men perceive and value their connection to the earth and other people. They do not want to be isolated and alone.
- It is an ethical spirituality. The men believe that actions are more important than beliefs.
- It is a spirituality of intellectual caution and integrity. The men are hesitant to trust what they cannot see and understand. They value the scientific, evidence-based paradigm for understanding the world. They want to be able to explain what they believe in ways that will be respected by the broader culture.

It was interesting to note the absence of biblical and theological language in the men's descriptions of their experiences of God. The men report experiencing God at church through music, singing, community support, honest sharing, and the open discussion of ideas. Sermons are less effective than discussions. There was little reference to the significance of communion and baptism. For the

---

7 This study was undertaken in the milieu of long-established urban Mennonite congregations of European ancestry. As mentioned above, members of these congregations tend to describe themselves as theologically progressive or liberal. While such designations can sometimes be unhelpful or misleading, they offer important context to the results listed here. Anabaptist men in other contexts would likely express their spirituality much differently.

8 By inner life I mean an awareness and attention to one's emotions, body sensations, motivations, and impulses. Inner life involves a discernment of one's calling, purpose, or direction in life and one's ongoing relationship to Christ. An active inner life would often include the desire to make regular times for prayer, reflection, and conversation with a spiritual director, guide, or friend.

great majority of the men interviewed, the idea of a personal relationship with God was a strange concept. God was not experienced as a personal being or presence. They did not speak about being personally addressed, loved, forgiven, or saved. They did not speak about their own sin, problems, addictions, or weaknesses. If I were to summarize their spirituality, I would do so as follows: *God may be real, but God is a mystery I cannot understand. I have received many undeserved good things in my life, and I would like to do my best to honor these gifts and be of service to others.*

Implications of the study for working with men

At the beginning of this chapter, I made the claim that primary experience of God is a necessary component of a vibrant Christian faith, especially an Anabaptist faith. The results of my study raises some questions about this claim: What exactly constitutes a primary experience of God? Are the men describing such experiences? What might their descriptions say to us as men and to those who seek to encourage men's spiritual growth in the Anabaptist tradition?

David G. Benner presents a helpful model of spirituality in which he situates Christian spirituality within the larger realm of religious spirituality, which in turn is situated within the encompassing realm of natural spirituality.[9] According to Benner, all people have a spirituality by virtue of being human. All humans have an innate desire for meaning, self-transcendence, and surrender. Religious and Christian spirituality emerge when these natural longings discover content and meaning within a particular religious tradition with its language, symbols, and rituals. The spirituality described by the men interviewed has more in common with Benner's definition of natural spirituality than it does with religious or Christian spirituality. The men clearly display a sense of transcendence and a desire to surrender through ethical living, but they do not as clearly interpret this within the language of the church.[10]

---

9 Benner, *Psychotherapy and the Spiritual Quest*, 104–107.

10 In a larger Lutheran study on the spirituality of young North American men, the authors come to a similar conclusion: "Whatever the final analysis, it is clear that the traditional language of the Christian church has not formed our 88 young men. . . . Their spiritual journeys and personal identities are, at the most basic levels, shaped less by Scripture and Christian tradition and more by personal reasoning and an assortment of personal, relational, and cultural experiences" (Anderson, Hill, and Martinson, *Coming of Age*, 164). It seems quite possible that the results of my study may reflect the spiritual lives of many men in Canadian and US society, especially in more progressive or liberal contexts. In talking with numerous male friends and

The Work of Interpretation

Traditional Christian language does not seem to be working for men like those I interviewed. I propose that if we wish to encourage such men in spiritual growth, we need to work intentionally at the *interpretation* of experiences of meaning. What does it mean in Christian language to be overtaken by the beauty of nature? What does it mean theologically to sense and respond to an ethical impulse? As a pastor, I try to connect biblical and theological language with current realities in my sermons. I try to make religious language accessible and understandable, but for whatever reason, this language of the church is not what these men are using to describe their experiences of God. Clearly, we need forums other than sermons and worship services to engage in this interpretive work. We need to find places in our churches where men can come together in less formal settings to share and interpret significant experiences.

Inner life

Men do have significant experiences of depth in their everyday lives. They are sensitive to questions of meaning and purpose. In order for these experiences to be integrated into a growing Christian faith, men need help in understanding and articulating these experiences through the lens of Christian language and spiritual tradition. For many men, this work will involve a growing awareness and articulation of an *inner* life. Experiences of depth touch our inner and subjective core. The language of the Bible is often connected to inner life. Jesus summons his followers personally. The apostle Peter is forgiven, and Jesus asks him, "Do you love me?" (John 21:15–17). The rich young man is challenged. A man in need of healing confesses his sin. The Bible at its heart is a story of people encountering God and being transformed from within. Encounters of depth, encounters with the mystery of God are indeed present among men, yet they often go unnoticed, unarticulated, and uninterpreted. They lie there as buried treasure. The work is to help men dig down into their experiences of meaning and to interpret them spiritually in ways they can own and understand.

---

acquaintances from various denominations, the majority indicated that the study results reflected their own spiritual lives as well.

Outer and Inner

The journey for men will often move from the external (concrete events and issues) to the internal (feelings, intuitions, and vulnerabilities) and then back again to external engagement with the issues of the world. In doing interpretive spiritual work with men, the goal is to stimulate awareness of the inner life since this is the less developed function. However, it works best to start where men are. It works best to start on the surface and gradually peel back the layers. In spiritual retreat settings, I've noticed that men are often chided about being more focused on the external than the internal—as if this is a problem.[11] Focusing on external observations is where many men feel most comfortable, and it is a perfectly fine place to begin in spiritual reflection groups, provided that the engagement does not remain there. The goal is to eventually move to issues of heart and soul.

The challenge of men's work (as well as women's work) is to find a healthy integration between the outer and inner. The inner is not better than the outer. The goal of an integrated faith is having them work in balance.[12] Anabaptist theology stresses a coherence between the inner and outer dimensions. We have always maintained that an inner faith without outward works is dead. We also know that Christ-like works without an inner faith are not possible. For believers to fully embody the ethic of non-violent love, there needs to be personal access to an inner spiritual fountain. It is not possible to follow Christ without knowing him in one's heart.

In conclusion, I offer four suggestions based on my study for working with men in the context of congregational or social life.

(1) Create places to listen and reflect with other men. Before we can work on the interpretation of experience, experience needs to be shared and heard. For the majority of the men interviewed, it was a completely new experience to be asked to reflect on experiences of God. It felt strange and vulnerable. Nevertheless, all of the men were willing and interested. There is a hidden hunger for encounters and conversations of meaning among men. Men long to talk about more than sports and the weather but are not sure how to

---

11 Could this be one of the reasons why men are not attending spiritual retreats? Could it be that the most common models of spiritual engagement are more stereotypically "feminine" in nature—in the sense of beginning with feelings and heart?
12 The integration of ways of knowing is a common theme in spiritual wisdom traditions. Cynthia Bourgeault describes the three knowing centers as movement/body, emotional/heart, and intellectual/mind. See Bourgeault, *Wisdom Way of Knowing*, chap. 3.

initiate such conversations. We want these sorts of encounters, and yet we fear them. Churches can have an important role in creating spaces for these sorts of conversations among men.

There are several important things to keep in mind. First, the space has to be safe. For some men, this will mean a male-only gathering.[13] While sadly having a history of dominating and excluding women, men are also intimidated by women. Oppression is often the result of fear and insecurity. Men are fearful of looking weak or foolish in mixed company. They are often less adept at naming feelings than women. They find it harder to cry and be vulnerable with one another. And so, in the early stages at least, it is a good idea to begin with male-only groups. Second, men benefit from space and distance in a group. A "talking stick" can be one way of providing this buffer.[14] Third, it is helpful to make a ground rule of "no advice or fixing." A common temptation for men is to try to solve problems. We must be trained to sit patiently and compassionately with unresolved issues. It is enough just to listen and hear one another. Men can learn to share more openly when there is space for unfinished reflections. It can be an experience of freedom and grace (an experience of God even) to be heard and accepted without having to look good or successful.

One effective approach to personal sharing in a men's group is to invite reflection on a "third thing."[15] This allows for personal sharing in a more indirect way since the object of reflection is not the self or the presentation of another participant. Whatever the methodology, the goal is to get men together in a safe and non-judgmental environment to share and reflect on experiences of depth in their lives. I've included a few additional reflection questions for such groups in the note below.[16]

---

13 In the current cultural milieu there is some resistance to men's only gatherings. Some may wonder whether men are simply re-grouping for another round of domination. Under a cultural cloud of suspicion, men need encouragement to gather together to share their struggles and to work toward healthy and collaborative masculinity and spirituality.

14 A talking stick is an object that is held by the one speaking, ensuring that there are no interruptions and interjections as only the person with the stick may speak.

15 "Third thing" is a term used by Parker J. Palmer in his book *Hidden Wholeness*. It refers to a poem or object or short saying that becomes the focus for group reflections. Palmer writes, "Every practice that creates a circle of trust must keep the space between us open and free and yet focused on things of the soul" (92).

16 (a) Where and when did I feel spiritually alive this week? (Where and when did I experience gratitude? a sense of awe or reverence?) (b) Where and when did I feel spiritually distant or disconnected? (Where and when did I experience loneliness, resentment, negativity, etc.?) (c) Where and when did I feel a call, challenge, or

(2) Work toward the integration of spirituality, theology, science, and culture. It was clear from the men's comments that a critical, evidence-based, scientific worldview is a central part of their consciousness. A significant obstacle to experiences of God and reflections on those experiences has much to do with unresolved understandings of how God and the current scientific worldview can coexist. Most men in our local urban congregations share the current modernist or postmodernist paradigms.[17] The work of integrating current paradigms with a spiritual, theological world-view is a significant challenge. Unless we have been able to work at this deliberately, the Christian language can sound ancient and otherworldly. It appears that for many men, the language of the church is used only on Sundays and disconnected from daily life.

In order to make sense of Christian language, we need to understand it within its social and cultural context and relate it to other language systems in which we live. There are ample resources for this sort of work and opportunities in sermons and in the education hour, but it takes considerable effort.[18] Lecture series, book groups, and open discussion forums can be more meaningful components of church life for many men than the typical worship service. Churches can be hesitant to wade into these discussions because they are fraught with challenge and controversy. Nevertheless, we avoid these conversations at our own peril. It may be that the church needs to adopt some new theological understandings and insights into the Christian spiritual path, but this should always be done with a deep understanding and respect for the language and tradition of the past.

(3) Explore with one another the use of biblical and theological language. As men share their experiences with one another in groups, it is good for pastors or facilitators to ask the following questions: How might this relate to a biblical theme? Where is God in this?

---

invitation? (Where and when did I feel nudged or guided? Where and when was I encouraged to act ethically?)

17 "Modernism" is the term used in philosophical circles to describe the rise of the scientific method, the historical critique of mythical stories, and the commitment to democracy and equality of all people and the values of progress, order, and institution. Postmodernism builds on these developments but critiques the "sins" of modernity, such as colonialism, patriarchy, and the marginalization of social and sexual minorities. Postmodernism tends to distrust grand narratives and objective truth claims.

18 Some good resources for this include the work of Richard Rohr, John F. Haught, Ilia Delio, Cynthia Bourgeault, Ken Wilber, Denis Edwards, and Celia Deane-Drummond. See, e.g., Haught, *Making Sense of Evolution*; Edwards, *God of Evolution*; Wilber, *Integral Spirituality*.

Might there be a theological way of reflecting on this? Such questions should be perceived as an invitation rather than a requirement. We grow in Christian spirituality as we begin to understand and interpret our current experiences in relation to the Christian biblical and theological tradition. The point is not to do it correctly or just as it has been done before but to practice doing it presently and personally. Christian spirituality is not static. It continues to find new relationships with the language of the church, while also questioning and proposing new meanings and words.

(4) Move toward the disclosure of vulnerability and failure. In the interviews I conducted, the men did not speak much about their suffering, brokenness, or failure. This is not surprising, as such sharing often comes only after much time and trust. However, this is a place we men should move toward if we wish to grow spiritually.[19] Christian spirituality is essentially about the mystery of death and resurrection. At its heart, the spiritual path of Jesus is learning how to deal redemptively with the suffering, sin, and pain of human life. Men, perhaps more than women, have been socialized to be providers and problem solvers. It is therefore difficult for many men to speak about their own personal weakness and failure. The natural inclination is to hide them and try to look strong. Safe places of support are crucial for this sort of disclosure. If men can find ways of naming their failure and pain in compassionate company, there can be new possibilities for experiences of God, including healing, grace, and redemption.

Bibliography

Anderson, David E., Paul G. Hill, and Roland D. Martinson. *Coming of Age: Exploring the Identity and Spirituality of Younger Men.* Minneapolis: Augsburg Fortress, 2006.

Benner, David G. *Psychotherapy and the Spiritual Quest.* Grand Rapids: Baker Book House, 1988.

Bourgeault, Cynthia. *The Wisdom Way of Knowing.* San Francisco: Jossey-Bass, 2003.

Brubaker-Zehr, Scott. "Understanding Men's 'Experience of God': How Men Experience God in an Urban Mennonite Congre-

---

19 Suffering and failure are most often the doorway into deeper spiritual experience, as they cause a crisis of the "false self" and an opening to the transforming love of God. Paul says that God's power is made perfect in weakness (2 Cor. 12:9–10), and Jesus says that a seed needs to die before it can bear fruit (John 12:24).

gational Setting and Beyond." DMin thesis, Regis College, Univerity of Toronto, 2013.

Charmaz, Kathy. *Constructing Grounded Theory: A Practical Guide Through Qualitative Analysis*. London: SAGE, 2006.

Edwards, Denis. *The God of Evolution*. New York: Paulist Press, 1999.

Haught, John F. *Making Sense of Evolution*. Louisville: Westminster John Knox, 2010.

Nelson, Dawn Ruth. *A Mennonite Woman: Exploring Spiritual Life and Identity*. Telford, PA: Cascadia, 2010.

Otto, Rudolf. *The Idea of the Holy: An Inquiry into the Non-Rational Factor in the Idea of the Divine and Its Relation to the Rational*. Translated by John Wilfred Harvey. London: Oxford University Press, 1957.

Palmer, Parker J. *A Hidden Wholeness: The Journey toward an Undivided Life*. San Francisco: Jossey-Bass, 2004.

Snyder, C. Arnold. *Following in the Footsteps of Christ: The Anabaptist Tradition*. Maryknoll, NY: Orbis, 2004.

Wilber, Ken. *Integral Spirituality*. Boston: Shambhala, 2006.

Becoming Men of Peace and Reconciliation

Chapter 15

John Powell

I begin this chapter with a disclaimer. I am not a theologian. I am a country preacher and practitioner of justice and reconciliation. I am a product of growing up in the South and experiencing the pangs of racial discrimination. I found avenues to grow into a peacemaker. The views expressed are born out of relationships and engagement with racial, social, and political reconciliation. This chapter is from one African American Anabaptist perspective, and it is both descriptive and prescriptive.[1]

I believe that our ability to achieve peace and reconciliation is predicated on how we interact with each other. Our worldview and response to our environment are defined by the place we occupy in society. What contributes to our welfare and self-preservation becomes prominent in our relationships with others and will determine our ability to change for the good of all.

Our Anabaptist-Mennonite tradition's focus on peacemaking has primarily related to our participation in war and the elimination of global conflict. Given the current realities of hatred, domestic violence, and racial division among us, it's time for us to address our participation in issues and structures that prevent God's peace and racial healing. This chapter is intended to help men become aware of the current realities of their relationships to the oppression of marginalized people. Addressing racial issues (or failure to do so) is a priority concern of our communities. My intent is to address boundaries in relationships that hinder peacemaking.

Since I am primarily addressing men, my comments are focused on men's relationships with each other. However, many observations can apply to oppressive situations in general, such

---

1 There is an adage that says that when the United States sneezes, Canada catches a cold. This assumes that the United States is dominant. I don't assume to know a lot about the power dynamics of Canada; however, I am aware that it shares many of the same racial and ethnic dynamics as the United States, though its ethnic issues are related more to First Nation and Caribbean peoples. While my writing explores men's relationship to race and reconciliation in the United States, many observations may be applied to the Canadian context.

as gender injustice. I hope to provide insights into how men can overcome exclusionary tendencies and become instruments of reconciliation and peace.

Historical background

When I was growing up, I lived in a closed community that valued family and community relationships. Being proud of who God made you was emphasized. Fathers conversed with sons about racial pride and ways to handle racist acts—how to take care of oneself when confronting racist behavior. Spiritual expression was important, and a Baptist articulation of faith was dominant. The church was the center for spiritual, social, and political life. Not only were members taught how to live in a segregated community, but youth were encouraged to take their rightful place in leadership. There was some emphasis on justice and equality, but it wasn't outwardly visible to the white community. We protected each other from white folks. Things changed as black folks moved north.

Blacks began an exodus from the South in 1916. This exodus, known as the Great Migration, witnessed the arrival of black folks to urban centers in the North. Jim Crow had relegated black folks to menial jobs, poor education, inability to vote, and lynching in the South. Blacks thought that they were leaving the South for a better life. Mexican migrant workers began coming to the United States in the 1890s; however, as industrialization increased between 1880 and 1929, migration to urban centers increased. Beginning in the 1970s, the lure of economic opportunities led to the arrival of Chinese people. As the population of each group increased, so did violence toward them.

I moved to Detroit, Michigan, in 1964, and I quickly discovered that racial segregation was rampant. Blacks, Mexicans, and Chinese had begun to move into designated white communities, and their presence threatened the status quo. When I started looking for housing in what was considered a white community, I was often asked if I was black or white. I understood that race was pivotal in keeping people of color in their place.

Even though northern communities have been viewed as more liberal than the South, racial inequality was and is rampant in the North as well. I maintain that the difference between the North and South is a matter of semantics. The difference is that in the North the attitude is, "I don't care how high you get, as long as you don't get too close," whereas in the South the attitude is, "I don't care how close you get, as long as you don't get too high." Both understandings of racial relationships have had the same devastating effect on racial reconciliation.

Setting the stage

A friend of mine once said that he was nonviolent by choice, not by nature. If this is true, we understand that overcoming our violent nature is difficult. Most likely we think of cessation of war and physical combat when we talk about peace. We seldom discuss peace as the absence of psychological and emotional violence as a result of racial hatred. This form of violence is just as devastating as war and, indeed, forms the backbone for war.[2] The lack of peace, no matter the form it takes, originates from our inability to be reconciled with each other. Masculine socialization, especially male entitlement and permissions to utilize violence or threat of violence as a means to an end, leads to hostility. Peace will not be achieved as long as men continue to embrace male dominance.

Let's explore the dynamics of race, inequality, and exclusion as a dynamic for achieving peace. We are a nation that separates people by skin pigmentation: white and colored. This has created hostility and division in families and nationalities. Even among persons labeled something other than white, there's tension. As people of color, we are often at odds with each other. From my perspective, an essential denominator that brings us together is that we breathe the same air and share a common perceived enemy: white folks. Many times when acceptance occurs at the table of power, relationships erode. We struggle to find our center and many times relegate each other to the margins. At the same time, we struggle to find a common identity with those we see as the majority community.

Our reality

Our communities have changed over several decades. Hence, we are surrounded by different ideologies, customs, and peoples. This has significantly changed the way we interact. We are more divided than we have seen in decades. Exclusion has taken roots in our relationships. We can't deny that exclusionary acts are real and have a voice. That voice dominates Western society. It speaks loud and clear into everyone's psyche. Racism is not silent and

---

2 See Marty Troyer's chapter on the gospel of peace above.

has had a devastating effects on people of color. As the voice of racism becomes more vocal, the soil under our feet shakes from the discontent of people of color and marginalized people. There's anger, pain, and alienation. We have been awakened by the unrest of those who demand that people in power change. Marginalized people's actions proclaim that they are neighbors and are here to stay. Racist tendencies and exclusion have affected all marginalized people; however, because African American men still experience the rudiments of slavery, they are often viewed as sub-human by many people. This has a chilling effect on the ability to achieve peaceful solutions. I believe that addressing the dynamics of competition, power, and forgiveness among men can open the doors to peacemaking. To this we now turn.

Competitiveness

According to numerous studies, men tend to be more physically aggressive than women. Men have dominated the landscape of violence, both internationally and domestically. Our aggressive behaviors lend themselves to exercising control over those who threaten our confidence and honor. With the rise of Western society, some women have gained political power that gives them the power of war. Even so, historically most women have attempted to find peaceful resolution before going to war.

Men generally are competitive with each other. There's a need to outdo each other in being manly. Our psyches seem to compel us to exert an alpha dog effect aimed at gaining the upper hand. Our ego gets in the way of expressing humility, and it's difficult to admit error. Competitiveness is complicated by distrust. This tends to create hostility when different racial groups come together. Men of color are often seen as subservient in the relationship. Given these issues, conflict resolution often becomes untenable for many.

Both white men and men of color are affected by acts of exclusion and racism: white men benefit materially, while men of color are harmed materially. There's a perception in Western society that a man of color poses a threat if he's competent. If he is perceived as a threat, he is deemed insolent and incompetent. If he is assertive he's considered pushy. Trying to remain non-threatening while demonstrating competence often creates emotional disharmony. Sometimes this leads to self-devaluation. These issues also can create negative family dynamics.

In a similar situation, if a white colleague is pushy and exhibits similar behavior as their colleague of color, he is often viewed as self-assured and powerful. While I can't speak definitively about the emotional pain of white men, I believe that there's fear of losing the privileges that society bestows on them. The emotional pain and effects on white men are often hidden and unrecognized, but the pain is there. The emotional pain that white men and men of color experience are real and have a tremendous impact on how they respond to racial stimuli, but both need healing.

Having a self-checkup about one's involvement in racial turmoil takes courage. Doing a self-assessment requires discovering what's at stake not only for ourselves but also for the other. How we handle this will bolster or weaken our resolve to become a reconciler in the midst of troubled waters. When I became an agent for reconciliation, I recoiled from self-examination. But I learned that recoiling was not an option. Self-examination allowed me to face my community with the truth that it, like me, was in need of liberation.

The difficult journey of racial, ethnic, and religious inclusion is outside our doors. Chinese philosopher Lao Tzu said that a journey of a thousand miles begins with a single step. We are often faced with taking that first step. The journey begins with the single step of admitting that our thoughts and actions aren't the only things that dominate. Other folks' thoughts and actions also dominate. We are left to deal with the consequences of conflicting priorities.

Most of us are aware of the results of disharmony among us. We are a family with different ethnic groups sitting at the table. It's time to have an open and honest appraisal about how race impacts our relationships. Being vulnerable with each other, we can find common solutions that will give all of us hope for the future.

The centrality of power

Being male in Western society gives access to power and privilege. We men often refuse to admit that we have power while exerting it or find multiple ways of justifying the use of power without acknowledging the implication for others. Conversely, most women and marginalized people readily recognize that personal power exists and that men generally wield the power. Their histories of marginalization as a result of men's access to power has created voices among them that articulate the need for shared power. Women and marginalized people who have achieved the fruits of power, prestige, and privilege often successfully challenge power brokers. This dynamic has not evaded men of Anabaptist faith.

Core beliefs about faith, humanity, and justice were challenged during the Civil Rights Movement. Communities of color honed their principles of justice and equality that guided their thoughts and actions. Working with people of different faith traditions who fought for equality, a new generation was born.

A merger of faith, justice, and reconciliation had been missing for me. Encountering Anabaptism while searching for spiritual identity, I hoped to find acceptance of my black identity. Wasn't Anabaptism a religious expression that believed in peace and justice? I believed that an Anabaptist understanding of the gospel of Jesus could help me merge my home grown religious faith with justice and reconciliation. As a black man, I found that merger important. I thought that the Mennonite Church was the place for me to do that.

The Mennonite Church faced a dilemma in the wake of emerging racial pride among minority peoples in the 1970s. The church could make the necessary adjustments to address the rising tide against racial exclusion or it could keep the status quo. In a 1970 sermon I said that we were being made aware that the problem involved in racial reconciliation was two-sided. White people weren't committed to understanding minority peoples. There was a tendency to ignore the call for racial justice. The church embraced a "Can't we just get along?" attitude. At the same time, people of color were frequently unapologetic about their reaction to white folks' negative attitudes and responses. Resistance increased on both sides of the issue.

A coalition of blacks, Hispanics, Native Americans, and whites, dominated by men, was formed to confront racial and cultural biases in the denomination. There were disagreements, but they spoke with a common voice. Understanding and achieving common ground were their goals. They understood that their destinies were interwoven. The church reluctantly began to slowly change. Yet a power disparity remained. White men still wielded power, and people of color and women were left out. I have a T-shirt imprinted with the line, "If you don't have a seat at the table, you're probably on the menu." For many years people of color and women were on the menu. But the menu began to change as more people of color joined the denomination. Despite these changes, men still held the power.

Reflecting on the past, I think we are better off now than we were then. Mennonite Church USA has deliberately placed emphasis on multicultural transformation and peacemaking. It has elected persons of color as moderators and most recently appointed an African American as its executive director. Yet, I still have some concerns. Most places I go in the church, I hear discussions about intercultural transformation but very little about racism. Intercultural transformation can help move the pendulum toward racial reconciliation. However, I fear that if we are not purposeful about addressing racial inequality, this focus may be a way of avoiding addressing the dynamics that race have on peacemaking. If racial equality is to be realized, we must deal honestly with power disparity in our midst.

The desire to keep power that has accrued to us by reason of skin color is a barrier to racial inclusion. Ervin Stutzman, then executive director for Mennonite Church USA, wrote in the April 3, 2012, issue of the newsletter *Equipping* that he can visit most congregations without anyone assuming that he doesn't belong there. He attributed this to his skin color and accent. I call this the power of sameness, where everyone is alike racially, economically, and spiritually. Like churches, communities suffer from the power of sameness. Trust and welcoming acceptance is automatically extended. There's little problem if there are a few unlike us. It's problematic when there are many, and they threaten our settled way of life. This exists among all racial groups; however, it's more prevalent in white communities. Realignment of the power dynamics can lead to purposeful reconciliation.

During one conversation between African American and white men, issues of privilege and power were central to the dialogue. A white participant exclaimed, "What's this stuff about power and privilege? I don't have either. Nobody gave me anything. I worked for what I have!" This attitude denies the implicit advantage that society bestows for having white pigmentation. It hinders movement toward reconciliation. Those of us who are who experience second class treatment understand that privilege and power become apparent when racial, ethnic, and socioeconomic sameness controls the progress of others. Therefore, people who have power are reluctant to talk about it because it often upsets the status quo. If we are to realize the vision of a reconciled community, this must be addressed.

Ted Swartz says, "When you carry a wound, the greatest gift you have is someone who will help you carry it gracefully."[3] Clinging to the power of racial prejudice, racism, and domination are wounds that kill the soul.[4] For many, the need to release power is in the head. What I have experienced is that confessing and releasing power is not in the head but in the soul. Traditionally, men have been viewed as the accepted power brokers in most communities. This is changing as women and people of color gain power. However, in some cultures and contexts, men are still the dominant power brokers in their families and communities. A pivotal question for creating a non-racialized community is how power will be used to dismantle racial, cultural, and gender injustice.

Forgiveness

If we are to achieve peace, we must embrace the power of forgiveness. It begins with giving yourself permission to forgive. Forgive yourself first for carrying the burden of hatred toward the hater. When we forgive ourselves, we are able to extend forgiveness. After forgiving yourself, extend forgiveness to the perpetrator. It's hard but necessary. The power of forgiveness leads to an understanding of who we are and what the future holds.

The road to forgiveness began for me in 1968 when I became the executive secretary of the Minority Ministries Council, an advocacy organization for minority peoples in the Mennonite Church. I was the first person of color appointed to an administrative position at the national level of the church. Being a trailblazer wasn't easy. I was frequently bold and was met with suspicion and rejection. During a presentation on race relations in 1969, an Anglo pastor said, "If we do what John Powell says to do, the next thing they'll have me out of my pulpit and a nigger in there." That hit me like a ton of bricks, and my relationship with Anabaptist-Mennonites started a downward spiral. I left the church disillusioned and angry, promising never to return. After a time in the wilderness, I was led

---

3 Swartz, *Laughter is Sacred Space.*
4 The majority of white people don't believe they are racist. They may admit being prejudiced (having unfavorable opinion with prior knowledge) against a person because of a perceived attitude or action. Therefore, anyone can be prejudiced. When prejudicial attitudes are extended to a racial group because of skin color, racial prejudice occurs. In western society, white people have power and privilege because of their race. They extend their racial prejudice and domination toward people of color and enforce their attitudes and actions by any means necessary. Consequently, racism is emboldened.

back to my Anabaptist understanding by my need for resolution. When we believe that our position holds the truth, it doesn't allow for the other person's truth. The fact is that we all have part of the truth. Reconciliation began with understanding that I needed to forgive and to receive forgiveness. My path began by reconciling with the brother from my encounter in 1969.

The healing process continues. There are times I backslide, but I remember how my unwillingness to forgive prolongs alienation. My story is not unique. Many civil rights leaders confronted their anger, forgave themselves, and offered forgiveness to their oppressors. They understood that reconciliation can take place when forgiveness comes first. In his book *Why Forgive?*, Johann Christoph Arnold quotes Hannah Arendt on forgiveness: "Without being forgiven—released from the consequences of what we have done—our capacity to act would, as it were, be confined to a single deed from which we could never recover; we would remain the victims of its consequences forever."[5] We can't do anything else unless we do.

Forgiveness doesn't mean excusing and accepting intolerance. It means letting go of the pain, anger, and distrust that provoke a violent response. What we believe about the nature of God gives us the ability to let go. I believe that God resides in each of us and that God is truth. God's truth is that we are all part of each other. If I let God in me respond to God in my adversary, peace often ensues.

We desire to achieve a beloved community where fear and discounting others are replaced with valued and trusted relationships. That requires corrective head and heart action. No form of exclusion is known in a beloved community. Anabaptist believers have done a good job of disciple-making. This should result in communities that reflect the oneness reflected in Revelation 7:9: "a great multitude that no one could count, from every nation, from all tribes and peoples and languages, standing before the throne and before the Lamb, robed in white, with palm branches in their hands." While this is a futuristic image of peace and reconciliation, Jesus instructs us to live into the present as well, praying to our heavenly Father, "Your will be done, on earth as it is in heaven" (Matt. 6:10). If we are to live together in heaven, we must live together in peace on earth. Hence, disciple-making is also about the disciple who is doing the making. It requires living out the mandates given to us as we encounter individuals unlike ourselves.

---

5 Arnold, *Why Forgive?*, 19.

I have had numerous conversations about racial inequities. Economics and class tend to dominate the discussion rather than dealing directly with racial tensions. Many say that, given our current reality, these factors trump race. They believe that economics and class undergird most issues that separate us, both nationally and in Anabaptist circles. Yet, we have placed a high value on becoming anti-racist and racially inclusive. Many people have participated in antiracism training and engaged in racial reconciliation endeavors. But the ability to engage in constructive peacemaking toward peaceful resolution has evaded us.

Where to go from here

Speaking to an audience at the National Cathedral in Washington, DC, just days before his assassination in 1968, Dr. Martin Luther King Jr. declared, "One of the great liabilities of life is that all too many people find themselves living amid a great period of social change, and yet they fail to develop the new attitudes, the new mental responses, that the new situation demands." This is the state we are in today. Hatred, violence, and various *isms* of exclusion are deeply planted in the souls of our communities. We thought we knew each other. Divisive events have shown that we have pretended to get along.

Many believe that everything will be all right if we become a melting pot where race and class don't exist. I suggest that this is a pipe dream. Given modern societies' accepted definition of race, skin pigmentation is the norm for acceptance. As long as we use this criteria, the melting pot won't happen. That doesn't mean that we stop seeking utopia, but it does mean that we can't ignore that the conceived designation by race exists.

Michele Norris, award winning journalist and executive director of The Bridge, a program of The Aspen Institute, created the Race Card Project in 2010 to promote honest conversation by asking people to submit their thoughts on race in just six words. More than twenty thousand people have responded. Most submissions have come from white folks. They were transparent about their identity. Their responses ranged from defiance to acceptance. In past studies, people of color have been less clear about their identity. Several studies have given black children pictures of white and black people in different circumstances. They were asked who was the prettiest and who they identified with. Most often the child selected the white person. This racial imprint is hard to eliminate.

It creates inner turmoil about their racial identity that continues into adulthood.

People of color have come to realize that, given the current realities, becoming a colorblind society is not an option. It is a false hope to believe that we will achieve racial parity if we ignore racial identities. Even as marriage between the different races increases, children born to those marriages carry the racial identity of the partner of color. My advice to people of color is thus to be proud of the fact that you are black, Hispanic, Asian American, or Native American because you are going to be that way for the rest of your life. Rather than transcending racial identity, the way forward is to acknowledge your racial identity and change the conditions that your racial identity imposes.

I'm certain that every white male has experienced racist thoughts. It's unavoidable since the culture of racism is so deeply imbedded in society. Likewise, it's unavoidable for men of color not to have moments of hatred against white men since they exert power through privilege. We have all found ourselves helpless to these unwanted thoughts. I admit that sometimes I have fleeting moments of hate and distrust when I observe the violence perpetrated against people of color. I shared my thoughts and feeling with a group of intergenerational and interracial men a few years ago. They were surprised to hear my confession. They had pegged me as a reconciler. During our conversation, other black men revealed that they had similar feelings. Some white participants shared their pain of holding hateful ideas. One confessed that he felt ashamed since his family was biracial, and he didn't know how to talk about his feelings with his family.

We all deal with issues differently, particularly when they challenge our way of life. We tend to lose perspective and are unable to engage in logical discussion to arrive at logical conclusion. It's hard to argue with people who are obsessed. To advance a reconciled society, each of us needs to courageously deal with the following issues:

- Do feelings of racial superiority or inferiority affect the way I interact with other races?
- How do I understand the negative and positive experiences of my race and other races?
- What are the common experiences that I share with other races?

- What keeps me from owning my involvement in the problem?

Other questions and issues that are important, but I recommend beginning with these. Reconciliation is dependent on our recognition that we are part of the problem. How we answer these questions can determine our willingness to change our impact on peacemaking.

A spiritual mandate

The 1966 movie *A Man for All Seasons* chronicles the life of Sir Thomas More, who willingly lost his life for standing with his convictions against the aspirations of King Henry VIII. There was a moral choice, and he became the man for that season. Today men are facing a moral choice of leadership. Who are we choosing to be in the battle against the tyranny of injustice? It seems that women have taken the lead, with a few smattering of men mixed in.

If we are to take our position of equal leadership, we need to find a true example for what it means to be manly. For men who profess Jesus as our guide, Jesus shows us how to respond. He is our man for all seasons. Jesus acted out of unabashed love. That love redeems humanity, including those who don't profess a religious preference. It is completely different from what we often experience. The rejected and marginalized people of society were never abandoned. Jesus showed compassion on everyone. A vivid example is his encounter with the Samaritan woman, where Jesus listened to her concerns (John 4:1–42). He responded with care when others spoke. His listening, touch, and compassionate way of engaging people gave them hope. While he listened with compassion, he took care when confronting others. He lived, taught, and challenged everyone to seek forgiveness. His actions were focused on forgiving those who breached a relationship.

The Christian's primary task is peacemaking and reconciliation. The Apostle Paul instructs us that "in his flesh [Jesus] has made both groups into one and has broken down the dividing wall, that is, the hostility between us . . . that he might create in himself one new humanity in place of the two, thus making peace, and might reconcile both groups to God" (Eph. 2:14-16). Elsewhere Paul writes that, "if anyone is in Christ, there is a new creation: everything old has passed away; see, everything has become new! All this is from God, who reconciled us to himself through Christ, and has given us the ministry of reconciliation; that is, in Christ God was reconciling the world to himself, not counting their trespasses against them, and entrusting the message of reconciliation to us" (2 Cor. 5:17–19). This is particularly true for those who understand that Jesus's act of atonement, or at-one-ment, is central to peacemaking. Our peacemaking mandate is rooted in an Anabaptist understanding of the gospel of Jesus. We believe Jesus is Lord and is (or should be) the center of our lives. Being Christ centered, we have the opportunity to exercise openness to people unlike us. Hence, we are God's ambassadors of peace. If we take this seriously, we will demonstrate it with acts of peace.

Because Jesus provides the model, we are left to follow in his footsteps. Changing the way we respond to each other requires us to be vulnerable as Jesus was. Being vulnerable is difficult because it demands our honest response. White men who are willing to own their privileged position open themselves up to address issues that have been hidden in their psyche since birth. They accept that their status will be altered if this change occurs. For men of color, being vulnerable also has its downside. It often brings hostility and anger. What they see is an unequal playing field when they observe past and current marginalization. The future doesn't necessarily look bright. Their goals for themselves, family, and community are hindered by the people they are engaging. Being willing to engage the perceived enemy in themselves requires being vulnerable. When both open themselves to self-examination and confrontation, the road to recovery has begun.

An interracial group of men in Elkhart County, Indiana, has taken up the banner of vulnerability. They call their group The Beloved Community, a concept shaped by Dr. Martin Luther King Jr. They meet monthly to have a meal together and talk about issues that keep them separated. They address the *isms* in their relationships that keep them separated. They are committed to work through difficult relationships, even when it becomes extremely uncomfortable. The men understand that being a beloved community requires corrective head and heart action. Consequently, they are ambassadors for inclusion and reconciliation in their communities.

This example demonstrates that the power of sameness can be overcome by being willing to have your thoughts and actions shaped by others. In many ways, they are part of a resistance movement that is shaping among us. Similar encounters will happen when we discover our call to become peacemakers.

Join the resistance

Worldwide hatred and violence have substantially increased over the past decade. These acts are aimed at immigrants, religious groups, people of color, and marginalized people. Most of these heinous acts are committed by young men. Many articulate feeling displaced or alienated from society. What we are encountering is not new. As stated earlier, men are generally competitive and aggressive and exert an alpha dog effect aimed at gaining the upper hand. Hate, racism, and exclusion are a generational cycle that continues to repeat itself. How we respond becomes a measure of our desire for peaceful resolution. The pattern for violence and exclusion has been implanted as boys observe their male models interact with their environment. Even though women play a role, the men are often the influencers. Hate and exclusion are learned behavior. In the case of violence among men, boys primarily learn it from men. If it's learned, the behavior can be unlearned. The same things we've learned from transracial peacemaking can be transmitted to young men. But it takes courage and the willingness to be vulnerable.

There are young men who are agents of hate and young people who are working to find peaceful solutions. Both need mentoring. Young men who perpetuate hate and violence need to be invited into a change process that asks men what kind of people they want to be in this world. There are young people who have begun to take leadership for a peaceful and reconciled society. Their efforts are hopeful, but they need to be supported and instructed on strategies for reconciliation.

The power of peaceful resistance against intolerance has begun to take root. However, the voices and actions are more prevalent among women and people of color. Having experienced discrimination, they understand that peaceful resistance is central to a reconciled society. Their demonstrations around the world against the assault on human rights validate that we are inextricably linked together for the good of all.

In order for reconciliation to happen in a society that seems to be void of a moral compass, there's an urgent need for peacemaking and peacemakers. Humanity is in the midst of a moral crisis that has produced pain, mistrust, and destruction. Many white brothers have seen the injustice that the dominant culture has caused. Men of color, who have experienced the pangs of brutality, also have skin in the game. Whether we are men of color or white, the day of reckoning is here. I call this a time for at-one-ment, where we must come together to discover our role in creating safe, humane, and peaceful communities. We can turn the reckoning into a time for domestic peacemaking. In the midst of hostility, we must find common ground.

There are many questions that cry out for answers. In our search for peace and reconciliation, we must ask ourself tough questions such as these: Can we proclaim our desire for reconciliation if we are unwilling to come to the table to be reconciled? Can we call others enemies of peace if we are not ready to negotiate? Are we not also the enemy? Is the collateral damage to humanity worth the need to be the manly superior? If the answer to the last question is no, then let's come together to work out the kinks that are keeping us form being reconciled.

Releasing ourselves from societies' expectations of traditional manhood—with its defensive and self-serving tactics of competition and aggressive behavior—is the key that opens the gates to peace. Dr. King called people who were ready to be agents of peace and reconciliation drum majors. The drum major carries out the instructions of the band director and sets the standards for the band. A drum major for a reconciled people sets the standard for peace and reconciliation in our midst. Men need to join the cadre of drum majors so that right and just relationships can be restored.

If we believe that racial peace can be achieved, let's do something about it. Gather like-minded people who want a society unhampered by hate and exclusion. Establish a Council of Elders (because we have been made wise through years of experience) to share your wisdom and expertise with people who are ready to see a different future. You might be surprised about the difference it will make.

Bibliography

Arnold, Johann Christoph. *Why Forgive?* Walden, NY: Plough, 2010.
Swartz, Ted. *Laughter is Sacred Space*. Ted & Company Theater-Works, 2012. https://www.tedandcompany.com/shows/laughter-is-sacred-space/.

Conclusion

We set out in this volume to open a dialogue with men regarding a preferred picture of living well as men. We explored a broad number of expressions of masculinity both historically and in current contexts within North American life. We also brought into this dialogue reflections of a number of men within our Anabaptist community to develop a theologically supported vision of men thriving as Christian disciples, growing in community, and seeking peace in their inner lives, relationships, and world. In the back drop of this work of developing a positive vision for masculinity is the incredibly sad picture of the vast array of men falling way short of this vision. From good men who fail to live up to their own best intentions to those with explicit and determined intentions to rain down terror on others, it is not debatable whether men have caused much havoc and destruction through history and continue to perpetrate such horror.

The important work of examining the systemic and personal dynamics that lead to such destructive behavior of men in our society is critical in moving toward a healthier future. Calling out the behaviors, beliefs, and values that maintain systems of inequity and entitlement is a continuing challenge for all who desire peace and justice. As Christian men, addressing collusion with dynamics of dominance and destruction of others demands a practice of honesty, humility, and lament. It also demands taking on the ministry of peacemaking in all places where inequities leave the vulnerable among us at risk.

In February 2018 Mennonite Men, the primary underwriting organization for this volume, issued the following statement of commitment to participate in the healing ministry for men in our society:

A Time of Reckoning for Men and Masculinity

In recent months there has been unprecedented exposure of sexually predatorial men in high places, as well as unprecedented violence perpetrated by solitary men with little or no regard for human life. Whether acting out of a sense of entitlement to use women, children, or other men as objects for self-gratification and demonstration of power or raging at humanity out of what author Michael Kimmel calls "aggrieved entitlement," an identifiable group of men has triggered a reckoning for all men.

While the majority of males do not perpetrate these types of actions with such callous disregard for others, *all men* must consider how we participate in a patriarchal system that enables this behavior and respond. Victims, survivors and their advocates have called out to men for decades if not centuries to be more than bystanders, and too often defensiveness or an uneasy silence has been the response. In the face of the current exposure of a toxic masculinity in politics, entertainment and religion, our silence as men who claim to follow Jesus must not be our witness to the world.

The current spotlight on abuse of power offers an opportunity for healing, love and justice long overdue. This will not be easy or comfortable, since honest reflection might lead to admissions of our own unhealthy, maybe abusive, relationships and a need for restitution. It also may trigger memories about personal victimization at the hands of others.

We must start with truth-telling—naming the ways we are complicit in the dynamics of patriarchal privilege, how we've benefitted from it, how we've contributed to others' oppression. We must lament—for the pain inflicted by men on others through the exploitation of power—from forms of violence of mammoth proportions to expressions of power that are subtle and often unintentional. We must own what is ours to own, for only when we name our reality can we begin to work toward change. A thorough accounting of the breadth of abuse of power will lay the groundwork for much-needed alternatives.

Critical to creating change is the recognition that many men have also suffered under the burdens of patriarchal masculinity, as seen in the fact that men die on average approximately six years sooner than women, men are more likely to die a violent death at the hands of other men and that men die by suicide three to four times more often then women. The denial and suppression of healthy emotional life, repudiated by male socialization as too "feminine," leaves all too many men with a limited scope of experience of life—and specifically some of the tools needed to negotiate stress and conflict in positive ways.

We as men must not remain incapacitated, however, by the heaviness and shame of lament, but rather rise to embrace healthy masculinity. It's tempting to point fingers at the publicly fallen and to name their need for change. As we recognize that masculinity too often falls prey to baser impulses, we can begin to redeem our own masculinity and envision healthier expressions. As men committed to our personal journeys of healing we must join the critical work of dismantling oppressive systems and reconstructing ways of living that serve the well-being of all people.

Christians have clearly not been immune to the tragic dynamics of male-perpetrated sexual and physical violence. In truth, Christianity has been complicit in the development and maintenance of systems of inequity that foster such abuse. Some traditional interpretations of scripture, translating historical social constructs of patriarchy into prescriptions for all the ages, have blessed the subservience of people of certain classes (women, children, people of color, the marginalized "other") and of creation itself to the whims of males. Even our own historical Anabaptist ethic of yieldedness or quietness ("the quiet in the land") have tended to "shush" victims, heroize suffering, and leave leadership largely ineffective in calling out such evil in our midst.

The consistent message in the biblical narrative is to remember who we are as God's beloved children, respond to our failings with repentance, and follow the way of Jesus, who has broken down the dividing walls of hostility and is creating "one new humanity" of God's shalom (Ephesians 2:15–16). Christ calls us to be disciples, living in relationships of love, trusting that peaceful ways of living will bear fruit in our lives as people of God. It is critically clear that men, as participants in this invitation to faithful living, have much opportunity to change, learn and thrive, and to in turn bless the lives of all those with whom we do life!

The board of Mennonite Men has declared its commitment to address this urgent need for transformative change for men, recognizing the hopeful manifestations of God's loving kindness that can flow to men and in turn to everyone whose lives we touch. To this end, we are expanding our work beyond JoinHands (grant making) to men's inner and relational work with JoinMen— our program to promote healthy masculinity. We are pursuing opportunities to learn from and work with women in this effort. We call men to engage in this work to bring about God's healing, love and justice for our world.

For more about the expanding ministry of Mennonite Men, visit MennoniteMen.org. We invite men who are interested in engaging in this important work to reach out to the respective coordinators in the US and in Canada. We welcome your participation!

In the spirit of this "Time of Reckoning" statement, we invite readers to consider opportunities to join the dialogue and to invite others to participate in the journey toward God's peace. We especially invite those whose personal or professional lives have equipped them with wisdom to add to the important conversation towards healthy lives for men and those whose lives we touch. We acknowledge that this is only one step in a larger ministry of bringing healing and hope to our world.

In gratefulness,
Don and Steve

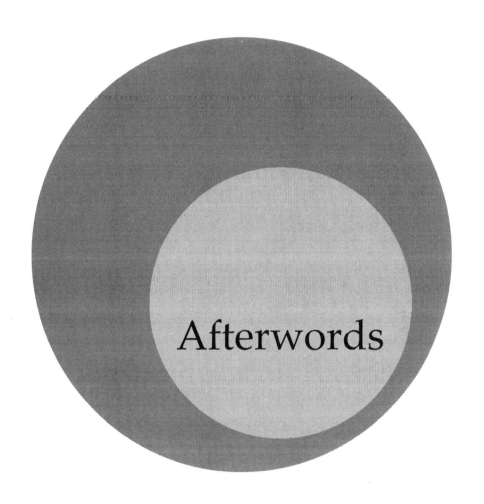

Afterwords

The Grace of Our Stories

I am impressed with men engaging the subject of masculinity in the way this book demonstrates. I am thankful for the stories shared with such honesty. Each personal story, regardless of the author's race/ethnicity, showed that this issue of masculinity has caused problems for men and women alike. I read a book years ago by Nathan McCall titled *Makes Me Wanna Holler*. In his book he shares the struggles of a black man growing up in America and trying to find his voice and respect as a man. Reading that book helped me to focus and provide a different level of care for my husband and sons. I realized through that book that the black man had a struggle I was unaware of as a black woman. This book provided that same type of personal growth. I realized reading this book that men not only struggle with the subject of masculinity but also have even less resources than women to help them deal with the issue in healthy and safe ways. It made me want more than anything to share each story with the men and women in my life and talk through these and other experiences. I came away from this book thinking that maybe it's time for all of us to shake off the history and tell the true story of our family and community.

This book also helps us see how different cultures experience the idea of masculinity and how tricky even within one's culture those understandings and norms can be to navigate. I was fascinated by the Asian American story of how, on the one hand, serving in the military is expected and seen as what men do, and on the other hand, fashion and culture are now dictating what a man should look and act like. I remember not too very long ago similar issues faced women and young girls. We still haven't figured it out completely, but, I dare say, young girls are getting better messages today about being free from letting societal norms and traditions dictate their own sense of self. We need to make sure those messages are directed toward all of our young people regardless of gender.

I appreciate the acknowledgement that gender roles changed over the years with little or no direction on what each gender should do in the new reality. Considering where we are as a society today,

I question whether the church is ready still to meet people where they are and offer grace as we figure out what is next. As we consider our LGBTQ family, can we take seriously the challenges that we the church and society has placed on them? Can we at least talk together about how our traditions and roles are evolving without fear of losing oneself or the church as a whole?

When I consider Leonard Dow's chapter and his view of the ordinary man, I was struck by the fact that these men would likely not acknowledge their ordinary status in our society. As Don Neufeld states in chapter 1, this false sense of self (even ordinary) is the problem. It is only when we are honest about our reality and, dare I say, fears that we will be able to change our circumstances. I can think of countless young men who have for all intents and purposes failed at life—mostly because they were ordinary, and being ordinary in this culture is like being invisible. We expect and encourage young people to be unique and to stand out. For those who do not have those characteristics or even desires, they are often looked on as undesirable or less than.

And let us not forget about what society in various cultures has deemed worthy of manhood: militarism, being a provider, and as stated in the book, *the temptation of being relevant, remarkable, and powerful.* We must begin to shape the next generation with an understanding that they are not responsible for wearing these hats and to give them the space to find themselves and not be ashamed if they are unable to provide or if they choose not to join the military. We must give them the understanding that they are fully accepted when looking to and sharing their roles with the women in their lives.

As Harry Lafond describes in his chapter, the Indigenous understand the role of the *ohtâwimâw* (the word that tells us about the man in the family), which teaches that the man is a partner to the *nôtokêw* (old woman) who wraps her arms around all her relatives. He is given to guide and bring along the rest of the family. This idea of sharing the care and guiding of our families and even of community in partnership is vital to healthy masculinity. We can use these various ways of looking at roles and find which one works best for our family. I would say my family has used this Cree model without even realizing that is what we were doing.

The challenge for the church is to abandon these gender roles and traditions; to educate society that the sky will not fall if men don't live up to certain standards; and to give one another grace if one family chooses one direction and another family choose a different direction. I love the idea of the father as guide and the mother as the one holding it all together. But just because it works for me does not mean it will work for every woman.

My hope for this project is that it will not only get men talking but also get women and men talking together. I pray we can provide space for one another to hear and challenge each other as we find our new normal. For me this book is about grace. It's about listening to one another and offering ourselves as spaces for grace and mercy. In the story of the Cree Elder who always brought gum home to his wife, a simple gesture symbolized the fact that he was thinking of her, that he loved her. We are called not only to grand gestures like Christ crucified but also to simple gestures like Jesus weeping with Mary and Martha. I carry your story, and you are asked to carry mine. Together we can overcome this toxic reality of masculinity and create healthy norms of masculinity and femininity.

Cyneatha Millsaps
Executive Director
Mennonite Women USA

Masculinity Close to Home

I read this book with fascination, with hope, and with some disappointment. The writers gave me new insights and food for thought. I sensed a deep and honest longing for God's leading. And yet there was something that I was looking for that I did not find.

I appreciate the discussions of power and the conviction that our ideas are rooted in our lives and in our stories. I value the vulnerability of so many of the writers and their engagement with Scripture and our tradition as they thought about what it means to be a man. They brought humility to the task; many of the writers talk about the fact that they are learning as they go.

The discussion of masculinities rather than masculinity is essential. For me, the chapters written by men on the margins were key. Perspectives of men who are gay, Asian, Latino, Indigenous, and African American gave me new vantage points for masculinity. Many of the writers made connections and intersections between different types of abuses of power. Violence takes many faces.

Over and over again, the writers talk about how masculinity is something that is learned. I was struck by how many of the writers talk about relationships with their fathers. The groundwork of masculinity is laid in childhood.

My Mennonite father was charming, outgoing, intelligent, and loved by everyone who knew him, including me. Stories from this book helped me think about him. My views of masculinity came first of all from him.

Like some writers in the book, I saw the dedication my father put into being a provider; his paychecks sustained our family. I also saw the toll that hard work in the factory took on his body. Being a man meant spending time after work with his buddies in the bar. Home was a place he retreated to, where everyday necessities were the responsibility of his wife and three daughters. I also saw how difficult life was for him and for our family when work dried up, and he had long months of unemployment.

My father was loving toward my sisters and me. He was warm and funny and tender. He spent time with us and loved us deeply.

I puzzled over this inherited blueprint of masculinity as I chose a life partner, a man who was in some ways different but in other ways similar to my father.

I learned about femininity from my mother, no doubt, but my adult understanding of what it means to be a woman was forged in the intimate relationship with my partner. I learned about this in the context of a committed sexual relationship with a long-time lover. We negotiated give and take, power and roles. How do we decide about two careers, about child care, about housework? How do we negotiate our masculine or feminine identity in the push and pull of daily decision-making and long-term directions?

I think that family relationships (not just family of origin) are a place where we construct our identities. My most intense wrestling about masculinity came when I had a baby boy. He was my second child, after my daughter. How would I raise him compared to his sister? How would I help him learn to be a man? How would faith in Jesus shape my choices? I was surprised that only a couple of writers mentioned their partners or their children. Are intimate relationships not that important for forming masculine identity?

The chapter on community focused on church community and stories about men in community with groups of men. Men's groups are significant; however, I haven't heard of any men's Bible studies where people have hit each other. Why is it that male violence so often happens in family relationships? What is it about family relationships that differs from other relationships in this regard? Why was this type of community overlooked in a book about peace and masculinity?

Violence is multifaceted in this book, which is important. However, violence certainly includes physical force and sexual abuse. How can we talk about peace and masculinity without talking about intimate partner violence and child abuse? This is the elephant in the room this book does not address.

My Mennonite father was violent with my mother and later my stepmother. When I was too little to remember things, my sister recalls my mother running into our room in the middle of the night crying, "Girls, help! Daddy is trying to kill me!" When I was old enough to have memories, I remember trouble at home. I remember hearing fights about money and too much drinking. I remember the sound of chairs being knocked over, my stepmother saying, "Don't you dare hit me again."

Good Mennonite men can be violent; wife battering happens in Mennonite homes at the same rate as in secular homes. In this book there are a few references to the need to work against domestic violence, but no one had a story to share about experiencing or being tempted to physical violence—except Hugo Saucedo who talked with great vulnerability about a close call with being violent towards himself.

Imbalances of power bring temptation to abuse. I know for myself that the people I have been angriest at in my life have been people who were in my power: my young children and my mother when she was in a nursing home. I really fought the urge to hurt them physically. And that is in spite of society telling me that to be a woman, to be feminine, means to be a nurturer, a carer, a person who is not physically violent.

As a pastor, I learned that a shocking number of my young female congregants were raped by men they were dating; some of them were Mennonite men.

Physical and sexual violence is a part of Mennonite men's lives, but it is barely mentioned in this book. How does masculinity play into violence in intimate relationships? I think it is easier to talk about Jesus and peace than to talk about our urges to be violent toward the people we love.

This is a very significant book. I find it immensely hopeful that Mennonite men are talking about being peaceful at heart. I think this book will stimulate countless important conversations between men and between women and men around kitchen tables, in small groups, and in churches. It's a book that invites further dialogue, further vulnerabilities, and further explorations about how being followers of Jesus makes us peaceful at heart. In this afterword, I have named one direction these further convesations must go—namely, how to go from being peaceful at heart to being peaceful at home.

Carol Penner
Assistant Professor of Theological Studies
Conrad Grebel University, Waterloo, Ontario

From Toxic Masculinity
to Peaceful Communities

What an achievement! This chorus of male voices represents, in my mind, a breakthrough moment for Mennonite men in particular—provoking an urgently needed conversation about what it takes to form and be peaceful men. At times I wept with the beauty, vulnerability, and honesty of the stories shared. Several chapters felt lacking—or a bit overdone—with a lot of variance in the depth and style with which the writers addressed a given topic. But it is a rare and precious gift to have the opportunity to listen to so many diverse and yet ultimately harmonious voices describing their experience of what it's like to grow up as boys in North America, the breakthrough moments in their personal journeys, and their call to us all to attend to the intentional communal formation required to nurture healthy masculinity.

The stories describe a toxic masculinity that prevails in varied, crippling ways in the diverse ethnic communities represented. Yet each chapter describes relationships and insights that show the way toward liberation, integration of heart and mind, restored generational love within families, and the embrace of a wholehearted humanness as men and women together. And what is perhaps most exhilarating is that despite the vast array of different culturally constructed masculinities and social locations described by the authors, there is a swelling resonance that gathers force throughout the chapters as the attractiveness of healthy masculinity comes into clearer focus and finds deep rooting in rich communitarian, spiritual, and theological soil.

Most mornings I receive an electronic newsletter entitled *Higher Ed Hot Topics*. It addresses all sorts of live topics on college and university campuses. This week one arrived entitled *Masculinity Crisis*. It began thus: "College men are in crisis due to a lack of positive male role models, declining academic success, poor conduct, social media attacks and stereotyping. To overcome those obstacles, ensure your institution provides strategies and programs that make men feel valued, safe, a sense of belonging and supported through their educational experience."

While all identities, male and female, are socially constructed, from study I've done over the years I've long assumed that male identities—particularly men's involvement as fathers in the lives of children and partners in parenting—are relatively fragile and re-quire (in general) more cultural reinforcement than do female roles. There is the elemental reality that women's bodies are designed to bear and suckle children, which gives women a biologically rooted meaning and tangible function in life that men lack. The father-child bond is more physically removed and less obvious. The father-involved family is an achievement of culture and requires mentoring, encouragement, and cultural reinforcement. If mascu-linity and ways of embodying maleness are socially constructed (as is said in these chapters), and the peace-filled, empowering presence of fathers with their partners, children, and communities requires cultural reinforcement, then the absence of intentional formation of healthy masculinity in our congregations, schools, and families is devastating—and that devastation is evident on every hand.

Why have we let this happen? Why does even talking about these topics tend to set off landmines? This is far too complex a social reality to get into with any adequacy here. But given the overwhelming toxicity of so much of North American assumptions about maleness, and how women and people of color in particular have experienced the oppressive and systemic burden of domi-neering white men, we must learn to talk about it respectfully and openly. We must learn to talk about what healthy maleness looks like in our congregational, academic, and community discourse.

Descriptions of systemic problems associated with patriarchy and male-dominated institutions abound in our educated circles. Systemic analyses of power provide important lenses for critical analysis, self-awareness, and reform. Yet sweeping condemnations of male leadership and men in general don't name the heart of the matter, in my view, and too often leave us impoverished and weakened as communities of real people. Rather than a simplistic tendency to stereotype maleness itself as the problem, how might we as communities of faith become more intentional with what is required to form peaceful men? How might we love men and invite them to do their personal work and practice life-giving ways of being male—in partnership with women?

I deeply appreciated the acknowledgement by David Evans of the "deep inner misery of men" and the bell hooks observation he notes that to create loving men "we must love males." This isn't about loving men for living up to what hooks calls "sexist-defined notions of male identity." It is all about helping men see, as Hugo Saucedo and other authors in this book describe so powerfully, that whatever culturally defined notions of male dominance or control are prominent in a particular community, they become a "prison" that traps men in crippling ways. With the difficult work of recovery over many years, restoration is possible—as beautifully described by Harry Lafond—restoration of the life giving identity of the father role and the knowledge that being a father is precious "with gifts and responsibilities from the Creator to ensure the well-being of generations to follow."

It is urgent that we learn to talk with each other about what it means to be healthy humans as men and as women—not pushing and shoving in counter oppressive moves. We must find persuasive, loving ways to intrigue men to pursue spiritual insight and bring to voice their questions, longings, and experiences of God in nature, at work, in families. We must model how to reflect out loud and with each other to make sense of the ways God is at work in the world, to show each other how to make down-to-earth theological sense of the meaning of life. We must urgently work to create spaces for brave, honest, hard, and liberating conversations to happen.

I appreciate the repeated acknowledgement in these chapters of how women have helped to show the way toward a more fully human, loving, empowering, and emotionally attuned way of partnering as men and women. As a woman, I am deeply grateful for many male partners and colleagues I live and work with who are "peaceful at heart," have done their inner spiritual work, and embody a diversity of masculinities that exhibit the fruit of the Spirit.

Above all, I love the way Jesus exemplified maleness. After his prolonged, stinging rebuke of the religious leaders—"Woe to you, scribes and Pharisees, hypocrites!"—he speaks with a powerful love for those he has just denounced: "Jerusalem, Jerusalem, the city that kills the prophets and stones those who are sent to it! How often have I desired to gather your children together as a hen gathers her brood under her wings, and you were not willing!" (Matt. 23:37–38). Is there any more tender image in all of Scripture?

I give thanks for this volume, hoping it makes us all—men and women—more willing to do what personal and spiritually grounded group work we need to do to better prepare for whole-hearted partnership so we will all, as John Powell writes, more fully "discover our role in creating safe, humane, and peaceful communities."

Sara Wenger Shenk
President
Anabaptist Mennonite Biblical Seminary, Elkhart, Indiana